Max Hartmann

A Cry of Despair

Danylo Movchan's Watercolors on the War in Ukraine

With a foreword by John A. Kohan and Mateusz Sora

UKRAINIAN VOICES

Collected by Andreas Umland

81 *Olga Khomenko*
Ukrainians beyond Borders
Nine Life Journeys Through the History of Eastern Europe
With a foreword by Zbigniew Wojnowski
ISBN 978-3-8382-2007-9

82 *Mykhailo Minakov*
From Servant to Leader
Chronicles of Ukraine under the Zelensky Presidency, 2019–2024
With a foreword by John Lloyd
ISBN 978-3-8382-2002-4

83 *Volodymyr Hromov (ed.)*
A Ruined Home
Sketches of War, 2022–2023
ISBN 978-3-8382-2008-6

84 *Olha Tatokhina (ed.)*
Why Do They Kill Our People?
Russia's War Against Ukraine as Told by Ukrainians
With a foreword by Volodymyr Yermolenko
ISBN 978-3-8382-2056-7

85 *Mieste Hotopp-Riecke, Sarah Reinke (Hrsg.)*
Die Krimtataren
Geschichte – Kultur – Politik
Mit einem Vorwort von Nariman Dschelal
ISBN 978-3-8382-1986-8

The book series "Ukrainian Voices" publishes English- and German-language monographs, edited volumes, document collections, and anthologies of articles authored and composed by Ukrainian politicians, intellectuals, activists, officials, researchers, and diplomats. The series' aim is to introduce Western and other audiences to Ukrainian explorations, deliberations and interpretations of historic and current, domestic, and international affairs. The purpose of these books is to make non-Ukrainian readers familiar with how some prominent Ukrainians approach, view and assess their country's development and position in the world. The series was founded, and the volumes are collected by Andreas Umland, Dr. phil. (FU Berlin), Ph. D. (Cambridge), Associate Professor of Politics at the Kyiv-Mohyla Academy and an Analyst in the Stockholm Centre for Eastern European Studies at the Swedish Institute of International Affairs.

Max Hartmann

A CRY OF DESPAIR

Danylo Movchan's Watercolors on the War in Ukraine

With a foreword by John A. Kohan and Mateusz Sora

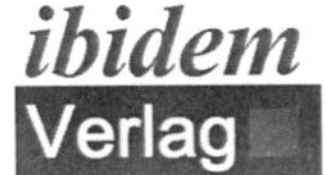

Bibliografische Information der Deutschen Nationalbibliothek
Die Deutsche Nationalbibliothek verzeichnet diese Publikation in der Deutschen Nationalbibliografie; detaillierte bibliografische Daten sind im Internet über http://dnb.d-nb.de abrufbar.

Bibliographic information published by the Deutsche Nationalbibliothek
The Deutsche Nationalbibliothek lists this publication in the Deutsche Nationalbibliografie; detailed bibliographic data are available on the Internet at http://dnb.d-nb.de.

Cover picture: Angel of Death (ангел смерті), Aquarell, 47cm x 40 cm, © Danylo Movchan 2024

Portrait Julian Chaplinsky:
1) https://commons.wikimedia.org/wiki/File:%D0%AE%D0%BB%D1%96%D0%B0%D0%BD_%D0%A7%D0%B0%D0%BF%D0%BB%D1%96%D0%BD%D1%81%D1%8C%D0%BA%D0%B8%D0%B9,_2015.jpg
2) https://commons.wikimedia.org/wiki/File:Юліан_Чаплінський,_2015.jpg
Licensed under CC 2.0 BY-SA, s. https://creativecommons.org/licenses/by-sa/2.0/deed.en

ISBN (Print): 978-3-8382-2051-2
ISBN (E-Book [PDF]): 978-3-8382-8051-6

Leuschnerstraße 40
30457 Hannover
Germany / Deutschland
info@ibidem.eu

Printed in the EU

Shunning realistic details,
Mochvan elevates the conflict in his homeland
to a cosmic battle between good and evil.
What sets these works apart is
that they evoke hope in times of despair.
John A. Kohan

The experience of war forces Christians
to reconsider the message of the Gospel,
raising questions about fundamental themes
such as forgiveness, mercy, and justice.
These questions are precisely
what are at the forefront of the watercolors
that Danylo Movchan has been painting
since the beginning of 2022.
Mateusz Sora

Content

Foreword

Whenever I sit down at my desk to write, I make eye contact with Andrey Sheptytsky. A friend from the western Ukrainian city of Lviv, knowing of my interest in collecting contemporary sacred art, decided that the venerated Metropolitan of the Ukrainian Greek Catholic Church and noted patron of the arts would be the perfect holy intercessor for me in my artistic pursuits. The icon of Sheptytsky, with his piercing stare, is the work of Danylo Movchan and is far from traditional. The Ukrainian cleric's face appears to float in a boundless white space, sculpted in an abstract manner. A golden half-circle at the top of the panel suggests a divine presence. My eyes and heart unite before this austerely simple image.

Is Movchan a minimalist? A symbolist? It's hard to say what exactly sets him apart from other icon makers in the new sacred art movement centered in Lviv. I know Movchan is an accomplished watercolorist, yet nothing could have prepared me for the flood of wartime images I first encountered in the German edition of this beautifully presented, contextualized overview of his art. Page after page features water-impelled colors bleeding across the paper. Shunning realistic detail, Movchan elevates the conflict in his homeland to a cosmic battle between good and evil. Here, we catch glimpses of balletic formations of amorphous shapes in ambiguous spaces, blurred by watercolor washes—so different from his sharply defined Sheptytsky portrait that hangs on my wall!

While news reports describe Russian "meat wave assaults" on the battlefield, Movchan dignifies the human body, encompassing both flesh and spirit. His nude figures are spiritual X-rays. Those who are healthy in mind and body appear red and blue, their vascular systems pumping life. Those suffering from a sickness of spirit appear unhealthy, colored brown and grey. How easily they are torn apart by the weapons of war! Another central theme for Movchan is the physical suffering of the crucified Christ, in which the spilling of blood takes on the meaning of a redemptive act of self-sacrifice. The recurring image of the cross under attack reminds us of those who stand with the Lord in this unprovoked conflict. In this book, Movchan discusses his desire to find the perfect artistic form to convey the horror of what is happening in his homeland to the world. Judging by the watercolors in the following pages, he has succeeded in creating antiwar art that is universally accessible. I hope this English edition introduces his heart-searing wartime imagery to a wider global audience. When future historians seek an artistic memoir of the Ukrainian conflict, I believe Movchan's cycle of wartime watercolors will stand alongside Goya's etchings of the Napoleonic invasion of Spain in The Disasters of War and Otto Dix's prints of World War I in The War portfolio. What sets these works apart is that they evoke hope in times of despair.

John A. Kohan, Delaware, Ohio

Foreword

Danylo Movchan's time in Novica was also decisive for his development as an artist. Novica is a small village in southern Poland where I organized plein air workshops for icon painters for many years. Danylo participated in his first plein air workshop in the third session, which had the theme "God's Messengers of the Old Covenant." He came to us as a self-confident and well-trained painter. Since 2011, he has consistently followed the path he chose. His works are characterized by elegant forms and a search for synthesis.

The figures and scenes he paints against a white background draw our attention to the essence of the biblical message. Whether the subject is the Expulsion from Paradise (2011), the Last Supper at Emmaus (2021), the Sacrifice of Abraham (2024), or a saint, Danylo introduces us to the reality of divine grace in action. His works, created during plein air sessions, break with the template of the "traditional" icon. Danylo Movchan undoubtedly belongs to the generation of Lviv artists who broke the dogma of the immutability of Eastern ecclesiastical art at the beginning of the 21st century. They have "disenchanted" us.

For many years, we have considered the plein air workshops that take place every September in Novica to be a laboratory for contemporary icons. Looking back at our work, I see that it has another dimension. They represent the art of a spiritually independent Ukraine that, while relying on tradition, seeks its own language to express the experience of faith sincerely and emphatically. As organizers of the Plein Air Workshop, we were fascinated by the freshness and "attractiveness" of the sacred artists' works by Lviv. Over time, we realized that their search for a unique artistic voice is directly related to the political and social context. Thanks to our painters, we were able to visualize events that changed Ukraine and its people.

This was evident in the protest's corrupt authorities and in the manifestations of belonging to the Western world and Euro-Atlantic values. In recent years, we have also seen this in the heroic defense of political independence and national identity.

Has the drama unfolding in Ukraine since 2014—the brutal suppression of demonstrators in Kyiv and subsequent Russian aggression—influenced the work of young icon painters? No, it further strengthened their convictions. For the Lviv painters, the war period was a time of intensive work, discovery, and popularization of Ukrainian culture, as well as community consolidation and new artistic initiatives.

It was also a time of crystallization: artists associated with the Department of Sacred Art at the Lviv Academy of Fine Arts joined others, resulting in the "Lviv School of Sacred Painting" phenomenon. Its representatives combine local tradition with the achievements of 20th-century European art in their works. Today, some Lviv painters are defending their homeland as soldiers on the front lines, while those who stayed behind continue to work as artists. Proceeds from the sale of their artwork benefit victims of the war—the growing number of widows, orphans, and disabled individuals—as well as the equipment of defenders.

The experience of war forces Christians to reconsider the message of the Gospel, raising questions about fundamental themes such as forgiveness, mercy, and justice. These questions are precisely what are at the forefront of the watercolors that Danylo Movchan has been painting since the beginning of 2022.

Mateusz Sora, Warszawa

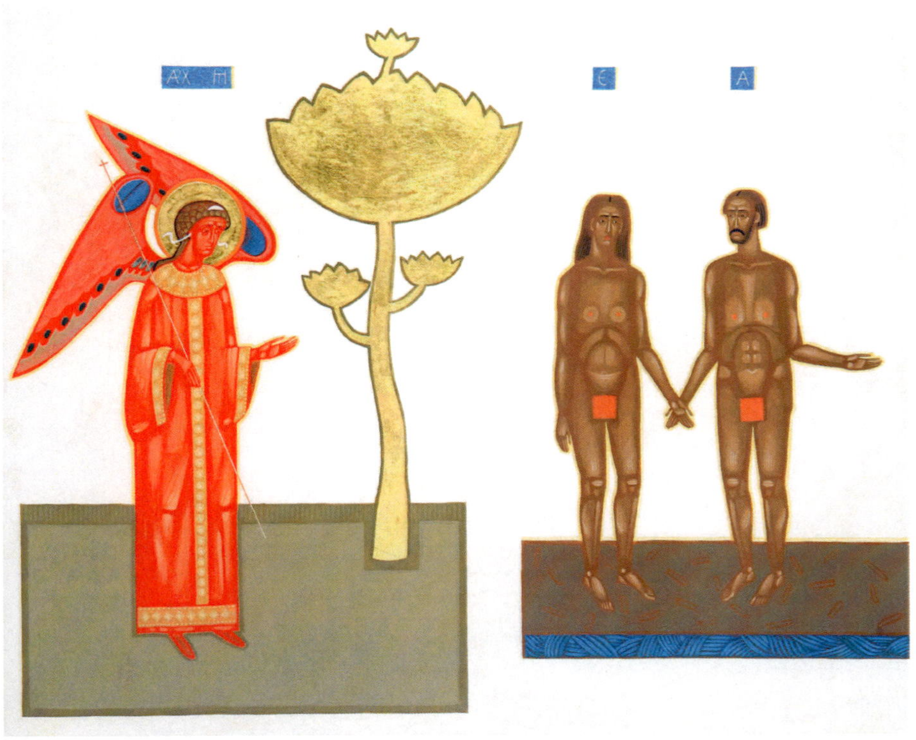

Expulsion from paradise. Icon on wood with primer.
Icon on wood, primer, colors on egg, white and gold, 2011

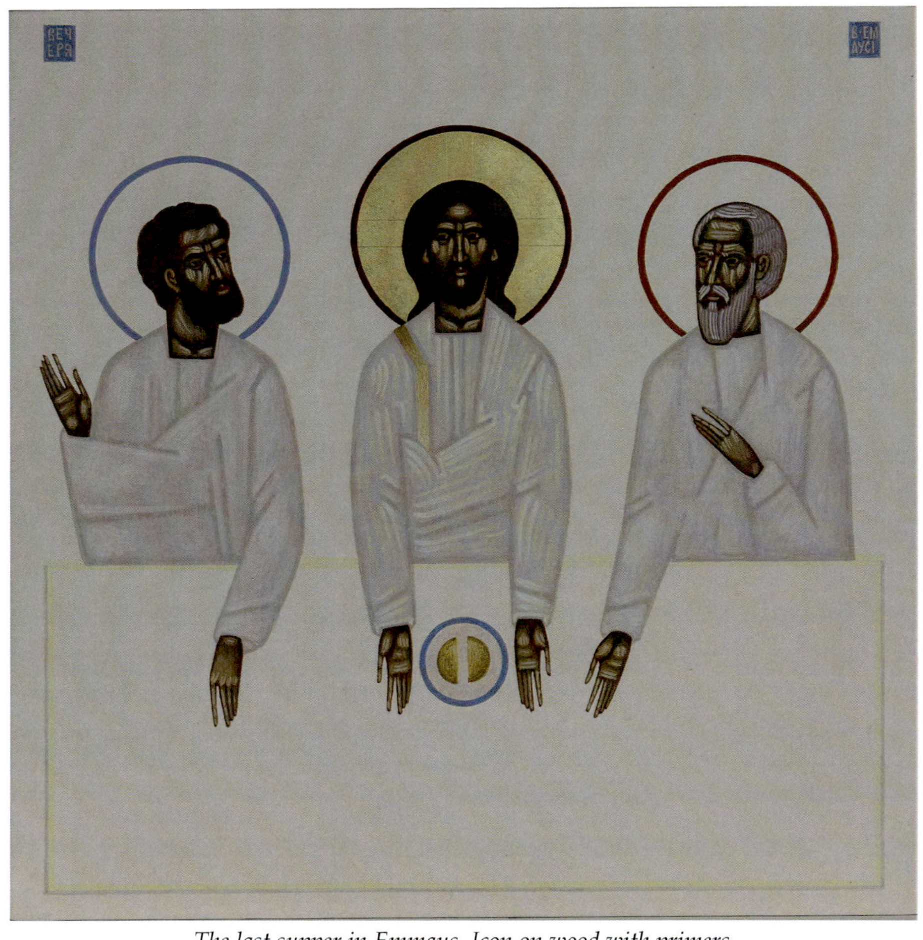

The last supper in Emmaus. Icon on wood with primers, color with egg, white and gold, 2021

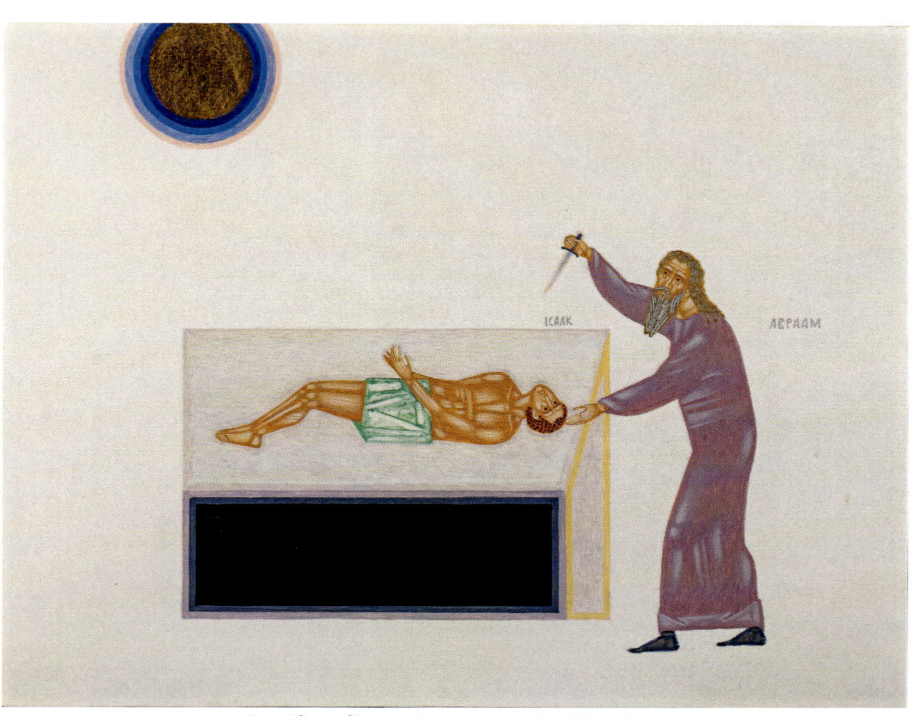

Sacrifice of Isaac. Icon on wood with primer, colors with egg, white and gold, 2024

Introduction

There is no doubt that February 24, 2022, will go down as one of the most significant dates in world history. Most of us reacted with shock and astonishment to the news of a major war in Europe. A major war in Europe? After all that has happened on this continent and beyond in the 20th century, how could that be? However, anyone who had been paying attention to recent developments was not at all surprised. Those of us in Ukraine and beyond knew it would happen. Russian troops were clearly visible on Ukraine's borders.

But would Putin invade the country? We thought it was just a threatening gesture. However, the unthinkable happened that day. Putin deceived us. Many heads of state sought talks to deter him. However, the six-meter-long negotiating table in the Kremlin spoke louder than words. They had to sit there while the same autocrat conversed casually with his allies.

However, Putin had completely miscalculated. He did not believe that his "special military operation" would lead to a major war. He did not believe the Ukrainians could defend themselves. He thought the operation would end in a few days and a government loyal to him would be reinstated.

Ukraine showed incredible resistance, not only from its army but also from its civilian population. The people of Ukraine, who are otherwise so divided, were suddenly more united than ever before. Many people who used to speak Russian have switched to Ukrainian. Most people used to speak Ukrainian but were forced to speak Russian during the many years of the Soviet Union.

The West had previously looked on in horror as Putin invaded and incorporated Crimea into Russia. They also helplessly observed the establishment of pro-Russian governments in the two People's Republics of Donetsk and Luhansk, which are only recognized by Russia, Syria, and North Korea. Now, the West has finally reacted.

However, military and civilian support are by no means assured. A new theater of war has opened in the Middle East, and a sinister alliance of autocrats is growing stronger. As we should have known long ago, Putin is not giving in at all. His lies and distortions of history are spreading among the many dissatisfied people in the West. They see him as a good alternative and believe his speeches.

But how many people here know the true history of Ukraine? Not just the crimes that this country endured in the 20th century, but all of them. How many know that fourteen million Ukrainians died in totalitarian attacks in the last century and what happened during the Soviet regime's many years of oppression? What was the reality? We could inform ourselves today, but few do.

Julian Chaplinsky, an architect, urban planner, and very wise intellectual, told me in his office at the Lviv city administration: "What we are experiencing today is the resurrection of totalitarianism, which may soon rule the whole world."

But what does the war in Ukraine look like for the local population? When the war broke out, the iconic artist Danylo Movchan was not initially surprised but was completely shocked. From then on, the shadow of death has hung over the entire country. However, he soon found a way to express through his art what words could not convey. For him, it was a way to express his feelings. For us, it was a touching way to empathize with the terrible reality.

How did this book come about, showcasing the many impressive works created since then? Like many things in life, it just happened. I had already met Danylo "by chance" seven years earlier when I visited the city and learned about the new kind of icon that had emerged after the country gained independence. I also met Danylo on Facebook later and bought one piece from him and one from his wife, Yaryna, who is also an artist. When I came across his new paintings about war on Facebook, they impressed me so much that I am still convinced today. People in our country should have the opportunity to experience them and understand what this war is like. Danylo responded immediately when I asked if he would agree to publish a book together.

However, I knew that I could not do it from a distance, perhaps with video calls; I also needed to meet him in person. Eventually, a group of four people came together: Danylo and his wife, our translator Solomia Horyn—who often participated in the conversations—and Julian Chaplinsky. I found Julian's vlog with Danylo on the internet, used AI to translate the words, and learned a lot of things that I would not have known any other way.

This also gave rise to the possibility of interpreting his early works. Real artists don't explain their own works; they're interested in what others have to say about them. As I am not an art scholar, I did not want to venture into interpreting his work on my own. However, Danylo often confirmed my impressions during our conversations. I believe others can also understand this art and its intention.

One special experience for me was the conversation with Julian Chaplinsky that Danylo organized. I thought it would be just a brief meeting, but I was surprised when he immediately engaged me in an important conversation that challenged me. His view of things is realistic and sobering. This encounter also led to the title of this book, "The Cry of Despair," which is fitting. This despair is often encountered in the printed conversations, the verbal nature of which has been deliberately preserved.

My visit to the grave of Danylo's brother, Mikhailo Movchan, also challenged me. It showed me the result of this war, the loss of so valuable people we are missing, and no one can replace. I'm at a loss for words, and all I could do was hug Danylo. I'll never forget that moment.

I would like to thank everyone who made this book possible, including our group: the editor of the Ukrainian Voices series, Dr. Andreas Umland, an Eastern European historian and observer of the war in Kyiv, the authors of the foreword: John Alan Kohan for the English version and Mateusz Sora for the German original Christian Schön and other participants from the publishing house ibidem. Thanks are extended to those who contributed corrections and suggestions for changes, including Andrew Sutherland of Salt Lake City and Eva Hartmann, who also reviewed and corrected the manuscript. For details on the main participants, see the first appendix. I recorded and translated the conversations with AI, and all published texts are authorized by the participants.

It is my hope that this work offers an art experience that deepens understanding of the realities of war and imparts meaningful insights into the human condition.

Max Hartmann, Zofingen

Dariusz Pago: Karina

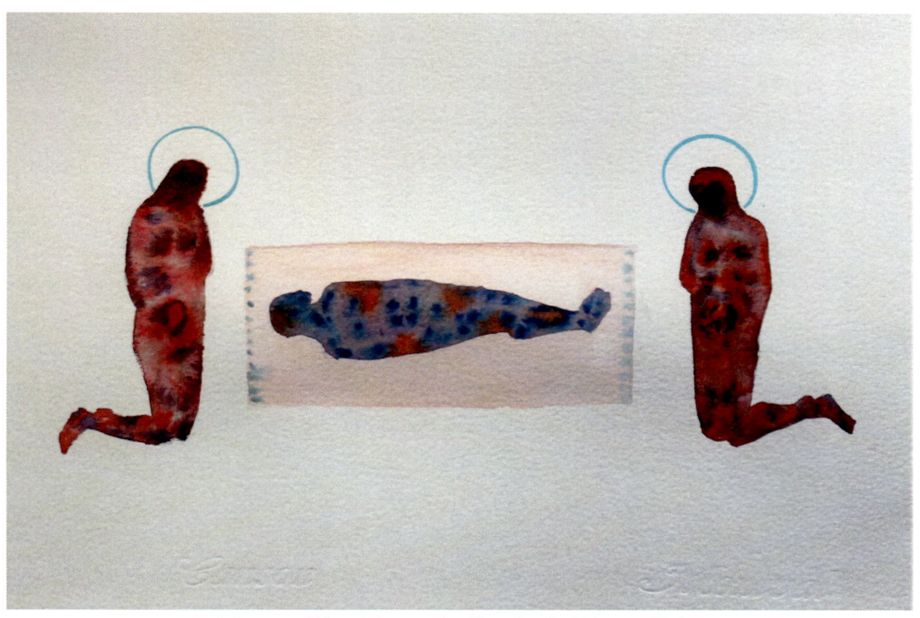

Adam and Eve Mourn the Death of a Human Being

Karina sewed a stranger's tattered coat
which she arrived yesterday
Today, she sewed two countries
together into a single cloth
with the scent of this earth

We know it is an old Ruthenian story
on this ground, once flourished
a meadow that knew no boundaries
which is now being crossed by strangers
trampling the grass, tearing along the mantle
the two edges of the Dnipro's banks

Interview with Danylo Movchan

In the spring of 2024, I spent ten days in Lviv for my first in-person meeting with Danylo Movchan. Due to the conflict, my travel plans changed. Instead of flying to the airport that was renovated for the 2012 European Soccer Championships, I took one of the available buses from Poland. Crossing the border requires passing through several checkpoints.

The Old Town and nearby areas remain vibrant. Unlike seven years ago when I first arrived, foreign tourists are now scarce. Consequently, some are surprised to find out that I am a foreigner. People often ask me about my origins and my reasons for coming during the war. These inquiries facilitate meaningful discussions. For example, I spoke with a young man who recently enlisted in the military to serve his country. Another young man plans to study fashion and design. City traffic has increased, making it more difficult to travel during rush hour. The cars in this area resemble those found in Western cities.

We have our first conversation in a cultural venue in the Old Town that offers various food and drink options. The Old Town is designated as a World Heritage Site. Danylo is waiting for me with his wife, Yaryna, who is also an artist. Solomia Horyn, who is proficient in German, is present as a translator and occasionally participates in the discussion.

There were four extended, meaningful meetings. As we parted ways, the couple, who live modestly with their two children, accompanied me to the adjacent military cemetery. Danylo's brother, who died fighting in Bakhmut several months ago, is buried there.

At the entrance, the names of more than five hundred fallen town soldiers are visible. A bereaved family, accompanied by several of the fallen soldier's colleagues, proceeded to the gravesite to pay their respects. An excavator prepares a new section of the cemetery. Each grave is marked with a photograph of the deceased. Their birth and death years are listed, and occasionally, a QR code provides additional information.

Danylo visits his brother's grave alone first. When we arrive at the grave, I notice the woolly hat Mykhailo wore during the war. Not knowing what to say, I choose to stay silent. This is the devastating outcome of any war. What is the death toll of soldiers and civilians in wars against Ukraine? Ukraine has experienced more bloodshed in the past century than any other place in Europe.

The current Russian invasion is a monstrosity that can never be justified. This war violates international law and the established rules of warfare. Will it never end?

Is pessimism the only perspective available when considering global circumstances? Is war an enduring aspect of human society that cannot be eliminated?

Experience in the Time of Soviet Ukraine

Please describe your experience in Soviet Ukraine. You were born in 1979, the Berlin Wall fell in 1989, and the Soviet Union dissolved in 1991, leading to the formation of an independent Ukraine. You spent your early years in Soviet Ukraine. Can you describe what that period was like for you?

Danylo Movchan (DM): As a child, I thought my life was normal. When Ukraine gained independence, I was in sixth grade and aware of the changes. In hindsight, I see that I was treated as insignificant, just part of the crowd. Currently, there is an understanding that individuals became integrated as Soviet citizens. Religious beliefs, along with Ukrainian customs and traditions, were systematically disregarded. Nevertheless, I participated in typical childhood activities and frequently played with my peers.

According to the regime, the school's main responsibility was to ensure ideological conformity among students rather than solely educating talented children.

DM: Looking back, that's exactly how it was. We were also forbidden to go to church. I often stayed with my grandmother while my parents worked. She listened to Radio Liberty, an American station that featured programs for Ukraine. She would turn on the radio early in the morning so that we could hear music, including popular American bands that we couldn't find elsewhere. She primarily used it to hear world events from another perspective rather than just local broadcasts. Many people did the same at the time, despite the ban.

Do you know why your grandmother regularly listened to these radio programs?

DM: I was too young to understand.

Do you recall any other experiences from that period?

DM: I remember my grandfather changing our surname from Movchan at some point during the Soviet era. From then on, he was known as Vovk. I still don't know why he did it. Perhaps our family name was seen as risky by the regime. My father originally went by Mykhailo Vovk, but he later changed his name to Yaroslav *Movchan.*

Could you explain why this matter was significant to him?

DM: I don't know, and I can no longer ask him. However, he did legally change his name, a decision also made by many others. He was required to manage a significant workload, including extensive documentation and numerous signatures. The reasons were likely political, as the government was concerned about his former name. He wanted to avoid exile to Siberia with his family, which was not an uncommon consequence during that period. The potential repercussions did not justify the risk. By changing his name, he sought to mitigate any further threat to his family's well-being. *I were him; I wouldn't want my family name associated with past dangers. No one wants to burden future generations with history.*

Yaryna Movchan (YM): Could you please clarify why this information was not communicated to me earlier?

DM: I didn't have anyone to discuss what happened back then with, and I wasn't interested as a child or teenager anyway.

YM: Did your grandparents use different surnames at various points in their lives? Did you have a different name when you were in school?

DM: I've been registered as Danylo Movchan since my birth in December 1979. However, my father appeared as Mykhailo Vovk in some documents from the 1980s. None of us ever used that name, so I was surprised when a former colleague called my father Mykhailo Vovk in the early 1990s.

Was one of your ancestors a priest?

DM: No, I don't think so.

YM: This means a lot to me, so please try to find out. Is anyone familiar with it? Could people easily change their names back then?

DM: Yes, that was possible at the time. I recall another Vovk who chose not to change his surname. He studied in Lviv, worked briefly in Russia, and then returned to Belarus to be with his wife. He found new employment there.

When I asked my Uncle Roman about my grandfather's experience in the war or his surname change, he refused to answer. My father was born in 1944. At that time, my grandfather and his wife lived near Zolochiv and later moved to an area near Lviv.

YM: This story is characteristic of your family. It's notable that there was a family secret.

DM: This issue spans three generations, each of which is quite different. I'm the only one interested in learning more. When my father was alive, I was too young to ask questions.

YM: Are you saying that this information isn't important to you? I believe it would be helpful for our family to learn more about our grandparents and share their stories with future generations. However, I would like to keep certain matters confidential.

DM: My grandmother didn't discuss the topic with me. At that time, people preferred to lead quiet lives. A friend mentioned that his mother thought he was too young for such discussions.

The Trauma of the History of Ukraine

The history of Ukraine is filled with traumatic experiences involving foreign powers. This is why the well-known historian Timothy Snyder titled his bestseller about eastern Poland, Belarus, and

Ukraine Bloodlands.[1] Before the current war began, hardly anyone in the West was interested in Ukraine, the second-largest country in Europe. If Ukraine was mentioned in history books at all, it was almost always in the context of Russian history.

This lack of knowledge means that many of us are unable to properly classify Russian propaganda claims on the internet. They often seem partially true at first but cannot easily be verified.

Half-truths are more dangerous than outright lies and distortions of the facts. This lack of knowledge means that many of us cannot properly classify Russian propaganda claims that we come across, usually online. They often appear partially true at first, but they cannot be easily verified. Half-truths are more dangerous than obvious lies and distortions of facts.

Anyone who takes a closer look at the criminal methods of the KGB/FSB will see that. Putin used to work in the KGB and now heads the FSB. Those who are aware of this also understand what is happening in Russia today.[2] He has never regretted his former work. It's certain that he still gives decisive orders himself today. Most of his closest associates are FSB members.[3]

Today's war is reopening old wounds in Ukraine and traumatizing new generations. The problem has finally been recognized. For example, the Greek Catholic University held an international scientific conference on practical psychology and offers corresponding training courses.

The Disaster of Chornobyl

The Chernobyl disaster, the biggest accident in the history of nuclear power plants, occurred on April 26, 1986. You were only seven years old at the time. The consequences of the radioactivity could be felt throughout

---

1 „Some 14 million died here through the 20th century in one mass slaughter after another. Ukraine is the crucible of the Bloodlands described powerfully by the Yale historian Timothy Snyder. https://time.com/6164810/ukraine-is-ourpast-and-our-future/

2 https://www.t-online.de/nachrichten/ausland/id_92002010/putins-schatten kaempfer-was-ist-ueber-den-geheimdienst-fsb-bekannt-.html

3 https://www.mdr.de/nachrichten/welt/osteuropa/politik/russland-sowje-tunion-kgb-fsb-putin-geheimdienst-spion-agent-100.html

Europe.[4] In Switzerland, for instance, we weren't permitted to consume the mushrooms we gathered. This catastrophe sparked a popular movement to halt the construction of new nuclear power plants and decommission old ones. The initiative was accepted.

DM: This radioactive cloud settled over Europe mainly due to strong winds that blew from the White Sea in the Arctic across Russia and finally reached us.

How did you feel when you found out about the accident?

DM: I was a child at the time and didn't really understand. You can't feel nuclear radiation. But the adults talked about it a lot.

Did people panic, too?

Solomia Horyn (SH): Not here. But in our main town, which is much closer to Chernobyl, there was a plant for a very short time. Officially, we were told very little about it. There was no internet at that time, so only radio and television were available. However, we were able to find out more through Radio Liberty and Voice of America. The local media was not allowed to publish additional details. Later, we heard that our workers were going to build a sarcophagus over the destroyed reactor to protect us. A few days later, the military arrived with buses to evacuate the entire city of Pripyat. The evacuees were given apartments so they could live safely.

DM: It will probably take about 800 years to fully assess the consequences of the catastrophe, such as the mutations that have developed in us. I was in school that day, but I clearly remember how hot it was. It was my first time participating in the May Day celebrations as a schoolchild. Everyone had to go to the parade.

SH: In cities and larger towns, all factory and business workers were required to attend the parade to demonstrate their satisfaction and enthusiasm for their work to the government. We were told that the extreme heat was the result of unusual weather for April—more like midsummer. Some people got sunburned at the parade. Any sensible person would have advised everyone to stay home.

---

4 https://fhs.ucu.edu.ua/en/documents/mizhnarodna-naukovo-praktychna-konferentsiya-psyhologichnyy-suprovid-do-pid-chas-i-pislya-viyny/

This would have been especially true in the immediate vicinity of the disaster because it would have been the only right decision. About twenty years later, we finally learned more about the people who worked in Chernobyl after the catastrophe. I had a neighbor who worked there, but we were only told that he died because he smoked too much.

Why weren't the possible consequences of the catastrophe discussed?

SM: Perhaps the belief at the time was that it would only affect those who participated in the cleanup after the accident. These people were not given protective suits or masks for their work. They were exposed to dangerous radiation for extended periods at the damaged nuclear power plant. To me, the fact that these people were treated this way in our country is another catastrophe. Everyone else had to go to school or work as usual.

What did your parents tell you about it?

DM: At first, they didn't say anything because they didn't know anything themselves. After a few days, when some people called us, they told us a few things. At the time, you could only find out more through these contacts.

SH: The accident occurred while Mikhail Gorbachev was president of the Soviet Union and attempting to implement his perestroika plan. When he realized it was impossible, he dissolved the Soviet Union and formed a new state.

What you are telling me shows the inhumanity of communism even today.

SH: Yes, that is true. We only received news of the accident and nothing more. Later, we heard from some people that a senior civil servant in charge of the nuclear industry committed suicide. He wanted to tell us something, but he was afraid. He knew the whole truth. Some in our media knew something, too, and could have told us.

DM: Of course, the children did not understand these things yet. My parents thought we were lucky to live in western Ukraine and said we should be grateful that we could continue getting our energy from the close-by Rivne nuclear power plant. They also said that experts from Japan had come to help us.

Now, people can go on tourist excursions there.

DM: In this contaminated area, scientists from all over the world are studying animals with unusual changes.

Collapse of the Soviet Union

The collapse of the Soviet Union was the next significant event.

SH: I know people in the West believed that it could become an independent state. A referendum on December 1 of that year confirmed this declaration, with over 90 percent of votes cast in favor.

After the fall of the Berlin Wall, did any of you think this outcome was possible?

SH: Not really. Some people in our country hoped that perestroika could easily bring about change here too and that more freedom would be possible. But we weren't particularly impressed by the fall of the Berlin Wall. However, we had a certain inkling that this special moment in our history might soon lead to Ukraine's revival. What happened to East Germany soon after made a much bigger impression on us. The execution of Ceaușescu and his wife on Christmas Day also made a big impression on us. Gorbachev was still a representative of the Soviet regime under which we had suffered, so we did not have much respect for him. So, we did not have much respect for him. To us, he was the epitome of the Soviet regime. Compared to previous leaders, he was new to us. However, we never treated him with the same respect that Europeans, particularly Germans, did. Under him, the government no longer seemed black and white, and we were no longer told only half the truth. Many things were kept from us, and we were often lied to.

This is why we weren't interested in news about current affairs. Of course, we could find out a lot from Radio Liberty about the heated debates in the West. So, when news of the sudden coup in Moscow came at the end of August 1991 while Gorbachev and his wife were on vacation in Crimea, we were shocked. We already knew that Gorbachev didn't have many friends in his government and wasn't popular with the people. This coup also triggered fears because it could affect us, too.

DH: I was almost twelve years old at the time. All I remember is that lots of people were talking about it. But I did not really understand it.

Ukraines Independence

One final question regarding these historical issues: The Soviet Union finally dissolved, and Ukraine declared independence. What was your experience of that?

SM: I attended all the demonstrations that had been organized in advance.

Was this the first Maidan?

YM: I still remember it very well. There was a big concert in Lviv with many choreographers. Some people even came to see us from Canada. We felt that a new era had begun for us. There was no mistaking it.

DM: I also remember a big concert organized by Ukrainian Youth for Christ in our stadium. There were many choir performances and lots of singing together. It was like the rebirth of our nation—everyone could feel it. It was a unique experience for everyone. There was also a big art festival in the city called Vyvych.

Becoming an Iconic Artist

Now, let us discuss your career as an artist specializing in sacred art. To what extent did your parents' religious beliefs influence your decision to pursue this field? How did your personal Christian convictions develop? During that period, it's important to note that the prevailing regime opposed religion and promoted the doctrine of "scientific atheism."

DM: We didn't grow up in a religious environment. I just recall visiting church with my grandmother in the early nineties.

YM: I recall you mentioning that, following the re-establishment of the Ukrainian Greek Catholic Church, you attended church with your family.

DM: Our family practiced Greek Catholicism and kept religious icons mostly out of tradition, not deep belief. I wasn't raised with strong religious values.

Have you been baptized?

DM: It wasn't commonly practiced at the time, but I didn't participate in First Communion due to restrictions. Nonetheless, some people attended despite these prohibitions. Subsequently, motivated by personal interest, I took Catholic instruction and received my First Communion. After that, I enrolled in a Catholic school and later pursued studies in art.

My father graduated from the Academy of Arts and worked as an artist-restorer at a museum. During my final year of school, I accompanied him to work several times. His responsibilities included restoring large objects at the Assumption Monastery in Univ, where he sometimes worked throughout the summer. Additional information about the monastery may be relevant. From 1934 to 1937, artists and monks painted the church and monastery walls. After the war, Soviet authorities destroyed or concealed these artworks until the monastery was returned to the Ukrainian Greek Catholic Church in 1992—a fate common to many Ukrainian churches of that era. The restoration process was complex and time-consuming. First, the paint applied over the church murals had to be carefully removed. Then, paint was skillfully reapplied to the residue remaining on the icons, successfully restoring their original appearance.

Were they not destroyed?

DM: The items were destroyed, but the remains were repainted with oil paints. The original icons could still be identified beneath the painted layers. In many cases, it was challenging to determine the previous arrangement. Restoration required careful work, millimeter by millimeter, using a scalpel to locate the correct positions. This detailed work demanded precision and patience.

Notably, the renowned Polish artist Jerzy Nowosielski also lived at this monastery for a time. He intended to gain a deeper understanding of the rites observed by the Ukrainian Greek Catholic Church. During the war, in 1943, Nowosielski developed an even greater appreciation for icons after visiting the National Museum in Lviv, where he was impressed by the artistry of the icons. While my father worked at the monastery, I learned to appreciate icons. I considered applying to the art academy like him, but he recommended that I start with a painter's apprenticeship in the restoration department at the renowned Ivan Trush Art School.

It was your father who introduced you to the restoration of sacred works of art, which later became your profession. Currently, however, you are no longer a restorer; you work as an independent artist. What led to this transition?

DM: Restoring works of art requires continuous learning. Based on my father's advice, I pursued a formal education in the field, completing a degree at the National Academy of Art in Lviv. Before making my decision, I evaluated different alternatives. I came across a video produced by the art academy that showed students painting icons in a contemporary and distinctive style. I enrolled at the academy to study sacred art. After finishing my studies, I worked as a professional artist. This transition occurred over time.

The Art of Danylo Movchan

How would you characterize your current professional activities? Currently, you work as a freelance artist, and your work has been featured in numerous exhibitions and has garnered international recognition.

DM: Initially, the purpose of learning art was to develop an individual style. Various techniques could be acquired, and foundational concepts for projects could be identified. Visiting exhibitions in museums and galleries helped me observe the themes contemporary artists were exploring.

My style is influenced by the tradition of old Ukrainian icons from the 14th and 16th centuries, as well as by elements drawn from 20th-century art history and aspects of contemporary life.

YM: While studying at the academy, Danylo practiced at home until he mastered a new icon-painting technique and began creating work he was satisfied with.

DM: Visiting European museums and participating in international plein air events provided opportunities for artistic growth. Both younger and more experienced artists participated, offering chances to learn from one another. Shared perspectives led to collaborations reflected in our artwork.

Do you mean the friends painting icons?

DM: We first met at a plein air event in Nowica, Poland, where we painted together. During these sessions, we realized that, rather than merely replicating traditional icons, we could also interpret them differently through our work. This marked a distinct shift from previous methods of painting icons. Our first major exhibition took place at the National Museum in Lviv in early 2010 and featured these newly interpreted icons.

It is assumed that each artist continually advances their work.

DM: I prefer to say that I am evolving, and I will leave the analysis of my development or thematic focus to art historians.

When did you first try to create a new icon?

DM: The Academy of Arts was the location. Only a few Fifteenth-century icons were copied there. I was interested in creating original icon compositions. After graduating, my work was exhibited at the National Museum in Lviv. Thanks to Ostap Lozynsky, I learned about a new icon, which I subsequently acquired from Iconart.

Do you work similarly to him?

DM: Although our perspectives align in many ways, we each have our own artistic approach. I was first exposed to his work at the plein air event in Novica. Collaborating with him and observing our painting process side by side is both stimulating and beneficial for our professional development.

Is it possible to earn a living from art in the current market?

DM: I am currently self-employed, and my work provides sufficient income to support my family. However, there are times when income is inconsistent, and payments may be delayed.

How would you characterize your style?

DM: It is challenging to articulate this precisely. Describing oneself or one's artistic work, and categorizing it definitively, can be difficult. In my case, I would characterize it as an integration of various styles.

A combination of symbolic elements and minimalist design?

DM: Not in all cases. A student may study this topic in a master's thesis. In my art, there are both sacred works and other types. Within my sacred art, I address themes related to human life as well as various subjects, employing multiple styles. In general, your assessment is accurate. My approach emphasizes minimalism and symbolism. Before painting, I examine the subject, gather inspiration, and consider my thoughts during the creative process. I strive to express these insights with originality. Nonetheless, it is often challenging for an artist to articulate their own practice; art critics are typically more adept at such analysis.

Your art powerfully conveys the reality of war and helps us in the West understand what is happening in Ukraine. Your new watercolors have a strong impact and offer meaningful insight. I'm impressed by your minimalist and symbolic style in both icons and watercolors. Using few elements draws attention to details and adds meaning, aligning with the simplicity central to my Protestant faith: "Christ alone, God's grace alone, faith alone." Your work also lends itself well to meditation and prayer.

DM: When painting icons, I pray. Painting only traditional icons limits the ability to create original designs. Traditional icons have always been marketable, but new icons do not require marketing to sell. It is not a priority whether people consistently appreciate art or not. The current approach is to paint based on what comes to mind. Some people resist new icons because they differ from tradition—certain Catholics, for example, are not receptive to this art. Yet in Poland, I find our work is generally well received.

Anyone can join our plein airs, not just professional artists. If you're interested in art, feel free to participate. However, to progress as an artist, some formal art study is recommended. Some believe icon painting must stay traditional, but history shows icons have evolved. Why shouldn't this continue? Simply copying old models limits creativity. True artists seek to express themselves, not just replicate tradition.

Artists today bring their own vision for color. You may wish to paint a figure in a new way, rather than following tradition. Icons from Ukraine in the early 20th century are a good example. These icons deviated from established conventions. Artists such as Mikhailo Osinchuk[5], Modest Sosenko[6], and Mikhailo[7] are examples of this style, Boychuk or Petro Kholodny? Later, all these famous artists were killed, and their works were destroyed.[8] However, some managed to escape to Europe or the U.S. and were fortunate to avoid our system of persecution and punishment.

When I observe global events, including those in Ukraine, I share Karl Barth's perspective. Discussing world dangers like the Cold War with Eduard Thurneysen, Barth remarked: "The world is dark. Don't let your guard down – ever! Governance exists not only in Moscow, Washington, or Beijing, but also on earth and from above. God is in control, so I am not afraid. God won't let us fall; we are governed." I asked you also to paint an icon of Christ as ruler of the world, so I could look beyond troubling news and conflict. The Bible ends not with the Apocalypse, but with John's vision: "Behold, I am making all things new... I am Alpha and Omega."

5 https://en.uartlib.org/ukrainian-artists/osinchuk-michael/
6 https://en.wikipedia.org/wiki/Modest_Sosenko
7 https://en.wikipedia.org/wiki/Mykhailo_Boychuk
8 The so called "Shot Renaissance". Under Stalin, the best modern artists in Ukraine were shot in a forest in Karelia in 1937: https://www.nzz.ch/feuilleton/erschossene-renaissance-wie-stalin-unter-ukrainischen-kuenstlern-wuetete-ld.1751792

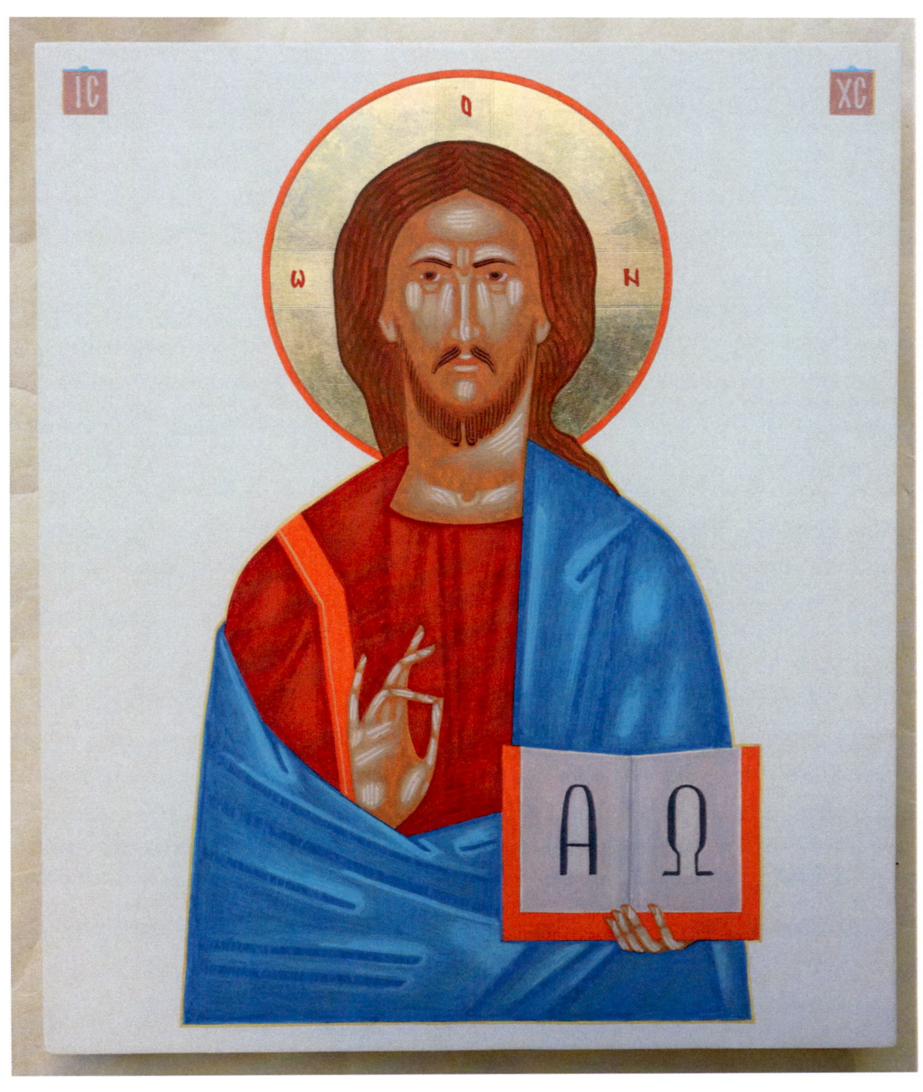
IC
XC
O ω N
A Ω

The Outbreak of the War

On February 24, 2022, the conflict began. On that day, you were at home when you received information that school was cancelled.

DM: The day began early. Yaryna initially intended to accompany the children to school; however, she was informed that all schools were closed.

Were you surprised by this announcement?

DM: Although we suspected it might happen, the news was still shocking. Earlier, we wondered if war was imminent.

SM: My daughter informed me about the outbreak of war. I acknowledged the news and subsequently observed long queues at banks and pharmacies, as individuals urgently sought to purchase fuel. It is surprising to witness such acts of aggression in the present day.

DM: Following Euromaidan (2013–2014), Russia's control over Ukraine weakened. The previous pro-Russian government was removed, reducing Russian influence in energy, art, and culture, as Ukrainian-language books and local music became more prevalent. You could feel everywhere that Putin had lost us.

Do you have friends in Russia?

DM: Yes, a few—just on social media. I asked a Russian friend on Instagram about Ukraine, and she said she couldn't understand Russia's actions either. My Facebook friends reacted differently: some were scared, some uninterested, and some supportive before eventually blocking me. A colleague who is also an icon painter initially expressed understanding regarding the distress caused by the Russian attack. However, he soon began writing me insulting words.

His reaction turned your friend into an adversary.

DM: I tried to tell him the truth, but he wouldn't listen. Few believed we could defend ourselves. First, there was a lie; then, responsibility for the war was incorrectly placed on Western nations, reflecting Russia's tendency to portray outsiders as adversaries. The

Russian government should focus on improving citizens' quality of life in line with public aspirations.

Yesterday, I read that the head of the Russian Orthodox Church stated support for the war during a synod.

SH: The view that Russia should pursue conflict with Western nations is also reflected within this Russian church. Historically, it has not been uncommon for the church to support or align itself with state ideology. The results of these actions are reflected in the current conflict involving us.

I know a Ukrainian woman living in Germany who trained as an interpreter in Russia. While in St. Petersburg, she met Putin multiple times. She wrote to me: "For me, this man has always been the Antichrist. I never trusted him. You could see it in his eyes."

SH: You should know that no one here can really understand the Russians. They repeatedly ask us, "Why do you oppose our politicians?" Why are you removing great Russian literature from your libraries and throwing it away? We Russians have the best literature in the world!" After all, Russian ballet is world-famous!"

They should also be informed that their bombs are destroying libraries in our country, eliminating our Ukrainian literature that we have only recently been able to publish again. Their bombs are also destroying the many famous Russian works in our libraries.

To me, Russians are simply chauvinists. They see themselves as superior and look down on us. That was the case in the Soviet era, too. Even then, Moscow was everything, and everything had to go according to Moscow's plan. Other nations were oppressed in the same way we are today. We aren't claiming that we're better than them. We are all the same and have many things in common. However, they are being outrageous against us again today.

Patriarch Kiril, leader of the Russian Church, claims Russian Christianity is the sole true faith. During church holidays, Putin publicly presents himself as a Christian by kissing icons and posing for photos while praying. He simultaneously spreads falsehoods and eliminates his opponents. To me, Putin is the devil – a "diabolos," as he is called in Greek – a perverter of the truth. Kiril states that Russian soldiers who have died in action will be granted forgiveness for all their sins and will be assured a place in heaven. This message does not conform to accepted norms.

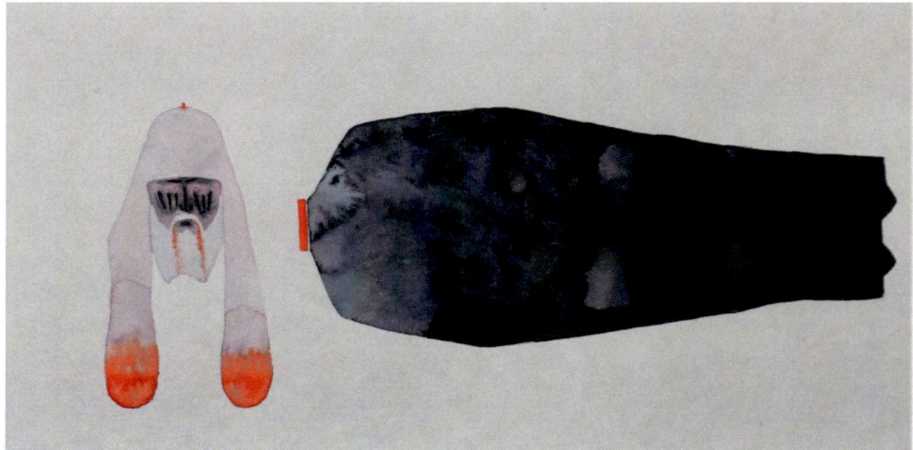

Death of Patriarch Kirill. Watercolor on paper, 20 x 40 cm

The Decision to Paint Watercolors About the War

Soon after the war started, I saw your first war watercolors on Facebook and wrote to say I was impressed.

DM: During the initial days, I found it difficult to paint effectively. My output was routine and lacked expression due to the persistent thoughts occupying my mind.

Were you confused?

DM: I was overwhelmed by fear and pain, unable to comprehend anything. Still, you need to focus and find a way to express yourself.

Experiencing this creates intense tension, making it hard to focus and triggering panic. Some people become closed off; others grow cynical or turn to drinking. After two years of war, people adapt and eventually grow indifferent as conflict becomes routine.

DM: Initially, I feared for my family's safety and felt responsible for protecting my children from danger. We were unconcerned about losing our house and never considered leaving the country. Millions of Ukrainians relocated to safer areas either within Ukraine or in Western countries. Ukrainian forces mounted a defensive effort, leading Russian troops to withdraw from several regions.

Your work today serves as a record of the experiences of war. When the conflict began, its impact on you became apparent. Rather than participating in combat, you choose to work with your brushes. During the first weeks, you created new pieces almost daily; later, your pace decreased. Over time, these works collectively became a public visual diary.

YM: Faced with a challenging situation, Danylo recognized the need to act. Upon engaging in watercolor painting, he experienced a sense of calm. This creative pursuit proved beneficial for his well-being.

Painting has also been beneficial for you. Your work helps others understand the situation. Other artists have also started portraying war in their art. Switzerland did not experience direct warfare on its territory during the major conflicts of the twentieth century. However, the country maintained defensive preparations in case of an attack. During World War II, the Swiss government made a series of agreements with Hitler's Germany, which are still debated today. The Swiss authorities communicated a consistent message: "The boat is full."

However, even those with Western comforts are not immune to hardship. We assume we're safe until a doctor tells us we have cancer and our world falls apart. You feel lost, wondering why this happened to you. You fight to survive, but the outcome remains uncertain.

SM: We say that war has no human face. Although war is said to lack humanity, people still intentionally kill each other. At the same time, people deliberately kill others.

Is humanity regressing? Why can't Ukraine achieve peace after enduring so many wars and renewed trauma?

SM: The loss of so many soldiers has a significant impact on society. Many of these individuals are highly qualified professionals and dedicated volunteers who contribute greatly to the community. Their expertise, as well as their potential future contributions—including their roles as prospective fathers—underscore the magnitude of this loss. Their absence will be particularly impactful during post-war reconstruction efforts due to the loss of their knowledge and experience. For us, this war will never end, perhaps it will for our children, but not for our generation. I truly believe that we will always be pessimists.

Danylo, you later wrote on Facebook: "Many people describe terrible events using this proverb: 'War destroys what people build, but it's not abstract. It's caused by millions of Russians willing to kill, rape, and maim."

DM: I recently spoke with someone who recommended several books to help me better understand current events. He recommended books about World War II. Reading about life before the war showed that people were unprepared. I didn't think history would repeat itself, but it has—with millions of deaths and people displaced. In 1938, the outcome seemed inevitable. It was only realistic to expect it.

Following that, even amid the Cold War, a period of compromise emerged. The West prospered, and the sentiment "Never again war!" prevailed. Currently, prospects for a world free of conflict are diminishing.

At the same time, Western societies lack a shared framework to distinguish truth from falsehood. Truth is increasingly regarded as subjective, with individuals determining their own standards of right and wrong. Russian propaganda can effectively target us, often leading to feelings of insecurity through its messaging. The current environment is rife with uncertainty about the future. Nevertheless, it is crucial to maintain hope and resilience in the face of these challenges.

SM: Evil arises alongside good and must be clearly identified and condemned. In Germany, Nazism and anti-Semitism are explicitly prohibited and penalized. In Russia, while some individuals act with decency, Stalinist views persist, and communist ideology endures.

DM: The current conflict can be seen because of the belief that Ukraine should be incorporated into the Russian Empire. This situation has parallels with events that took place in this region during the 20th century. Russia, for example, consider our "shot generation" murdered the country's intelligentsia in a forest in Karelia in 1937. Time will tell. The present war marks only the start of greater trouble. Many Ukrainian intellectuals have left to avoid repeating such experiences.

Ukrainian art has consistently reflected Ukrainian identity and culture. As a result, art and intellectuals in Ukraine have often been viewed as significant by Russia. In the present context, I continue to express my views and maintain my presence. I aim to uphold my Ukrainian identity and refrain from actions that would prevent its expression. When war began, my mind was crowded with thoughts. When I work on paper, I simply follow whatever inspires me in the moment.

What were the responses to your pictures?

DM: I received many responses from friends, artists, clergy, strangers, and people abroad who offered help and support. What helps me most is continuing to paint, as my art allows me to share the situation in our country.

Examples

Your watercolors blend minimalism and symbolism, featuring repeating motifs that reveal subtle differences each time.

DM: This is partly due to the recurrence of similar adverse events throughout this conflict.

You once said that you couldn't paint icons anymore, but I think you still do.

DM: To paint an icon, one must be calm and focused beyond daily concerns. One must also have inner peace to pray.

Your watercolors reflect the spiritual dimension of this war, which is influenced by the Russian Orthodox Church. However, since the conflict targets Ukraine and the West with an "anti-Christian essence," I consider some of your works sacred art. Some of your work could be considered sacred art, but I don't view most of it that way.

DM: I have noticed recurring themes in your work, including references to gunshots, bombs, explosions, destruction, casualties, injuries, and blood. These elements are commonly associated with war and include depictions of fatalities, injured individuals, loss of limbs, and visible bloodshed. For instance, you depict two individuals with severe burns, but their status—whether they are alive or deceased—remains unclear.

However, I also see works with Christian symbolism, like this one. Time and again, I see works of yours with very clear Christian symbolism, such as Christ on the cross. At the same time, the cross is in the middle of Ukraine. To me, this means that Christ knows about the Ukrainians' suffering through his own.

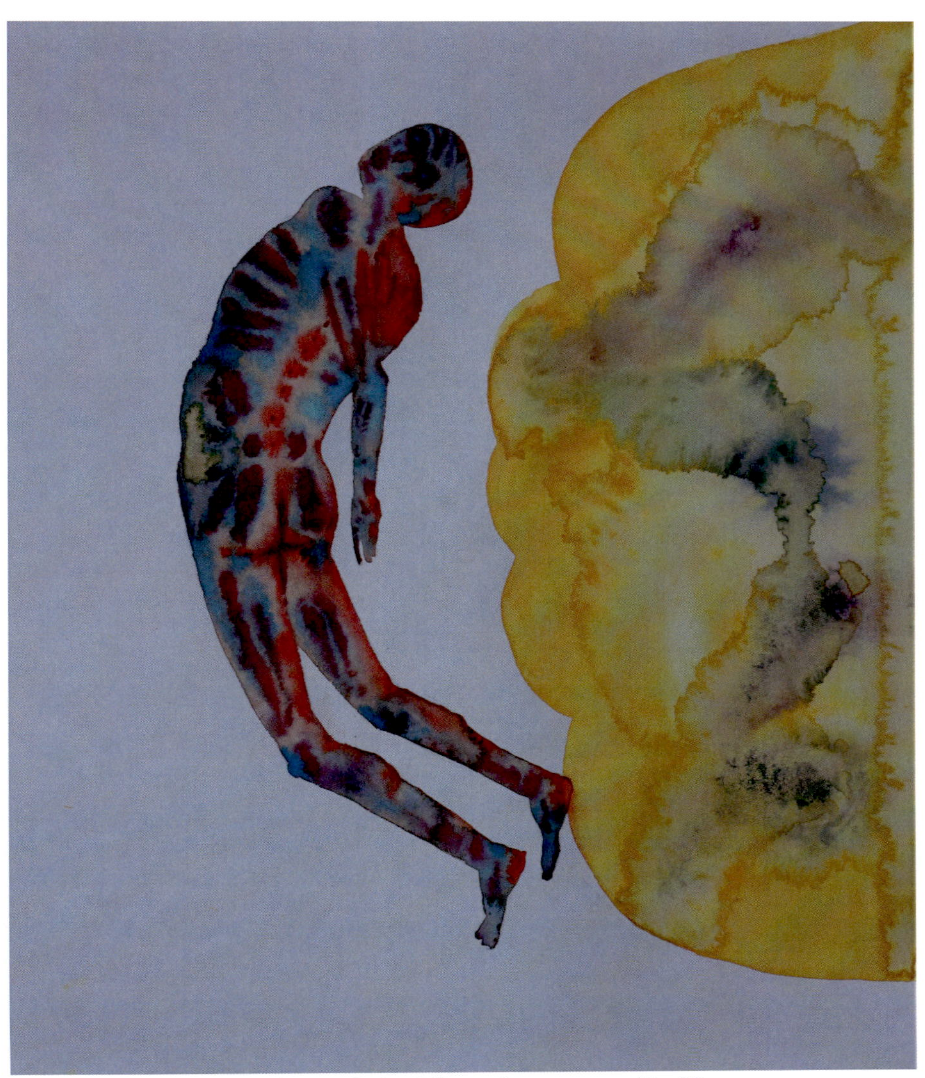

Embroidery explosion. Watercolor on paper, 40 x 35 cm

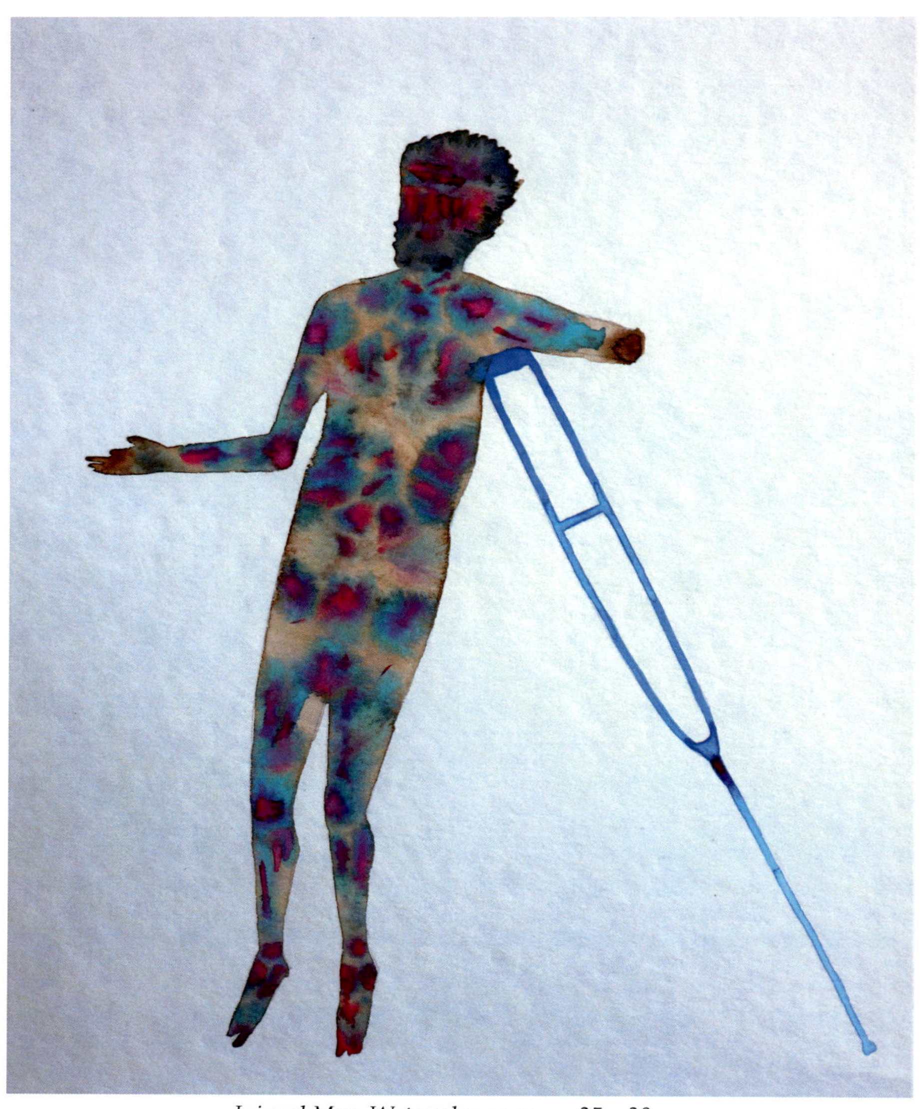

Injured Man. Watercolor on paper, 25 x 30 cm

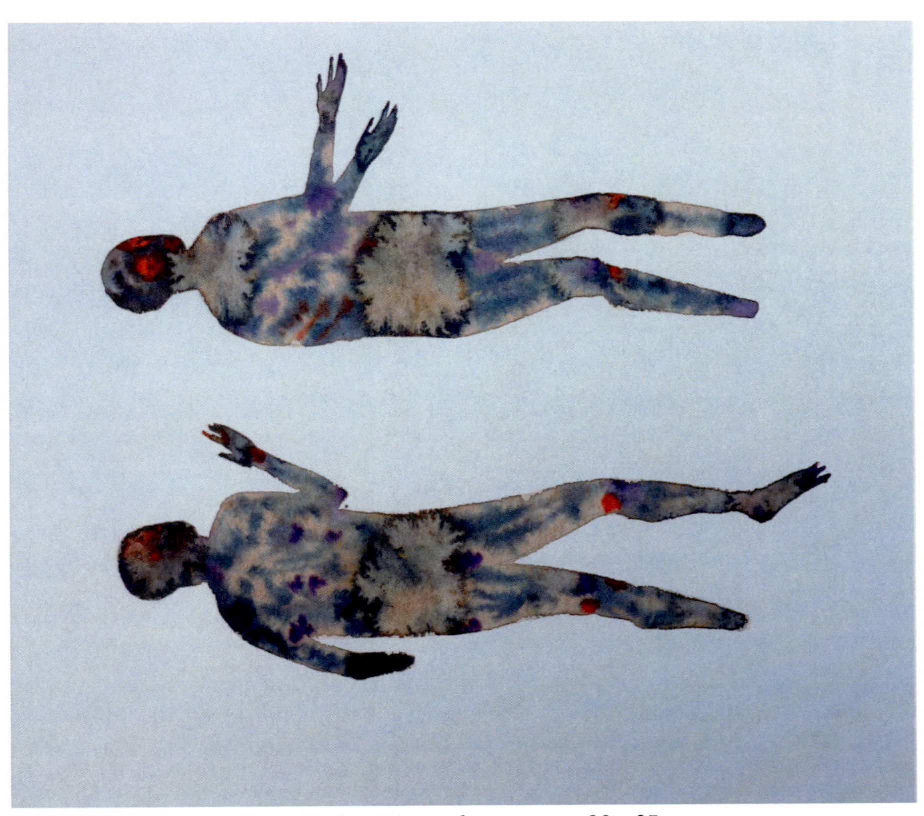

Burnt Bodies. Watercolor on paper, 30 x 35 cm

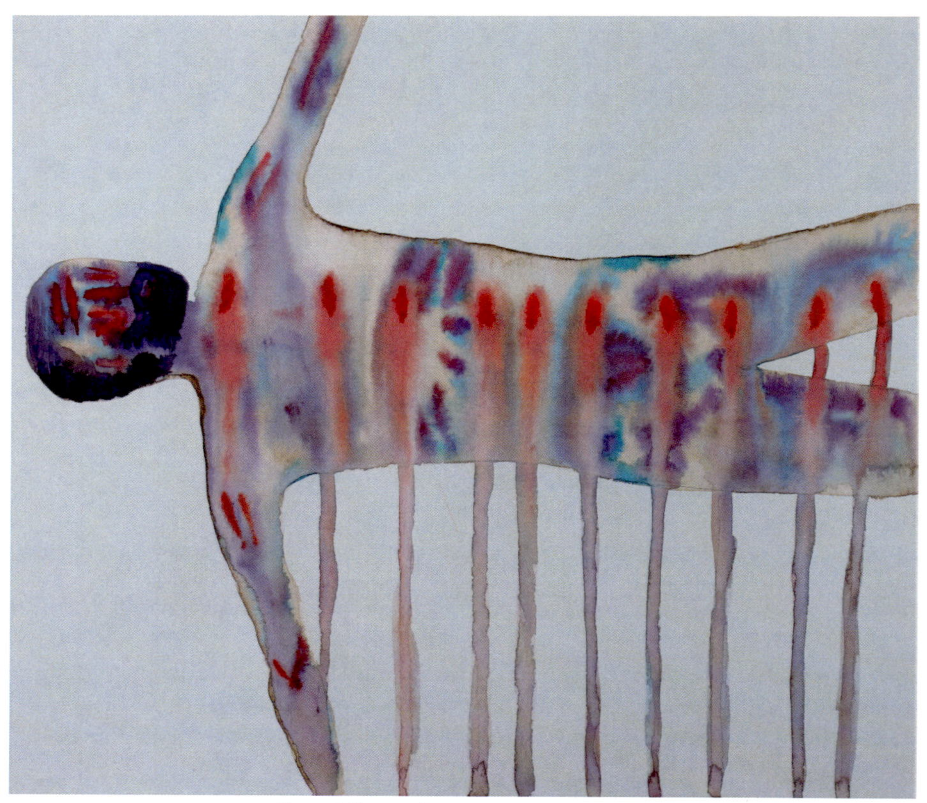

Shots. Watercolor on paper, 30 x 34 cm

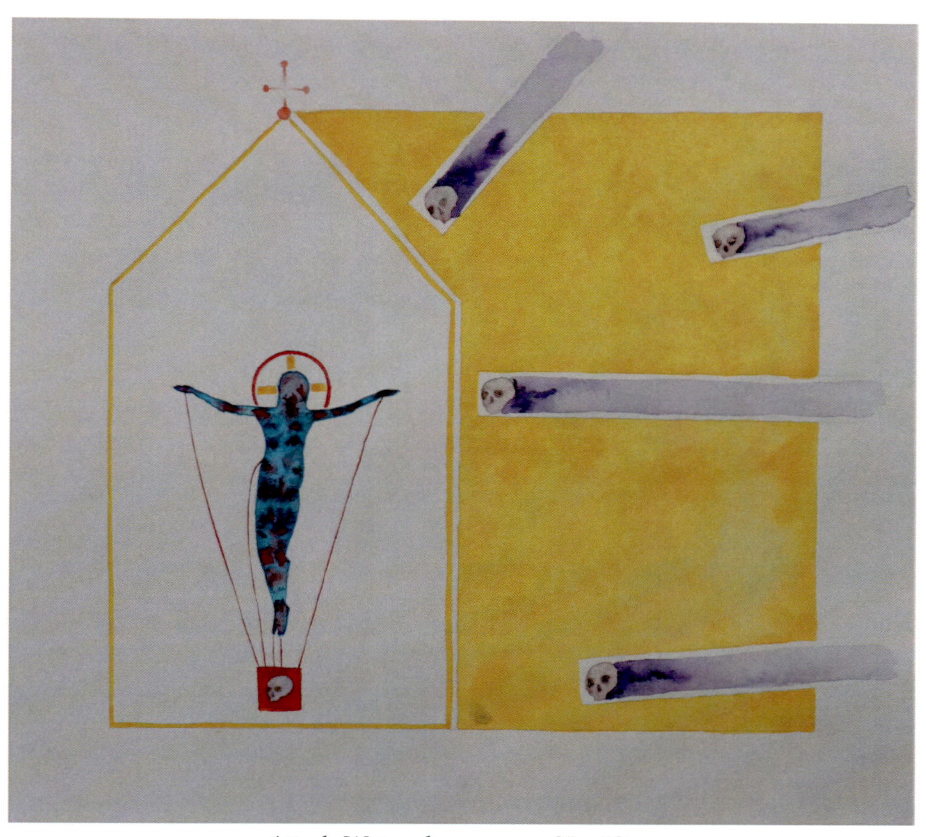

Attack. Watercolor on paper, 35 x 40 cm

You portray individuals in a manner reminiscent of Christ on the cross: completely unprotected, vulnerable to Russian attacks, and stripped of their dignity. One example is a tortured wife.

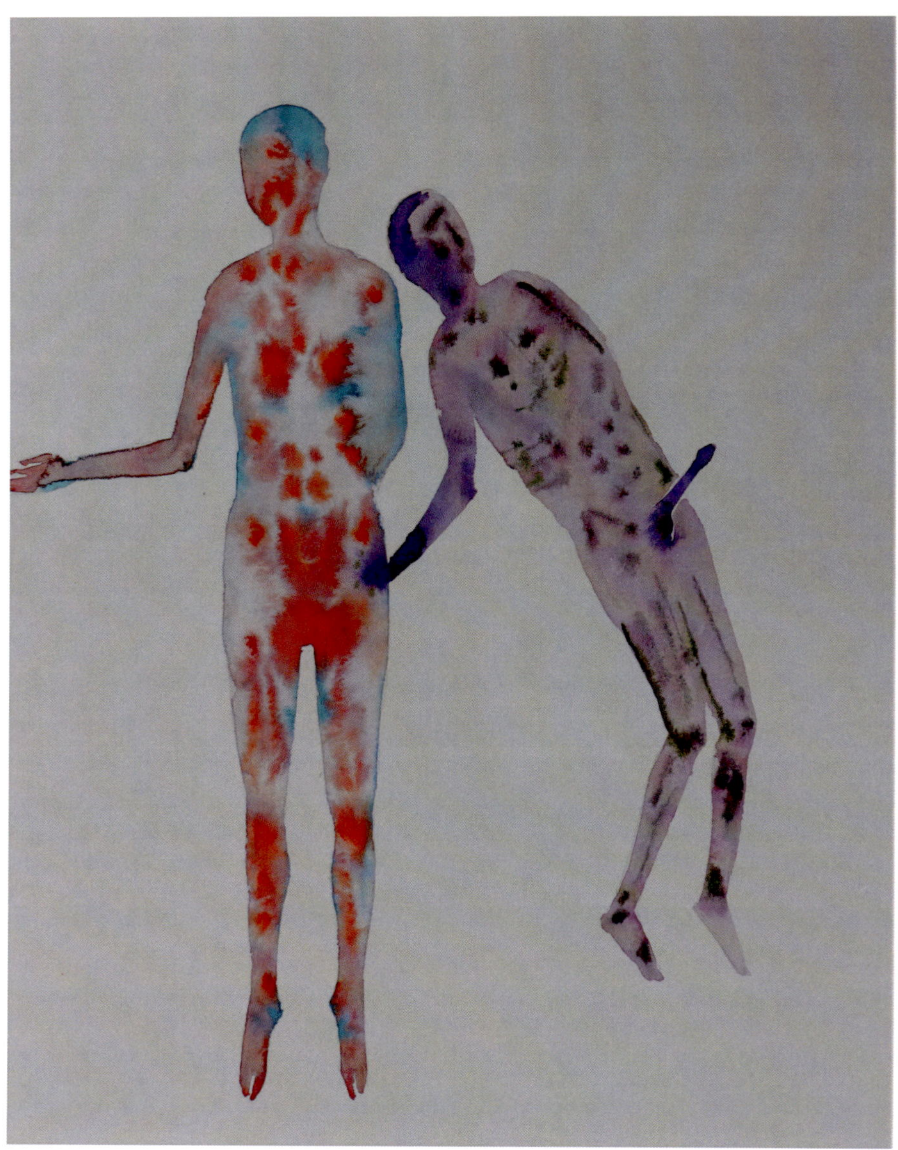

Russian raping Ukrainian woman. Watercolor on paper, 40 x 35 cm

The colors blue and yellow of Ukraine appear in your designs and color the cross before the skull.

This detail suggests that mortality has become a symbolic "cross" for Ukraine, representing a shared burden.

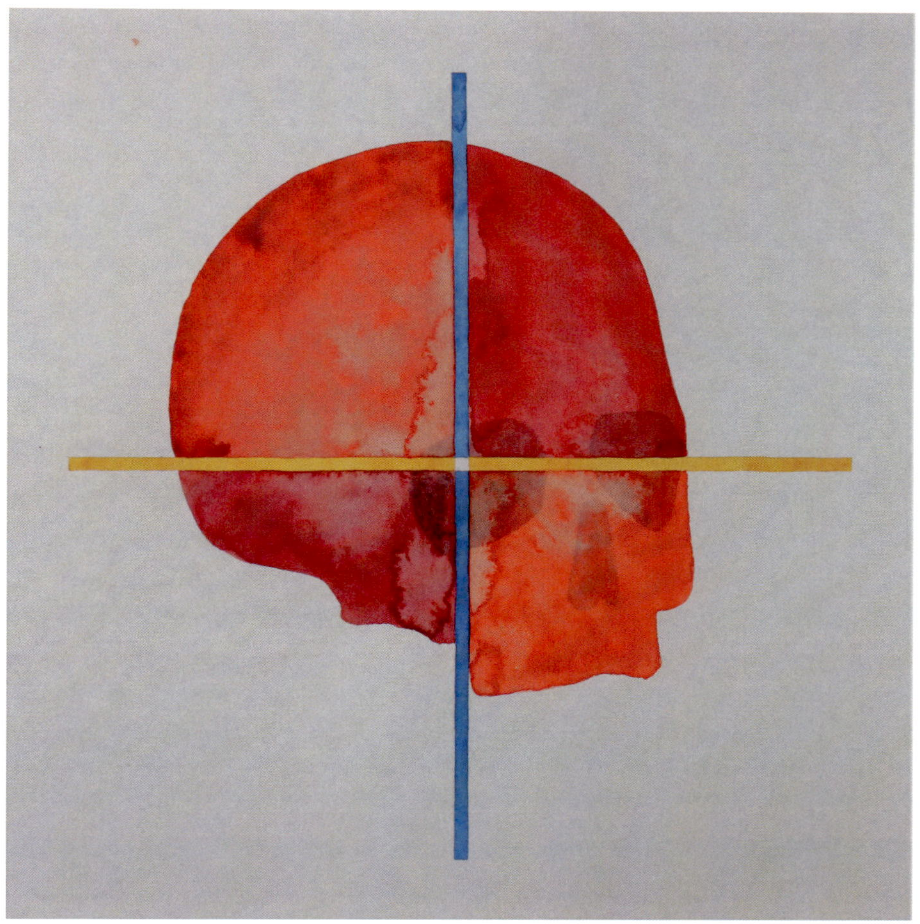

War. Watercolor on paper, 35 x 35

How did you hear about the war?

That morning, I heard the news on the radio and then watched Swiss TV broadcasts showing initial images of the incident and discussions about Ukraine's prospects for survival. Ukrainians quickly began supporting one another and their soldiers. Our country also quickly organized donation drives and private aid efforts. Russian troop movements to Belarus near Ukraine's borders signaled longstanding threats aimed at pressuring our government. Some officials sought dialogue with Putin to prevent conflict, but he deceived the West.

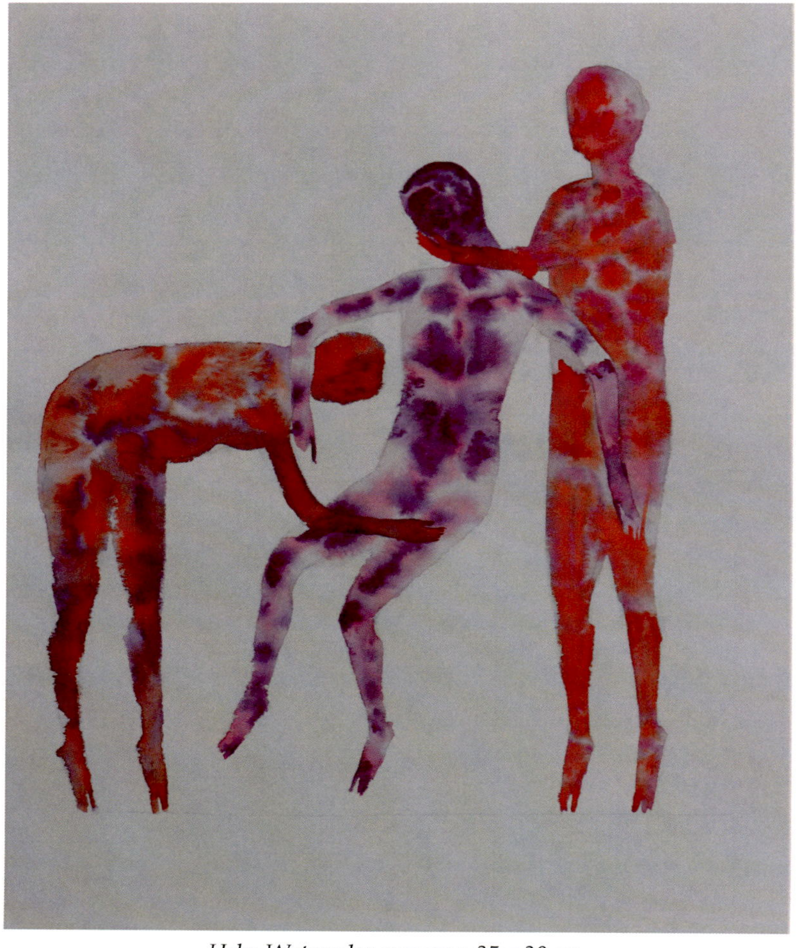

Help. Watercolor on paper, 35 x 30 cm

One of the watercolors is titled "Adam," which denotes "man" and symbolizes humanity as a creation. The artwork depicts an individual observing events in their country, such as explosions and fatalities. The person considers questions including: What has caused these events? What are appropriate responses? What possible future developments may arise? Will Ukraine continue as a nation?

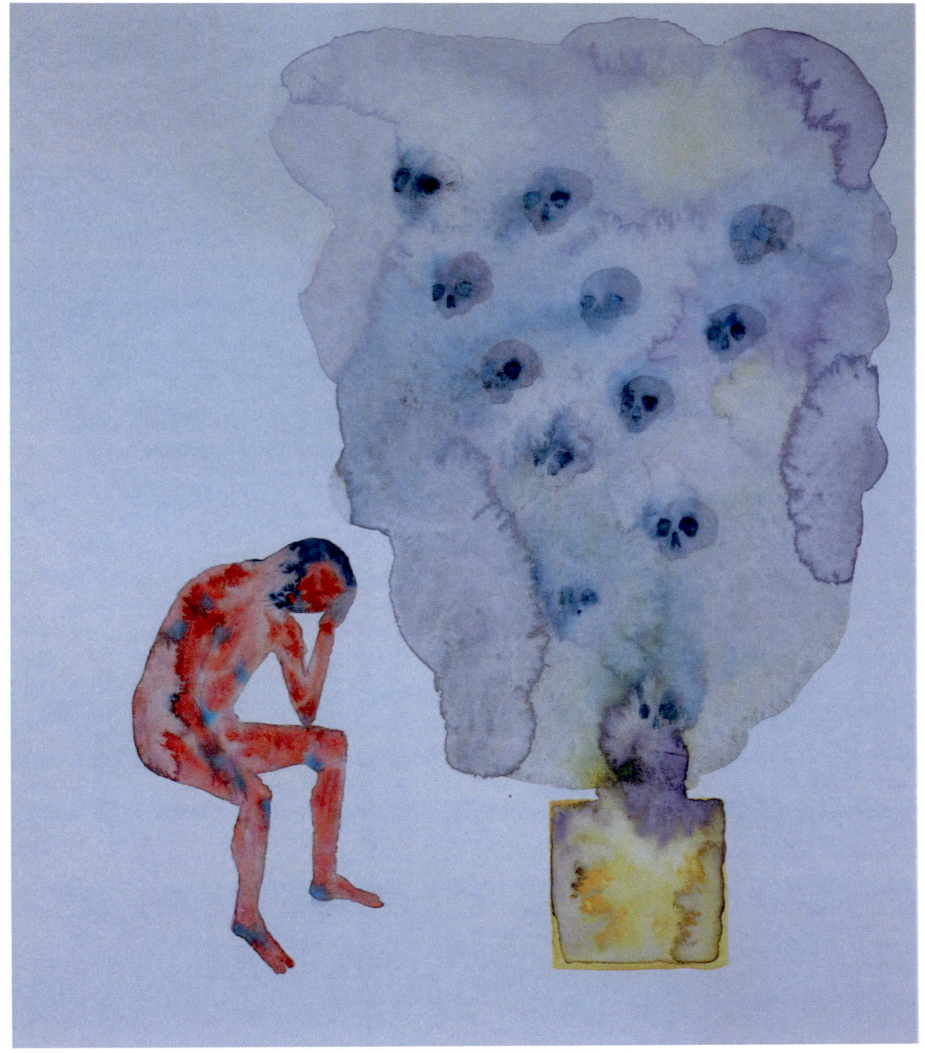

Adam. Watercolor on paper, 35 x 40 cm

The Lament Psalms in the Bible express feelings of despair through direct, unembellished language. These prayers offer candid reflections without omission and occasionally express doubt about divine action. Such approaches raise questions about their appropriateness. If I were to adopt a similar method, my prayers could provide psychological relief. (Refer to the appendix for a detailed analysis of my perspective on the concept of divine justice.)

How has this conflict affected your individual convictions? Have you experienced uncertainty about God's existence, or have your views on God changed? Were there alternative viewpoints that became more important to you during this period? Furthermore, did your faith offer support, and if so, how was this manifested?[9]

DM: Thank you for your thoughtful questions. I need some time to reflect, but I still believe that Christ is the Son of God.

9 See in the appendix the essay "Job and the Justice of God"

Dariusz Pado: Image Capture

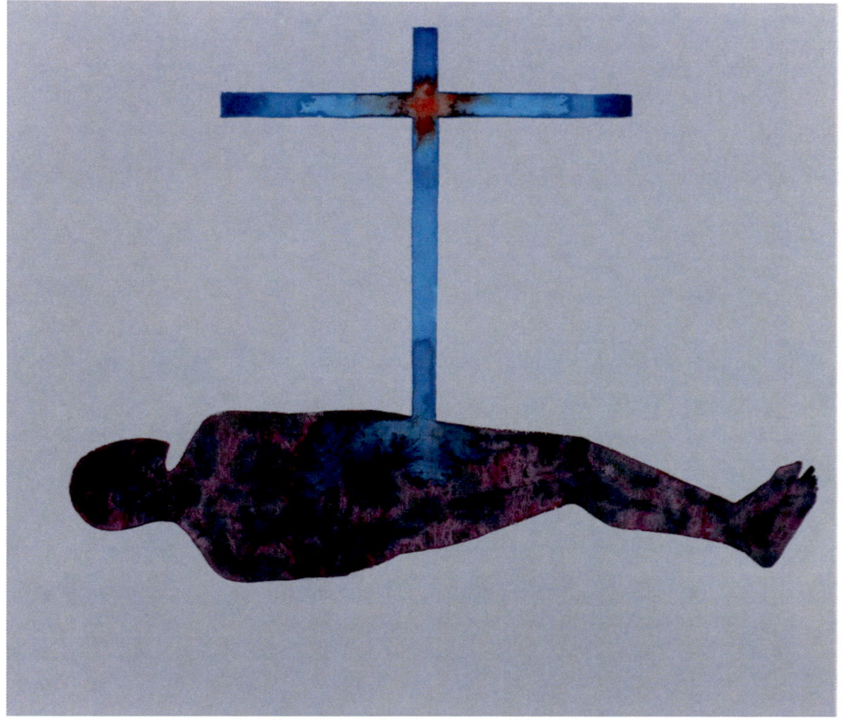

Death. Watercolor on paper, 30 x 30 cm

At an intersection a pedestrian
lying on the roadway
while a cyclist is positioned
near his bicycle

A smartphone captures several houses
with the cameraman
using a simple setup
for a natural background

A dog is watching
over a companion
but becomes
unsettled

Image Selection 2022

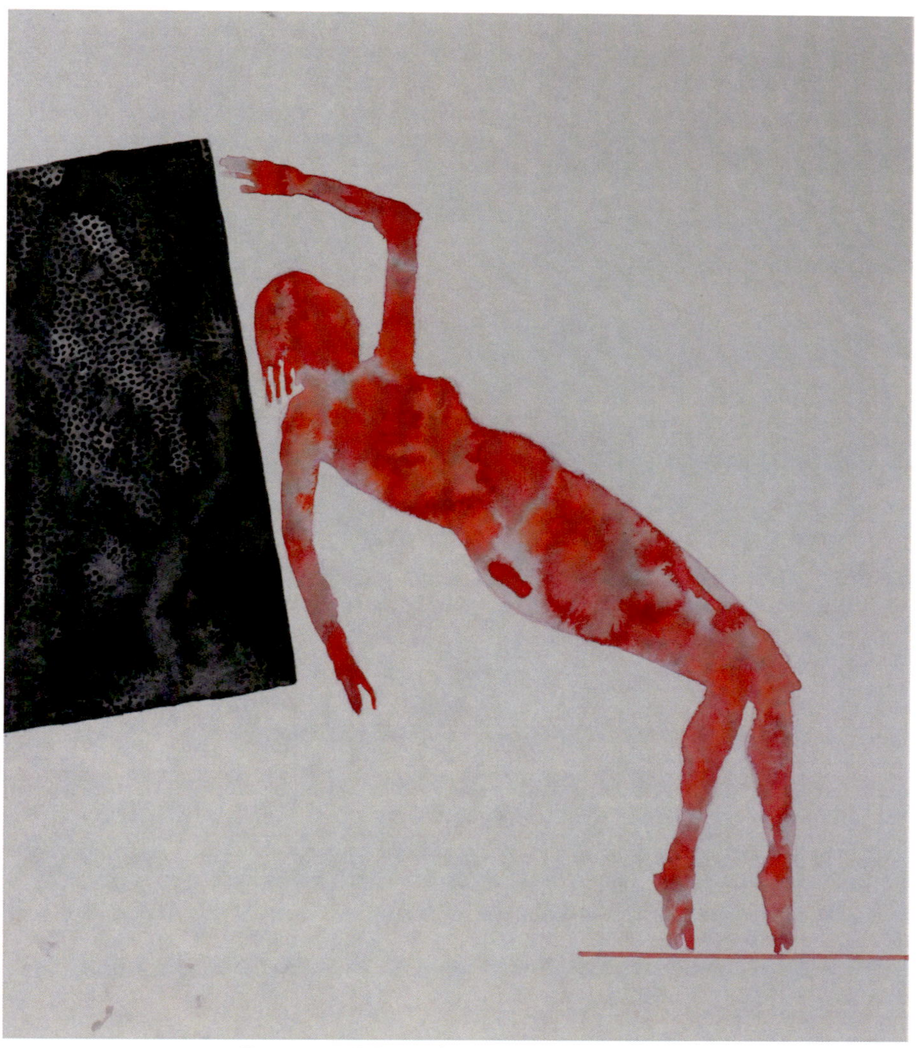

Deterrence. Watercolor on paper, 40 x 35 cm

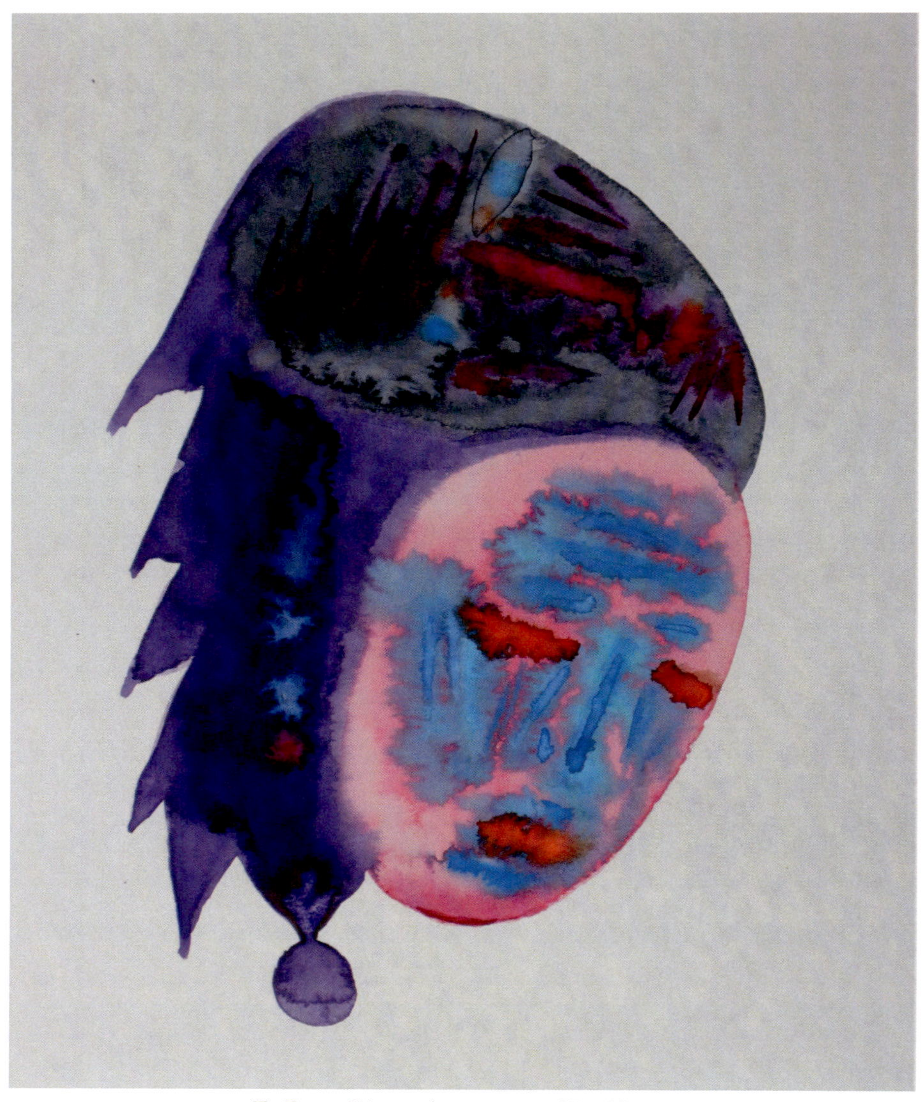

To Faces. Watercolor on paper, 35 x 30 cm

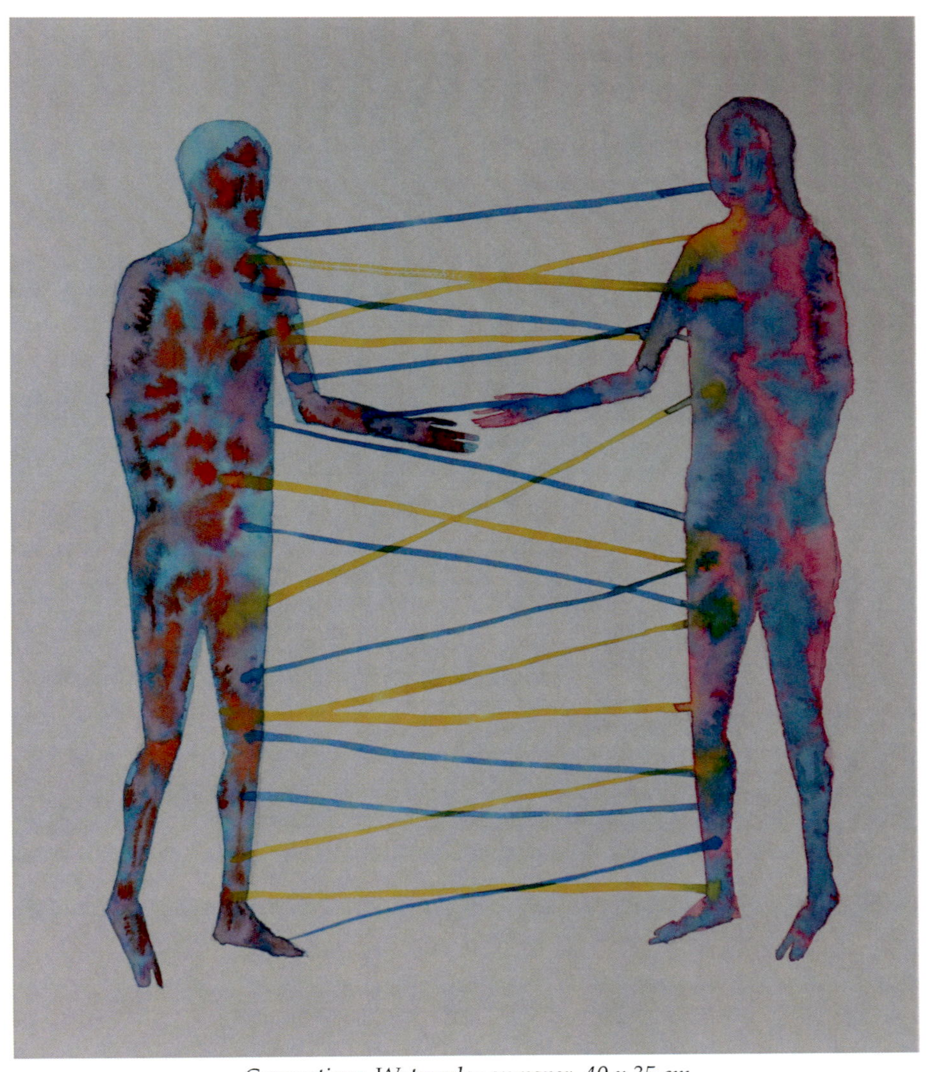

Connections. Watercolor on paper, 40 x 35 cm

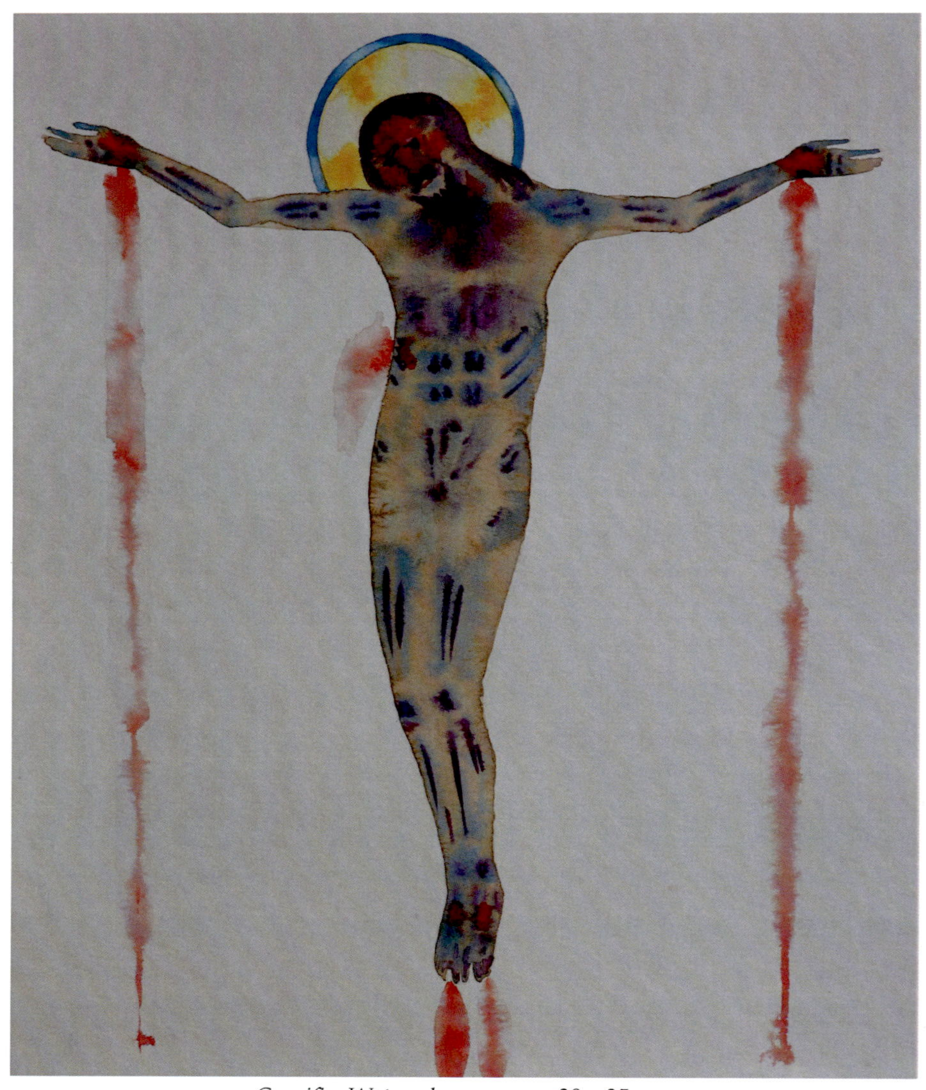

Cruzifix. Watercolor on paper, 30 x 25 cm

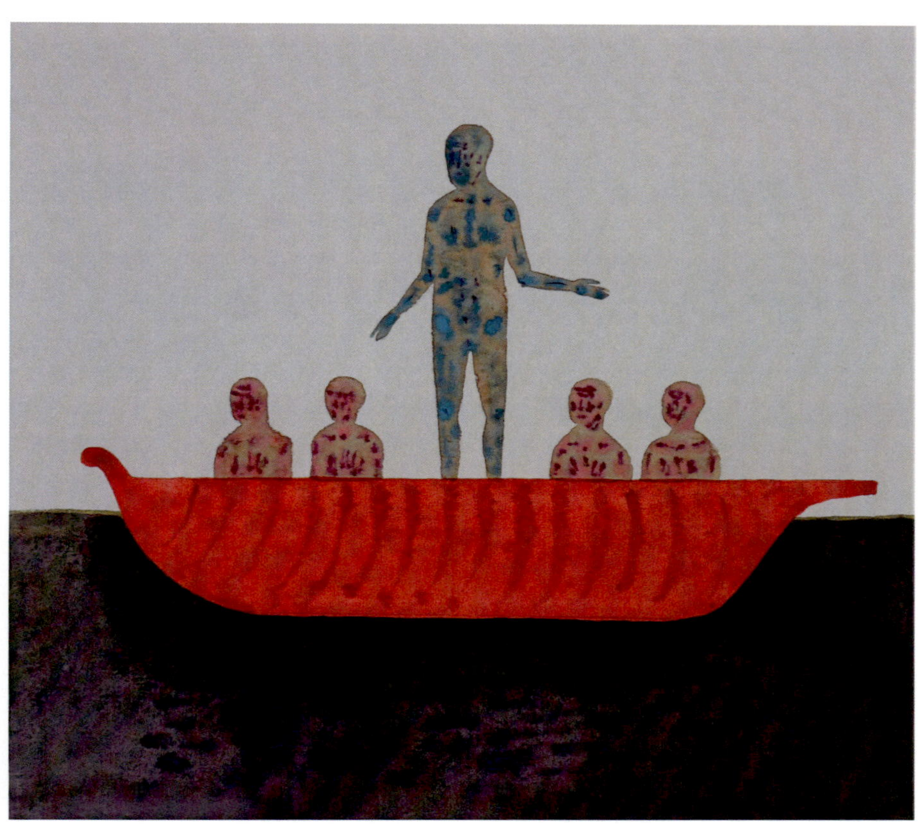

Charon. Watercolor on paper, 35 x 40 cm

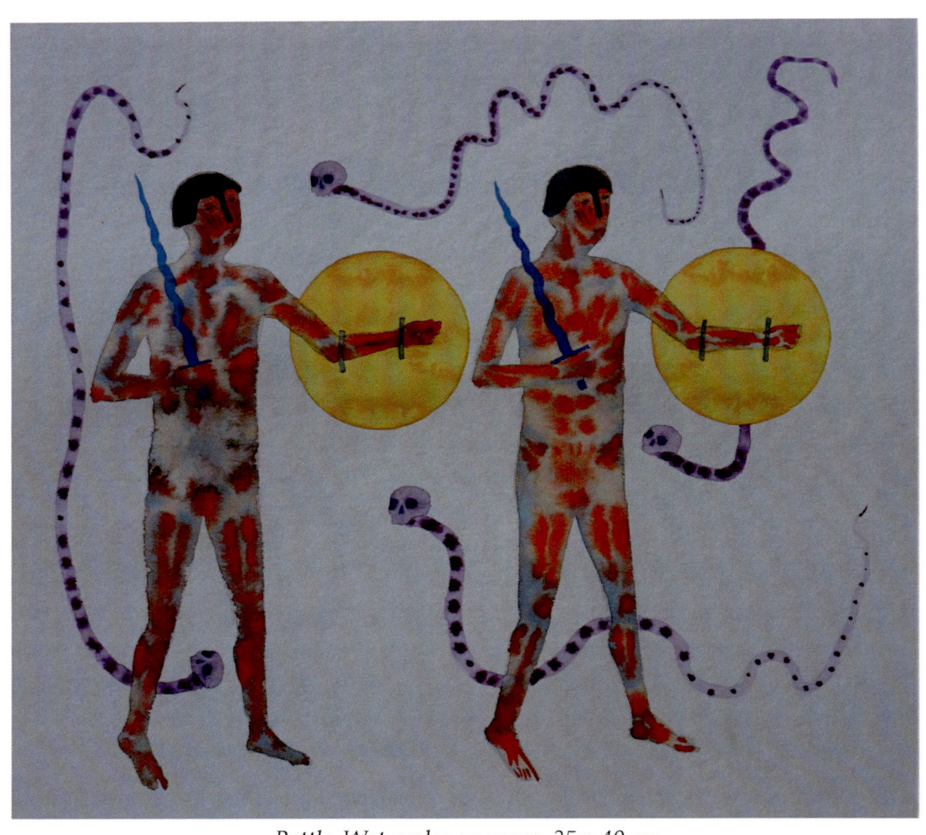

Battle. Watercolor on paper, 35 x 40 cm

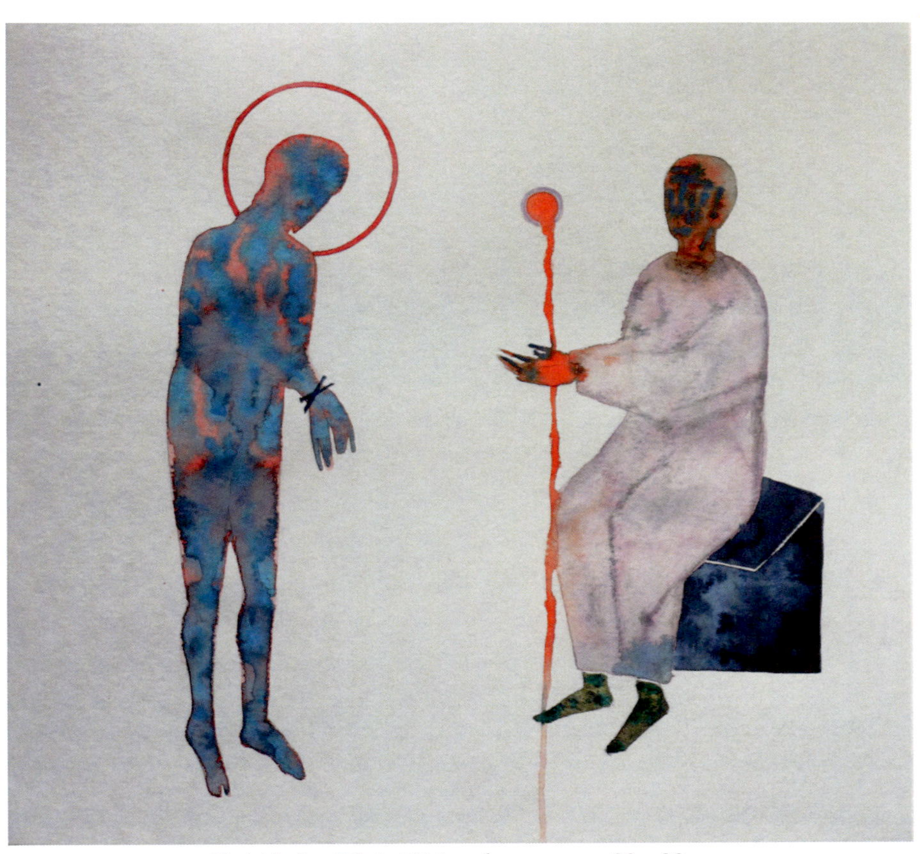

Christ before Pilate. Watercolor on paper, 30 x 30 cm

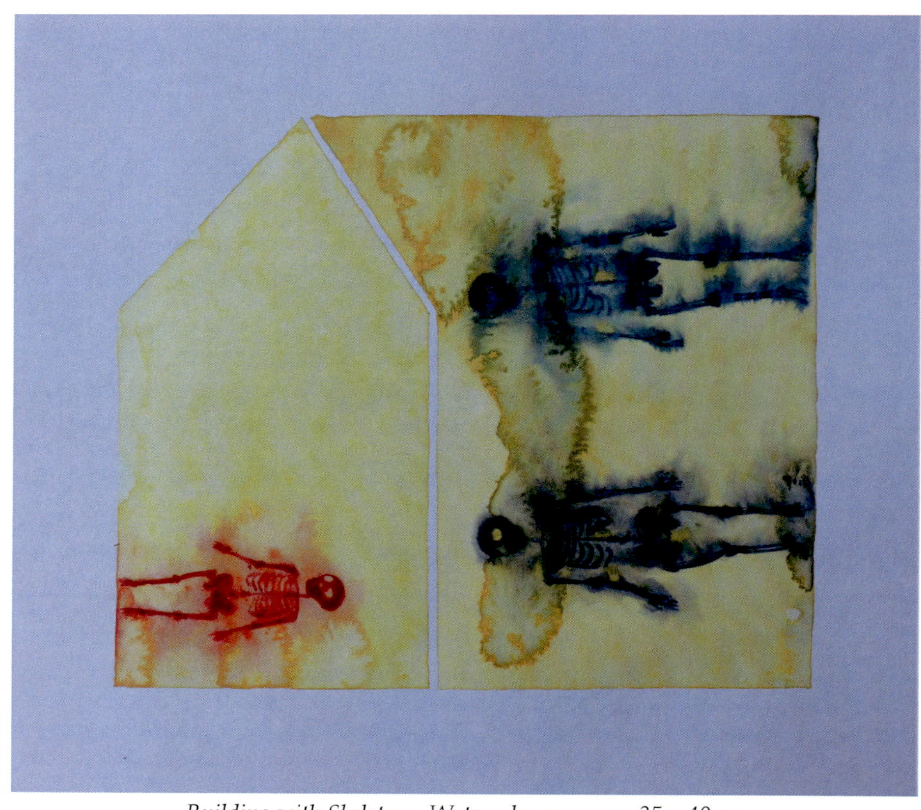

Building with Skeletons. Watercolor on paper, 35 x 40 cm

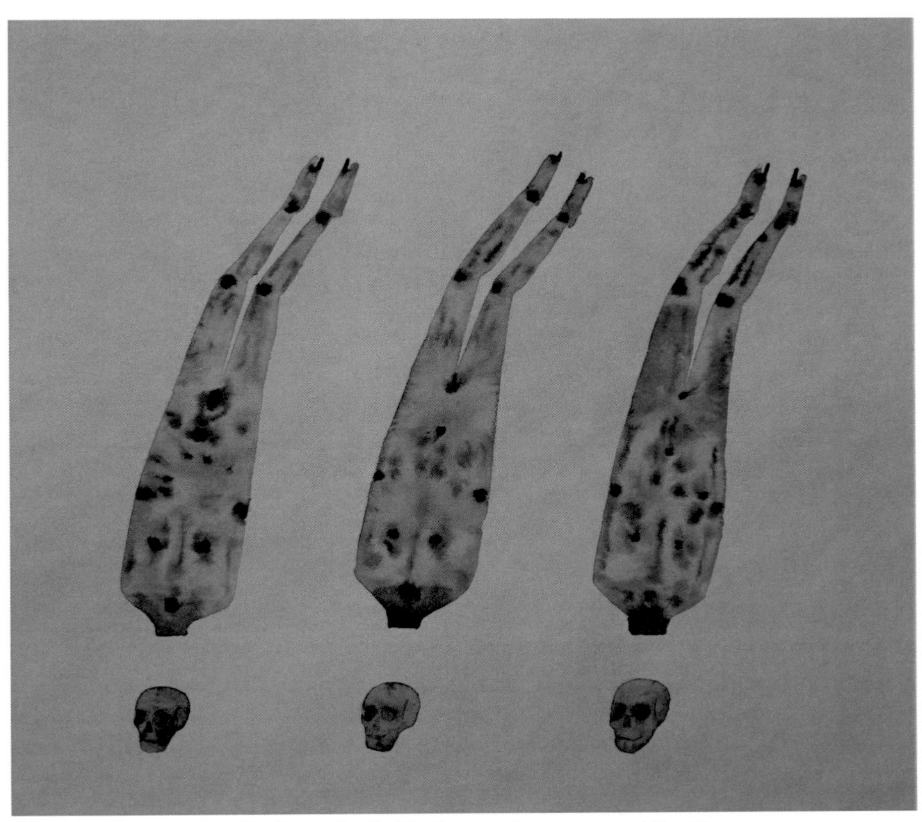

Three Bodies with Skulls. Watercolor on paper, 30 x 35 cm

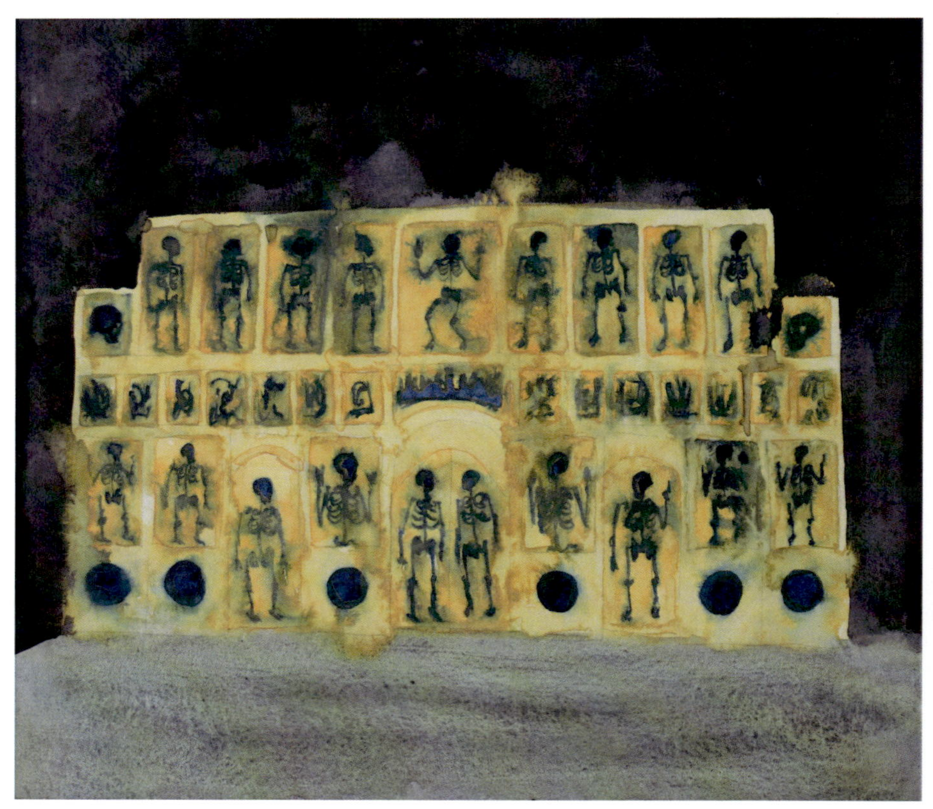

Russian Iconostasis. Watercolor on paper, 30 x 35 cm

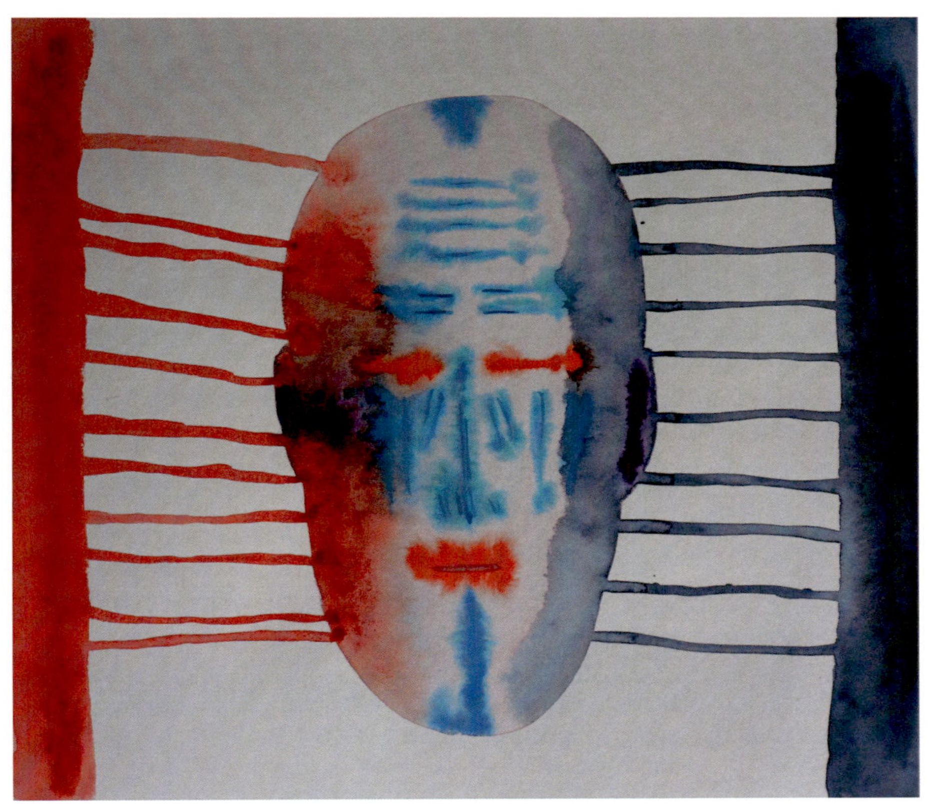

Red and Black. Watercolor on paper, 30 x 35 cm

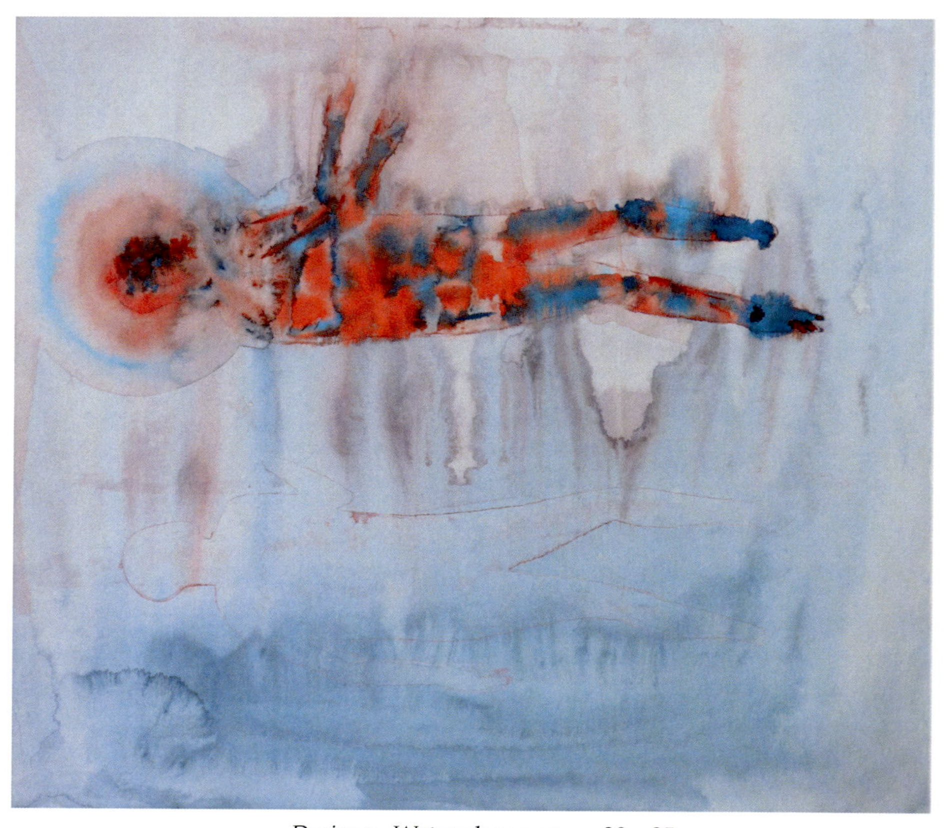

Drainage. Watercolor on paper, 30 x 35 cm

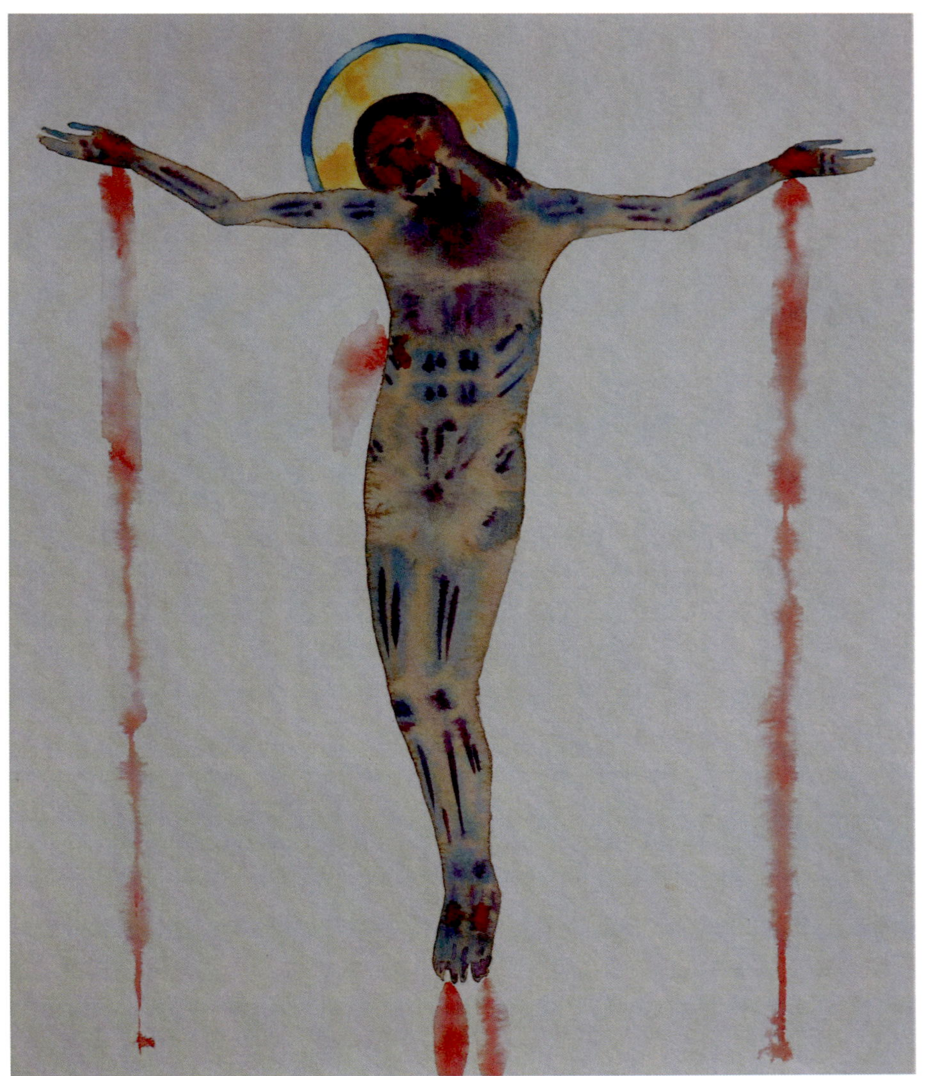

Cruzifix. Watercolor on paper, 30 x 25 cm

Chaplinsky & Danylo Movchan Vlog[10]

Today, I would like to highlight the notable and impactful artwork that Danylo Movchan has created since the war began. Several of your pieces have appeared as profile images on my account. Danylo primarily specializes in sacred art, which is why I consider him a distinguished figure among icon artists. Nevertheless, we appreciate your continued presence.

Yes, I'm still here.

One of my longtime friends who participates in my plein air painting workshops joined me. Lviv's relative safety during the conflict makes it easier for us to share our thoughts. Danylo's Christian-themed artwork, associated with the Greek Catholic Church, has reached individuals new to the faith, among other audiences.

His artistic style references Ukrainian icon art from the 14th and 15th centuries, during the transition from the Middle Ages to the Renaissance. His works utilize a childlike aesthetic to depict divinity while incorporating contemporary elements into this traditional subject.

When the conflict began, your impactful images quickly spread online and generated strong reactions. I've seen your work published internationally in places like Switzerland and Finland, and it seems this is only the beginning. Are you a quiet person? How would you describe your typical mood? Do you ever feel concerned?

I'm usually quiet, but because of the war, I've put my previous work aside and turned my attention to my current pursuits. This new area of focus is particularly significant to me at the moment.

Art portraying suffering can inspire empathy and compassion in audiences. During the Baroque and Counter-Reformation periods in Catholic culture, for example, artists painted saints being pierced with arrows. Echoing Caravaggio's realism, these works vividly depict suffering, blood, and fear.

Your artistic style is defined by minimalism and symbolic representation. I am interested in your perspective on realistic art that evokes an

10 Conversation with Danylo Movchan about his watercolors depicting the war in Lviv, 2023: https://www.youtube.com/watch?v=Qlljcwg8Hgw

emotional response. Do you aim to encourage independent reflection on the realities of war by depicting them symbolically? Furthermore, do you aim to demonstrate the characteristics of this conflict within our country and communicate the importance of preventing such occurrences in the future?

European art has always offered different perspectives on these topics. Personally, I prefer symbolism to realism in my art. I prefer to subtly convey the meaning of war rather than depict it realistically.

This type of presentation likely appeals to sensitive individuals. This is evident in the comments I have received, in which people mention how my work impacts them or ask specific questions.

Do you feel that your recent work demonstrates advancement over your previous accomplishments? If suffering were portrayed in the same manner as in your earlier esteemed pieces, viewers would likely not be so emotionally impacted by these images as to be moved to tears. Expressing such themes symbolically enables you to connect with a wider audience. Your artwork addresses themes of war without explicitly portraying suffering, bloodshed, or pain. In the context of contemporary global challenges, your pieces are highly relevant to a broad audience.

Like Le Corbusier's early modernist works, your approach can be seen as an important development in art history because it effectively conveys complex concepts through minimal visual cues. After the war, Le Corbusier's paintings focused on peace rather than conflict. The devastation of World War II made people long for its end and return to peaceful living. They sought peace instead of renewed conflict. This artist sought new ways to highlight the importance of peace. He achieved this with minimal brushstrokes, much like how you use a few drops of watercolor to evoke emotions such as fear, worry, empathy, and compassion. Was this your goal when painting?

No, I wasn't thinking about that. It's more about current events and the situation we were all experiencing at the time. Once I start painting, I find it difficult to know how my artist friends will judge it based on their experience. So, I just try to express my own feelings.

Could you explain why you chose to paint it as a watercolor?

Watercolor painting requires minimal preparation and is quick because no primer is needed.

Will you transfer these works to tempera later?

About three or four years ago, I tried painting quickly for the first time to see what I could achieve. Even now, I am not entirely sure what happens when I paint this way. The image seems to emerge on its own as I work, gradually revealing itself. I follow my feelings and whatever comes to mind.

Examples

Your first piece on the war, "To Victory," will be displayed from February 26. Created just two days after the war began on February 24, it marks an early artistic response to the event. This work reminds me of the early days of the war in Ukraine when explosions were commonplace and danger lurked around every corner. I knew right away that it would be violent. What was going through your mind as you painted it?

It was something like that. I just wanted to show that death threatens us all from now on and everything that will happen to us because of the war.

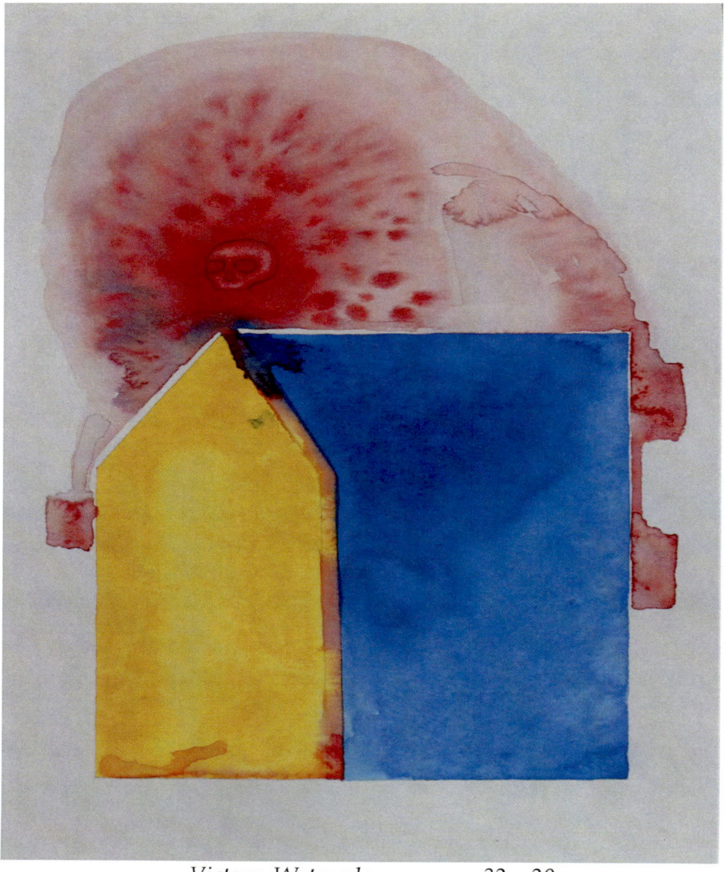

Victory. Watercolor on paper, 32 x 20 cm

In the second picture, I see someone crying over the death of a fighter on our side.

By that time, it was clear that many of our men had lost their lives. This realization was profoundly distressing. I was also seeking ways to express through my work, whether through color or composition, what words could not adequately convey.

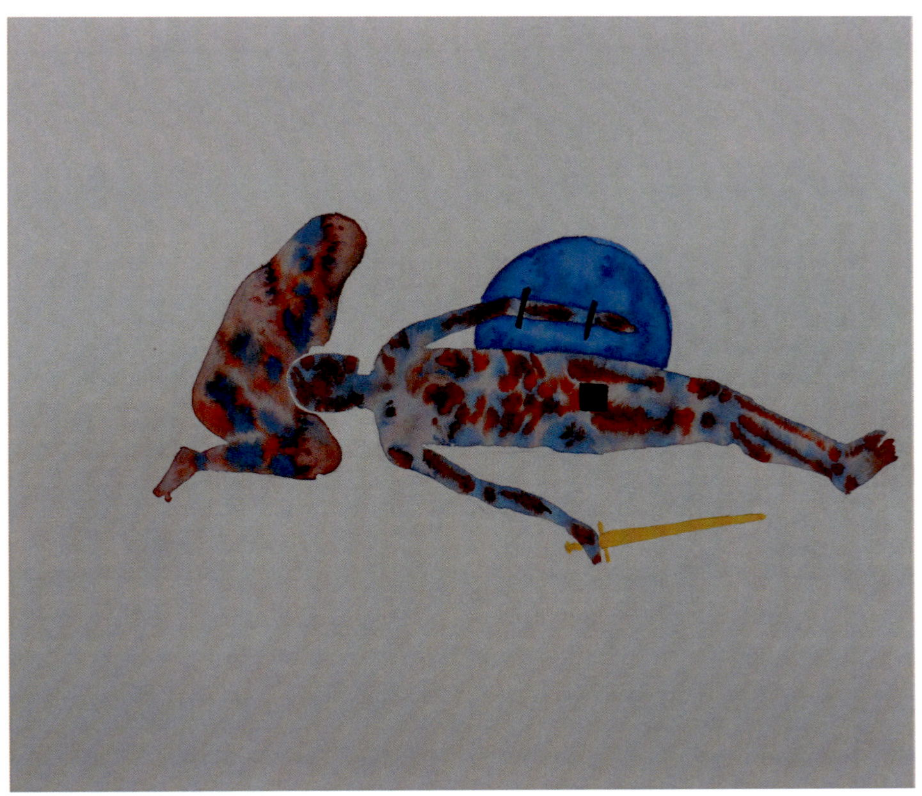

Mourning for a Warrior. Watercolor on paper, 30 x 35 cm

Because I know your children, who are also highly creative like you, I thought that they inspired you.

No, it wasn't like that. At that time, the museum of the famous Ukrainian artist Maria Prymachenko[11] had just been attacked, which made me incredibly sad.

I didn't even know that. Now, I understand it better. This woman was a great shining star in our sky. This Moscow devilry!

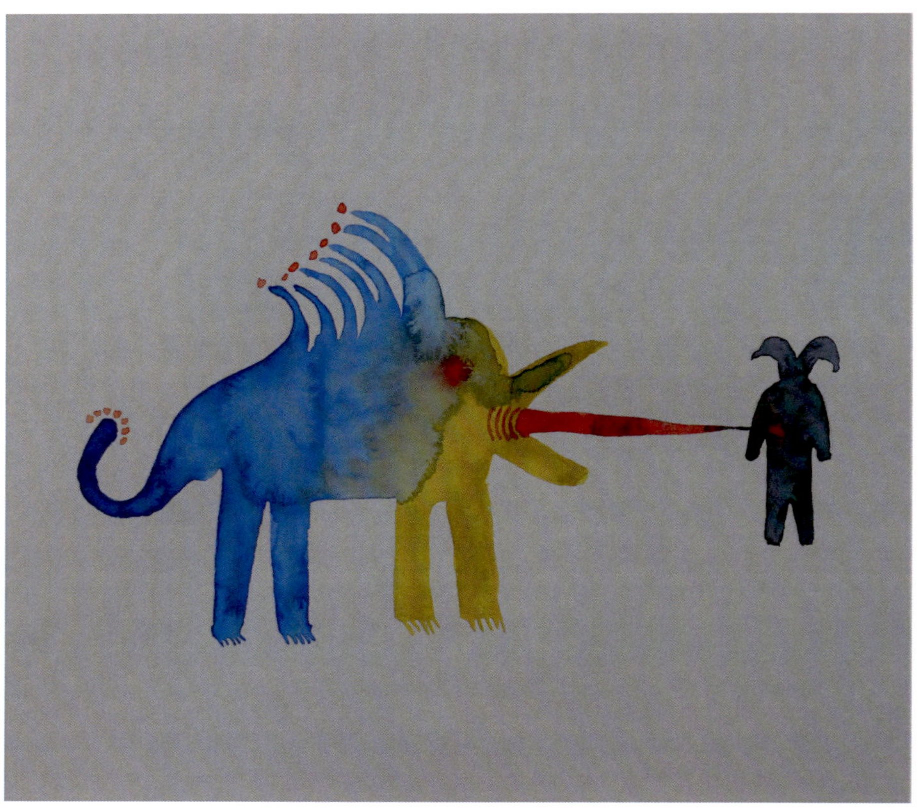

Battle. Watercolor on paper, 30 x 35 cm

---

11 https://en.wikipedia.org/wiki/Maria_Prymachenko

Could you please explain what you mean by "holds a cross" in this picture?

This image depicts someone holding onto a cross, symbolizing Christ's spiritual reach to the deceased. Christ understands the suffering of those killed in Ukraine and the burden of the cross. His prayers give him strength.

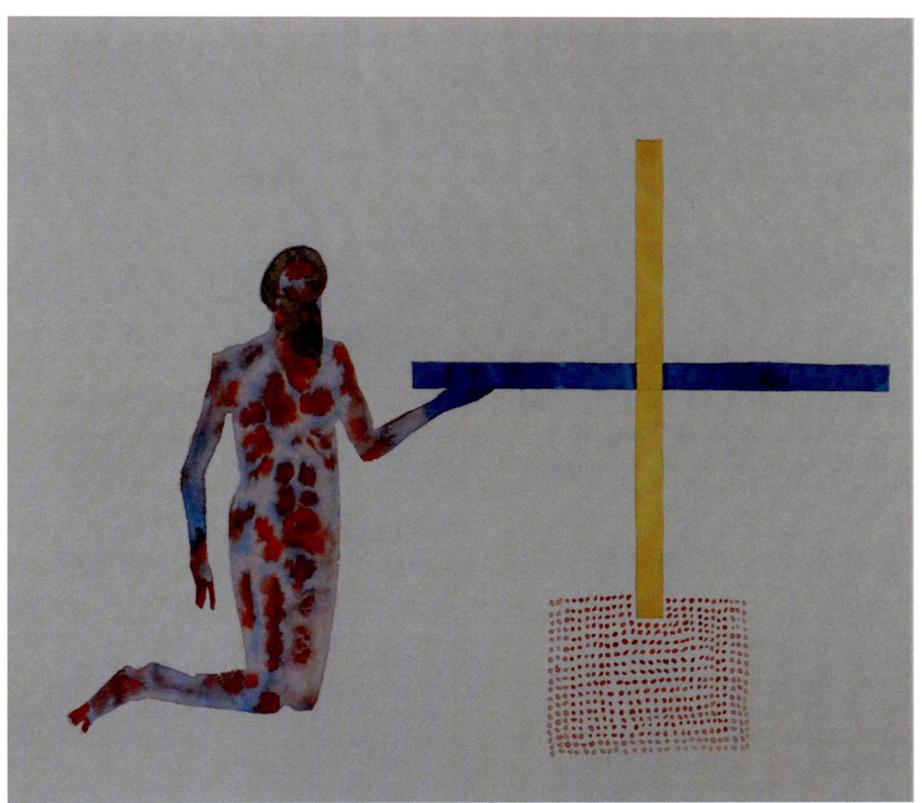

Holds a Cross. Watercolor on paper, 30 x 35 cm

The next image must have happened after the attack on the Zaporizhia nuclear power plant began.

Yes, that was the case.

Or is it also about the Chernobyl nuclear power plant?

No, it's about the Zaporizhian nuclear power plants, where there is dangerous radiation in the reactors. If we are not careful, it could be very bad for all of us.

I also find it impressive how the attacks depict skulls as symbols of death.

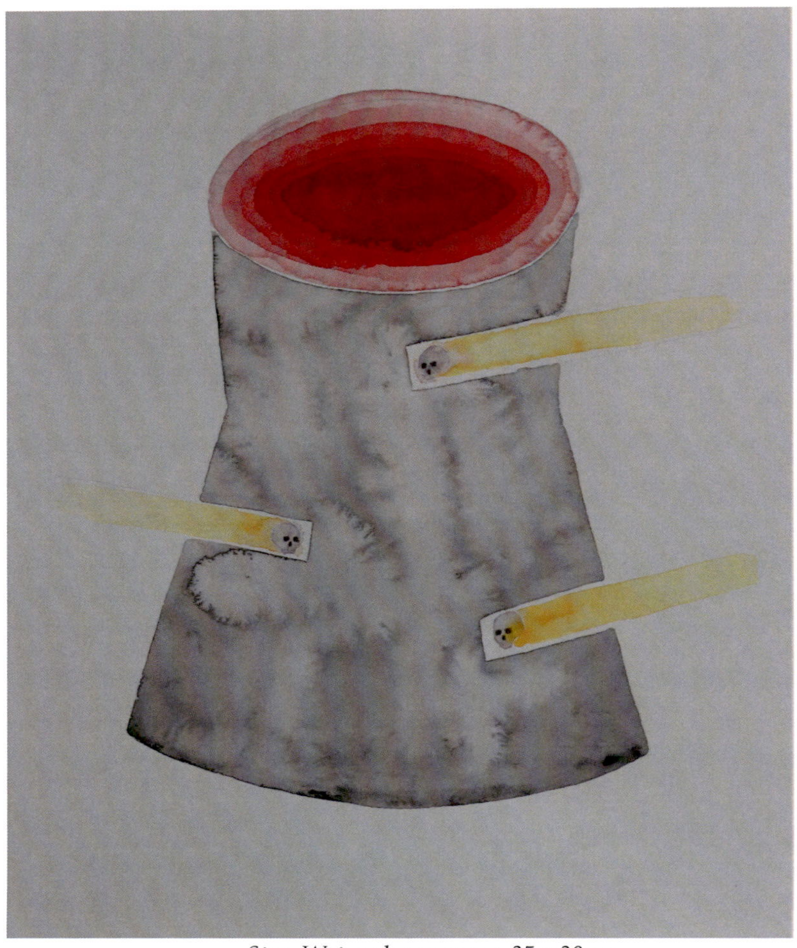

Stop. Watercolor on paper, 35 x 30 cm

This brave knight is killing a Russian occupier. At that time, you probably believed Ukraine would win quickly. After all, there are still smaller victories today.

Fortunately, they are still here every day.

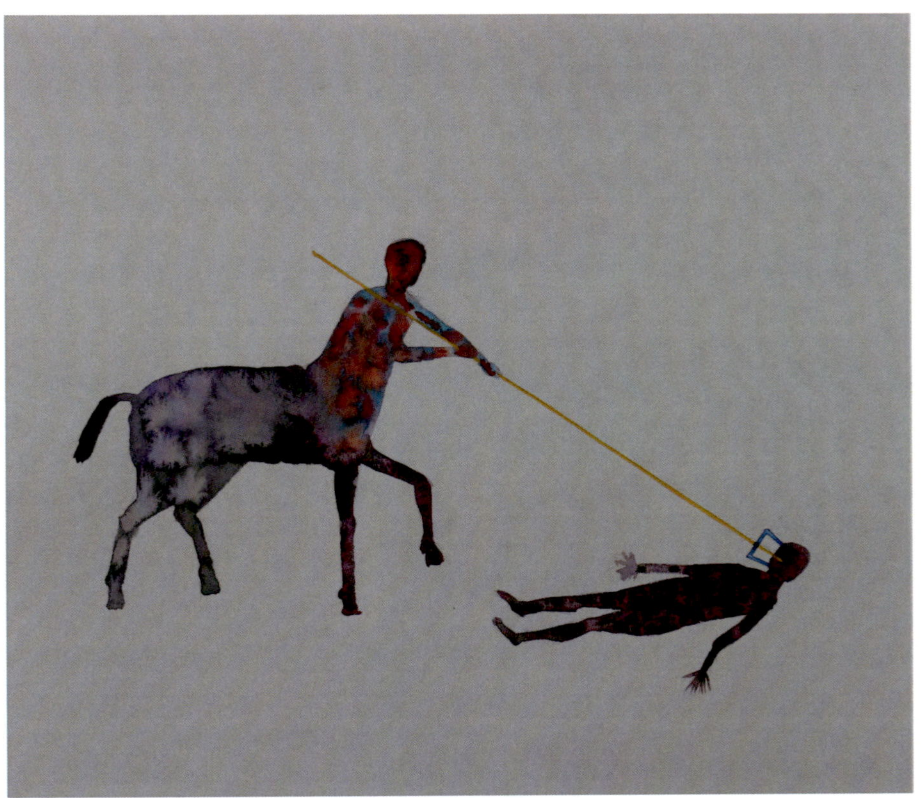

Death of the Russian Occupier. Watercolor on paper, 30 x 35 cm

As I look back on your early work, I see a development in you up to April: progression from initial shock to a certain calmness and great confidence in our army's fight.

From the start, it was clear to me that we would defend ourselves. However, reports soon emerged that countless valuable buildings in our cities had been destroyed.

"Migration" is another work that touched me deeply. We all remember it very well. How did you feel while painting it?

All of this hurt me very much. Nobody understands something like that. Someone spends a long time building something new for a better life, and then someone else comes along and destroys it all again.

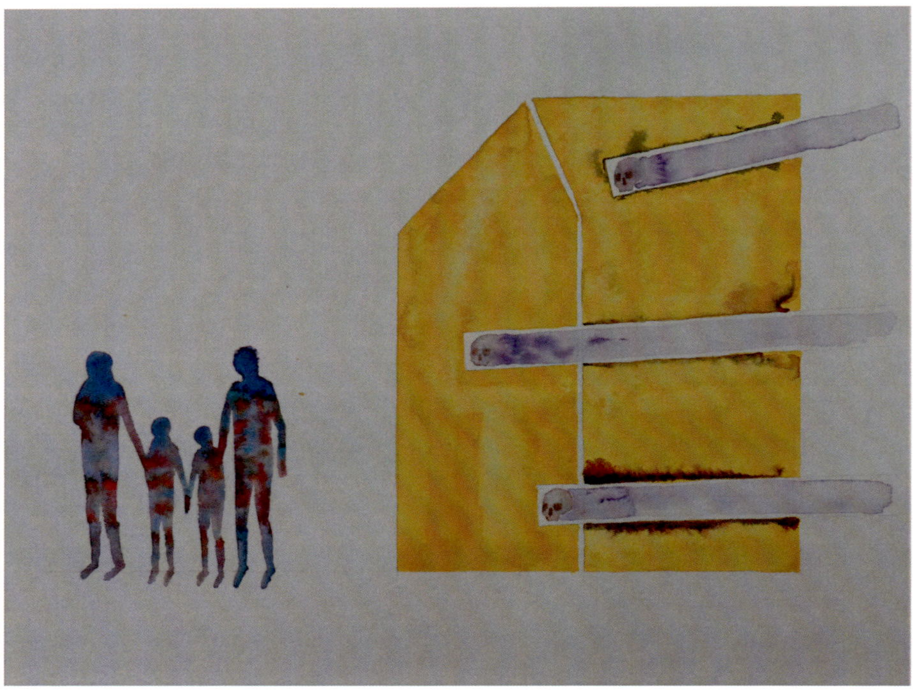

Migration. Watercolor on paper, 25 x 30 cm

Putin has us in his sights here, literally.

Yes, Putin. But I don't think this dragon is as big as we Ukrainians are.

Your watercolor technique is impressive. The facial expression and symbolic components proficiently convey the nuanced ambiguity associated with Putin.

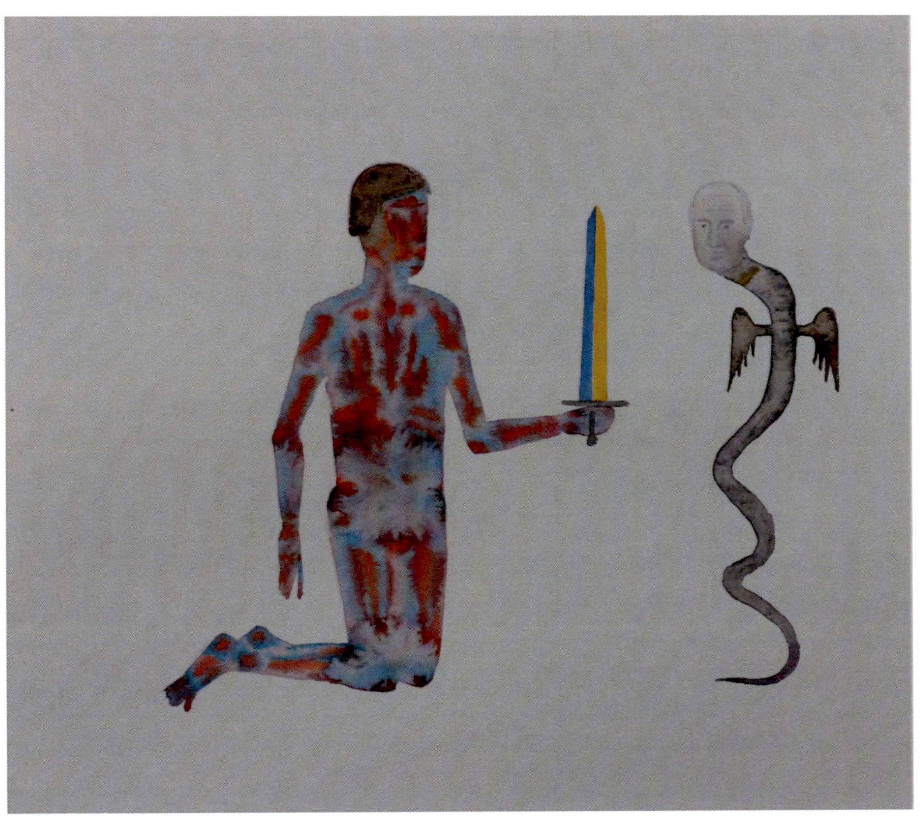

The End of Evil. Watercolor on paper, 35 x 40 cm

There's something new in your art again. Did you feel like crying at the time? This picture shows what can happen when painting a watercolor. The paints flowed away and created this symbolic figure with two faces. Is it a father or a mother?

We have received reports about pregnant mothers and their children being affected. I aimed to highlight this issue through this process. I utilized the watercolor technique for its unique capabilities. However, the outcome can be unpredictable. This process helps convey certain feelings.

It is an excellent piece that stirs our emotions. For the first time, we encounter a sacred theme from traditional iconography: the Crucifixion of Christ. His blood flows in streams.

At that time, the first reports of attacks on churches had just emerged, and some of the churches had been destroyed. I wanted to show that people who do this are monsters to me.

Where is humanity in that? This kind of things is just terrible. Where is humanity in this people? Which events shocked you most?

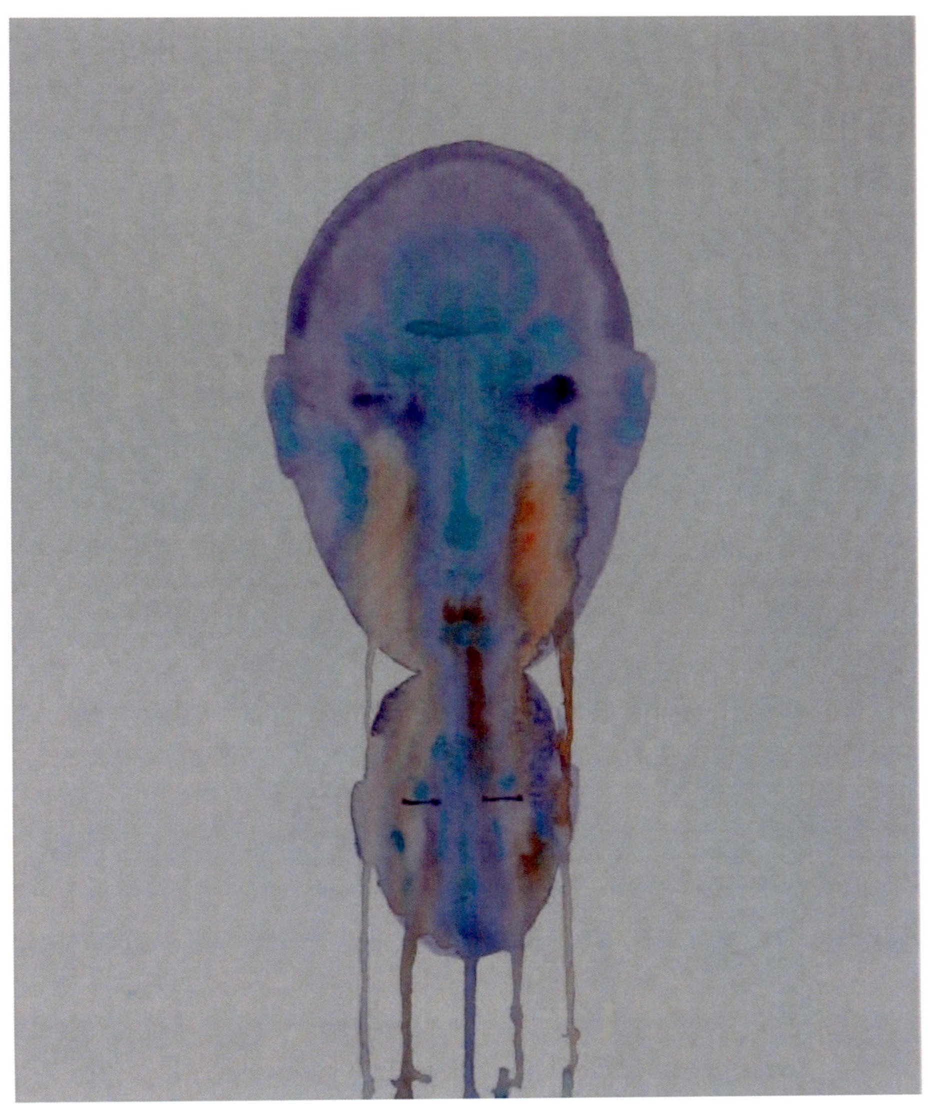

Crying. Watercolor on paper, 35 x 30 cm

They likely involved the death of Russian occupiers. It seems that the individuals sent to harm us may not have fully understood their mission. Additionally, Russia appears to be indifferent to its own casualties.

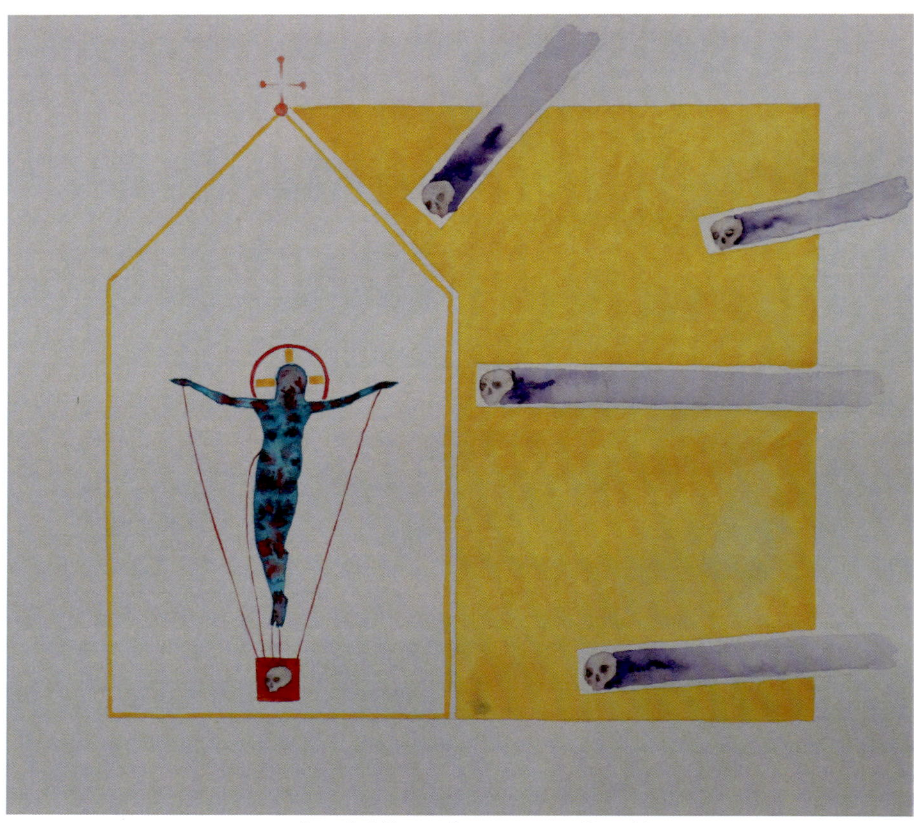

Attack. Watercolor on paper, 35 x 40 cm

I see our good Ukrainian black soil there, along with the bodies of our Russian occupiers, which are about to be swallowed up by it.

No one will ever remember them again.

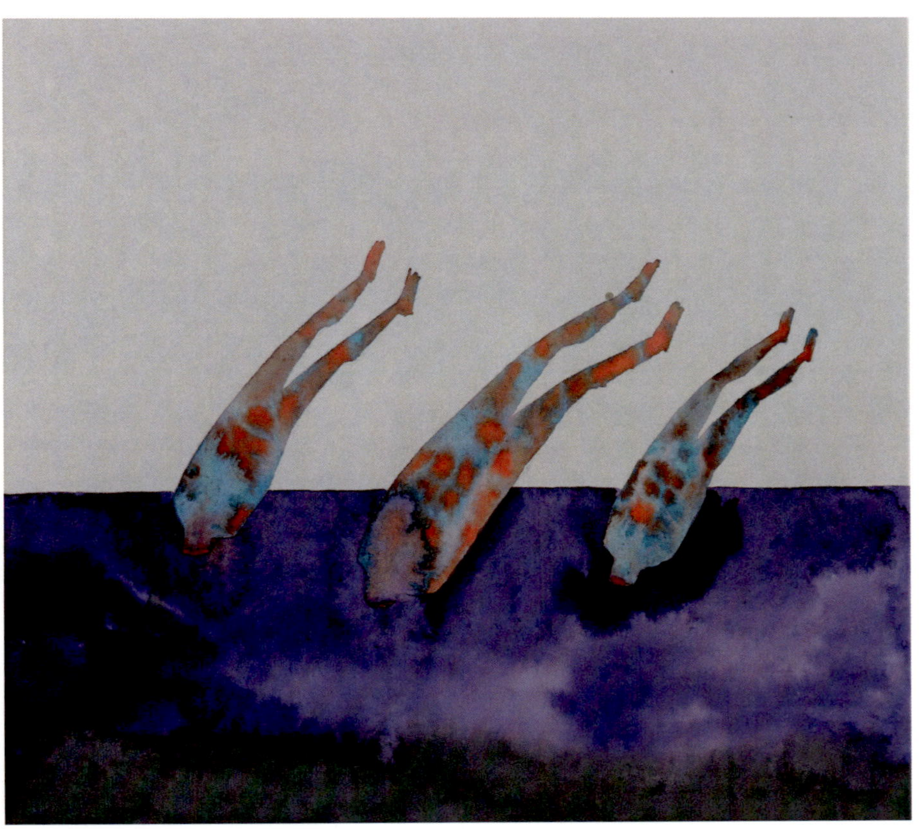

About the Occupiers. Watercolor on paper, 30 x 35 cm

Something new again. These 11 Connections with my own body seem to me to be something sacred. That is why it is called "11». It's probably about the pain that a suffering person feels.[12]

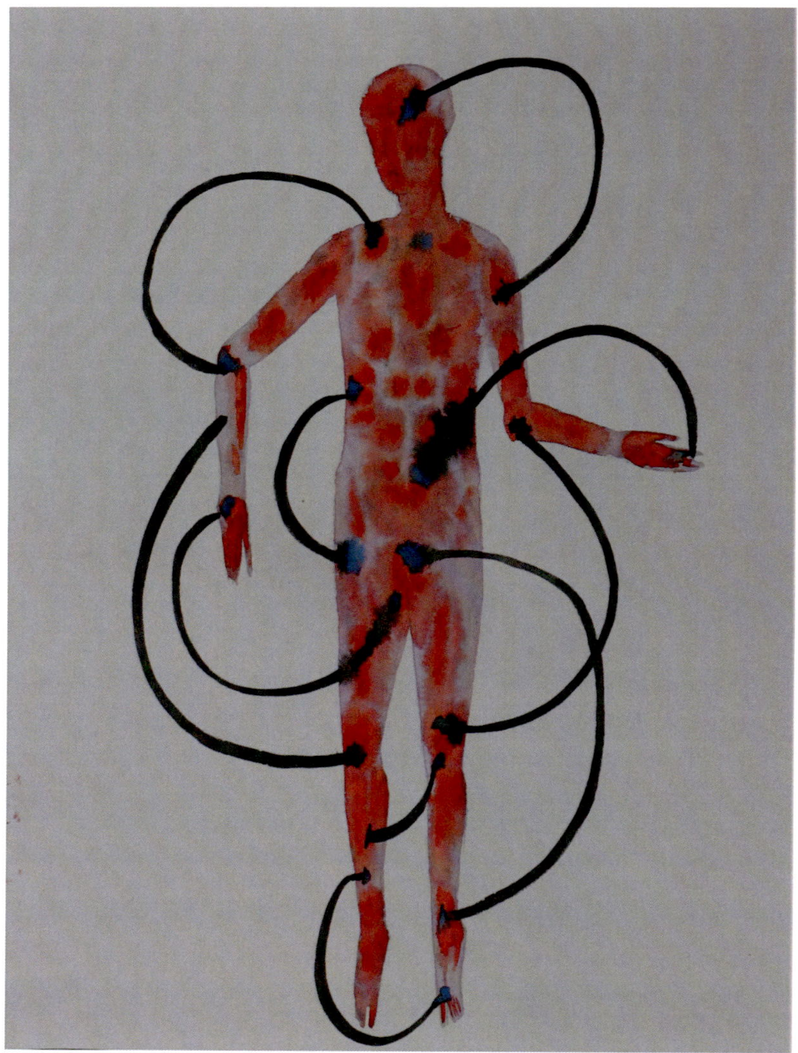

Connections 11. Watercolor on paper, 40 x 35 cm

---

12 In mysticism, the number 11 is understood as the number of the angels and stands for inspiration and enlightenment.

Today, science teaches us that everything in the human body is interconnected and that the brain can transmit pain throughout the body. I am also referring to Russian culture, which has always sought to dominate us. This culture used to benefit us all, but today it seems the opposite is true: it is completely brainless and sinister. The war we are experiencing now shows the consequences of this culture, which was once great, but is now terrible for us.

Would you describe Russian culture as entirely negative? Was it different for you before the war? Are there aspects of it that you have always disliked?

To be honest, I haven't paid much attention to Russian culture lately. There is absolutely no reason for me to pay attention to it anymore, because I am convinced that this corrupt Russian culture ultimately contributed to the war against Ukraine. Russian culture has always been hostile towards Ukraine and our culture. That simply must be said.

I also used this picture, titled 'Prayer', as my Facebook profile picture. Now, I understand what you meant.

During this time, many people sought refuge in bomb shelters and basements. Others turned to prayer, hoping for relief from their difficult circumstances.

Against this black-and-white backdrop, I see something reminiscent of Eastern spirituality: the unity of opposites in ying and yang.

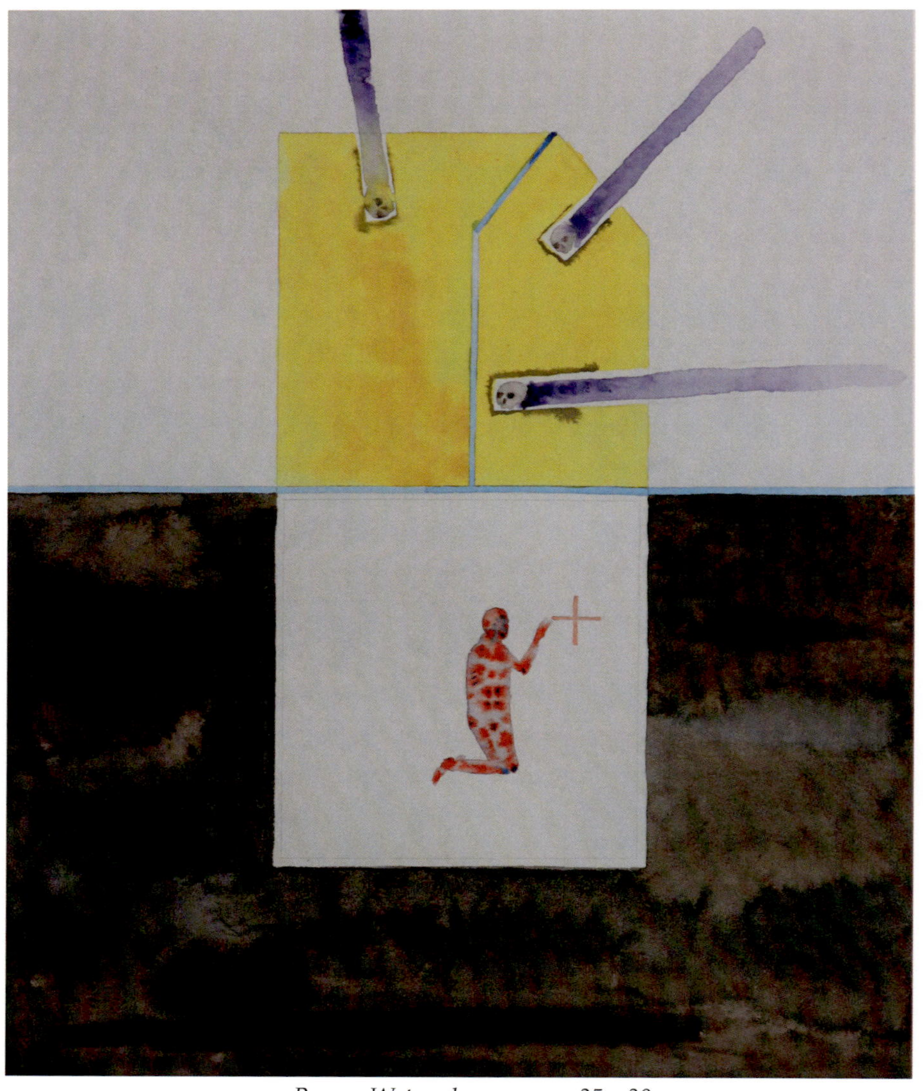

Prayer. Watercolor on paper, 25 x 30 cm

Once again, the theme is despair. Am I correct in thinking that we are seeing the face of a wounded man?

I wanted to show my pain again about what just happened to us. Everyone here is probably experiencing this pain throughout their body today.

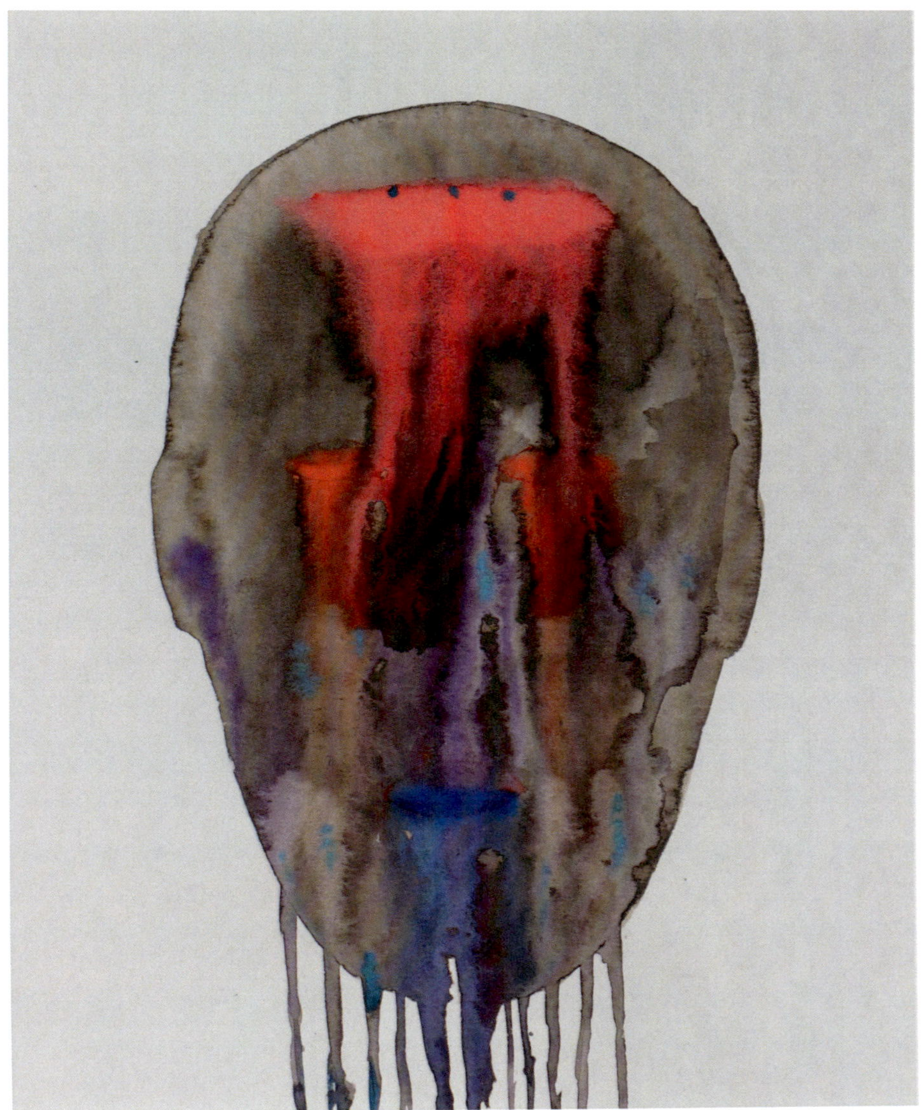

Pain. Watercolor on paper, 30 x 25 cm

Mariupol, for example, faced a prolonged attack for many weeks.

Yes, I was talking about Mariupol when the Russian dropped bombs on a hospital with a maternity ward.

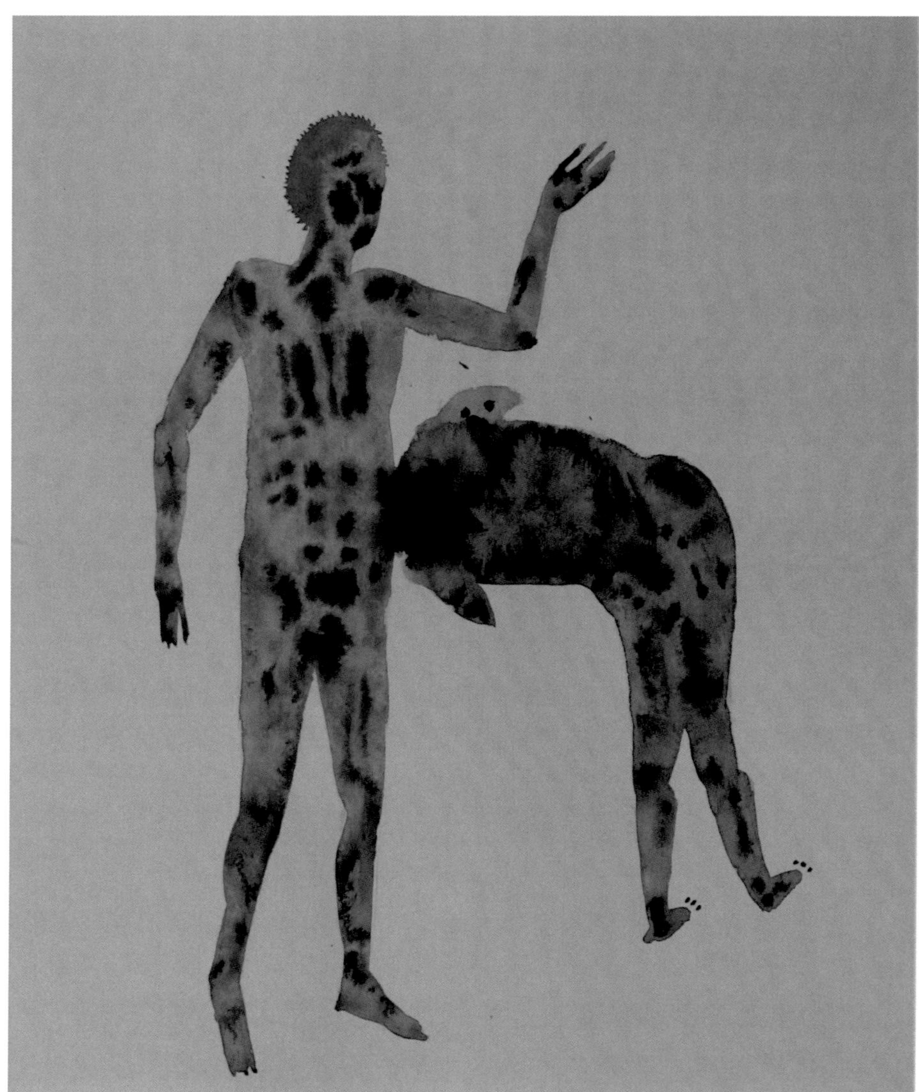

Intrusion. Watercolor on paper, 40 x 35 cm

This work depicts the silhouette of a pregnant woman who has experienced a loss. The piece conveys a strong message that evokes a sense of sadness for viewers.

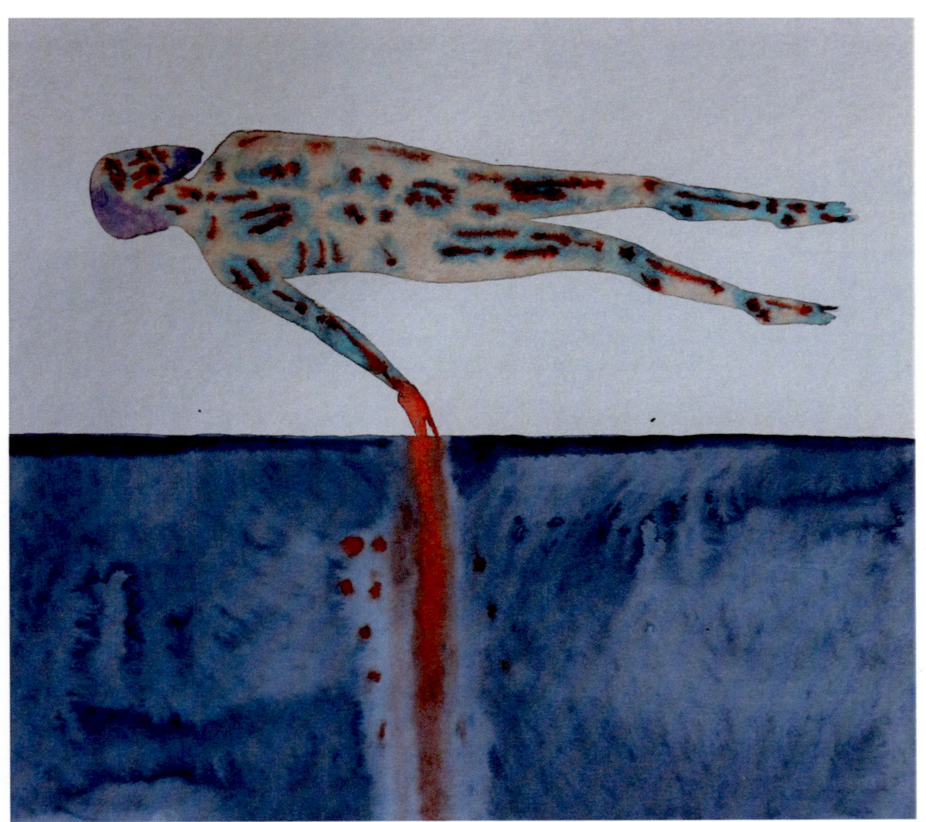

Mariupol. Watercolor on paper, 35 x 30 cm

The two of them are carrying something that appears to be sacred to them. It is probably a church. They are doing this in the hope that it will be spared during the resettlement process.

The one thing they cannot take from us is the light of our faith.

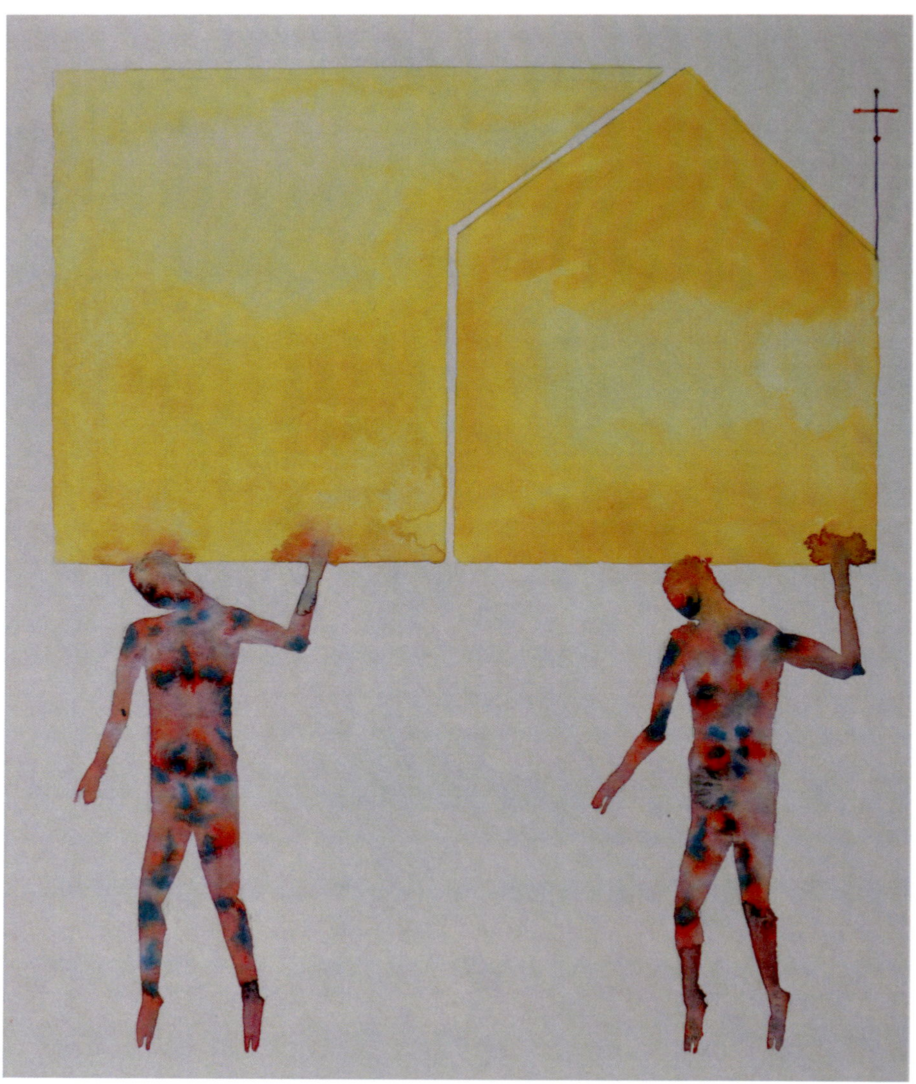

Migration II. Watercolor on paper, 25 x 30 cm

Here are the outcomes of recent military actions involving Russia and our country.

Today, it is important to inform the world about the consequences of the Russian invasion so that the international community understands the current situation.

What are your specific thoughts on this matter?

This reflects the challenges and circumstances faced by everyone in the region due to the ongoing conflict.

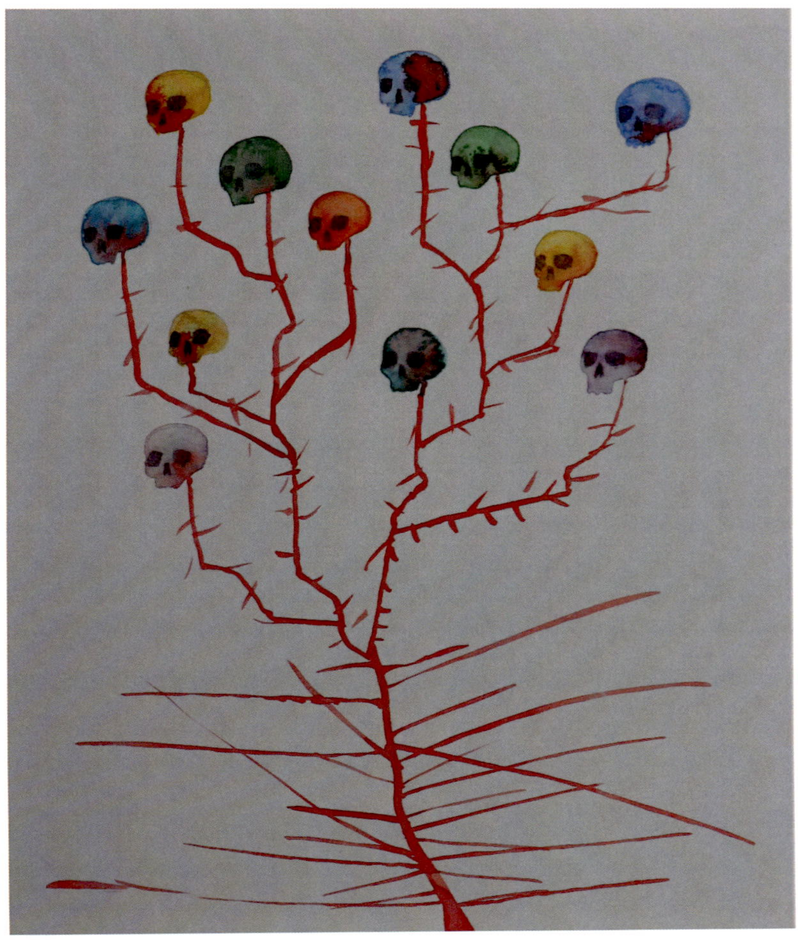

Flowers from Ukraine. Watercolor on paper, 30 x 25 cm

One of your minimalist artworks that I find particularly interesting is called 'Fear'. I see the dark color flowing onto the other side as a constant fear – this darkness that is increasingly determining our entire lives. Am I right in thinking that this represents the consequences of war for us?

However, everyone can take steps to avoid living in constant fear. We can find ways to protect ourselves so that fear doesn't dominate our lives. Some people inherently know how to shield themselves from fear, but it can permeate our entire being.

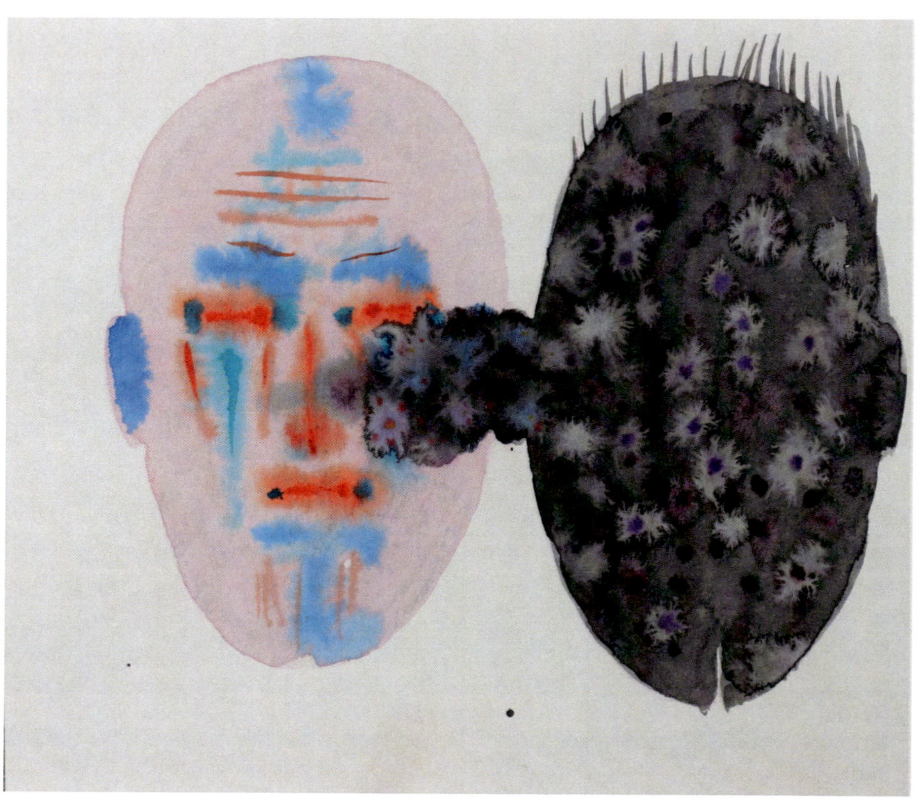

Fear. Watercolor on paper, 30 x 35 cm

A maternity hospital under attack. What more can I say?

All I can offer is a deep sigh.

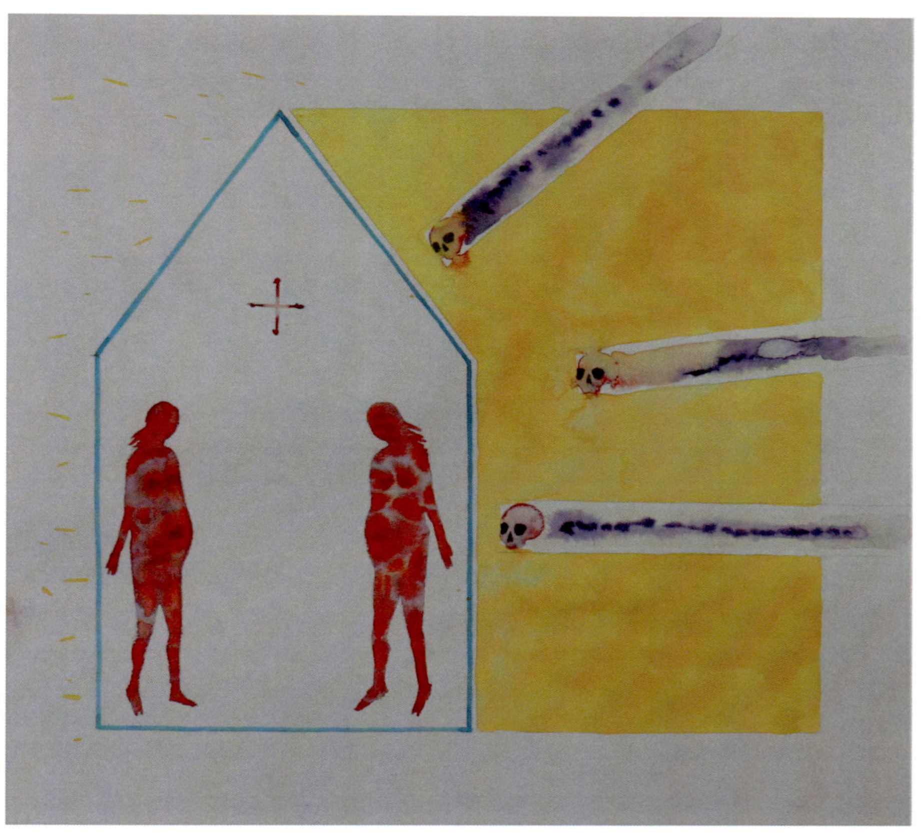

Hospital. Watercolor on paper, 35 x 40 cm

Another maternity hospital is featured.

A mother, having lost all her belongings, is present at the facility. Tragically, her child has passed away.

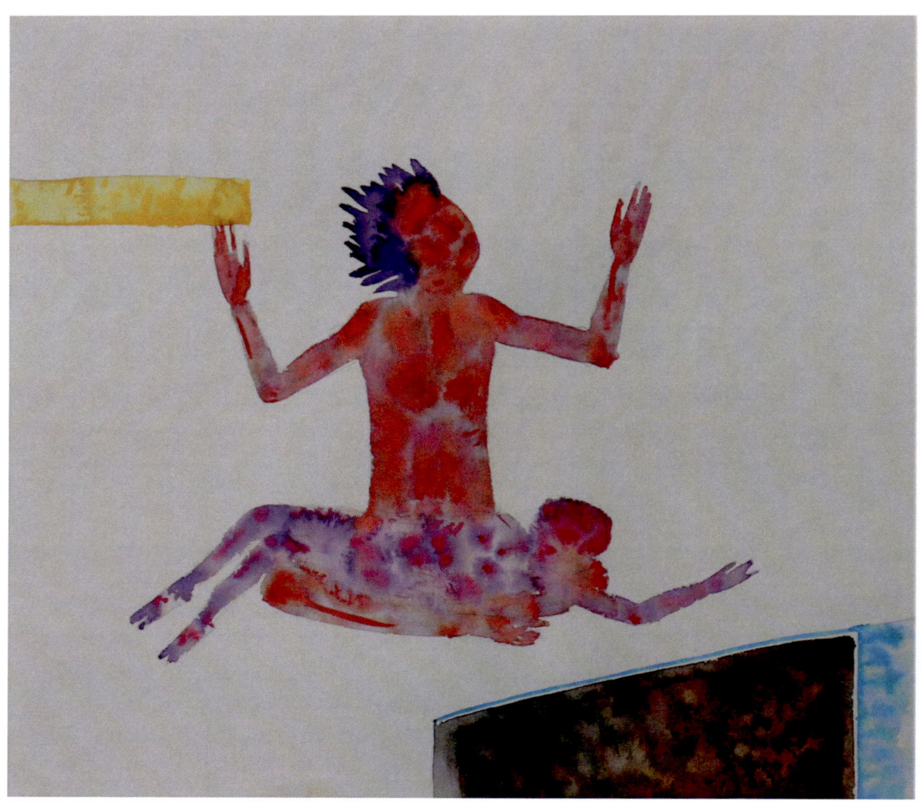

Mother and Child. Watercolor on paper, 30 x 35 cm

"Russian culture". What do you mean by that?

Russian artists who bring death with their silence, just like rockets.

Are there any Russian artists you are still in contact with?

No – they simply want to live safely, too, and therefore remain silent.

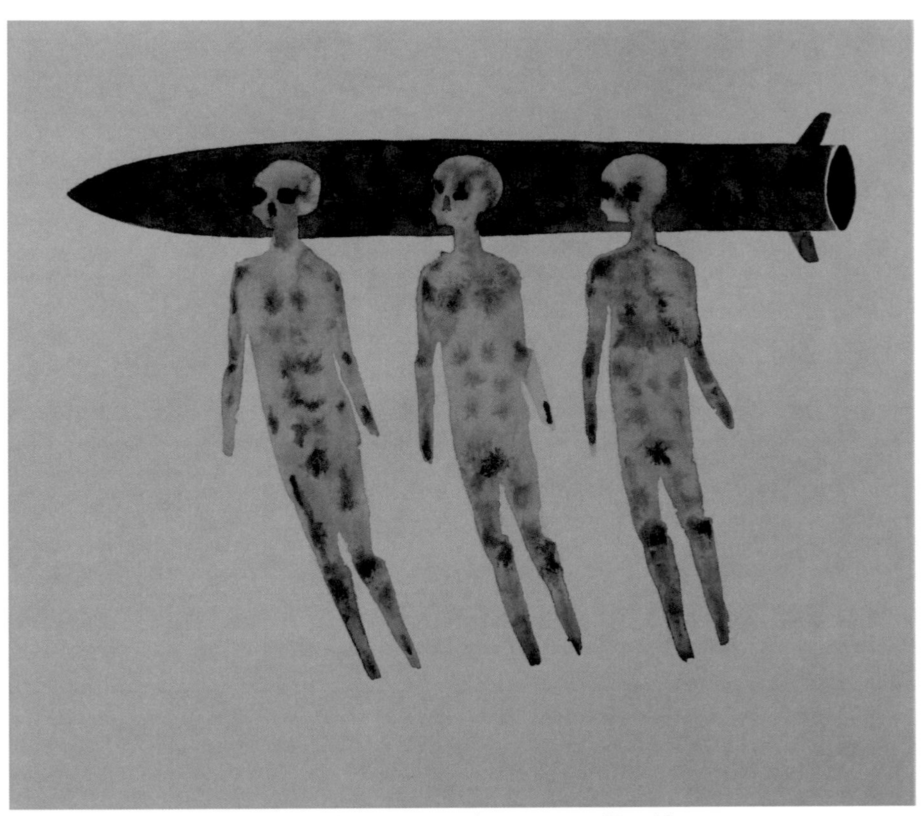

Russian Culture. Watercolor on paper, 35 x 40 cm

I'm not really allowed to say anything about that, because the patriarch who feeds on our blood wouldn't let me. He would just tell me: "Shut up! What is your name? What's your father's name? What's your family name? Who are you? To me, you are ... nothing. I your Patriarch, I can say whatever I want."

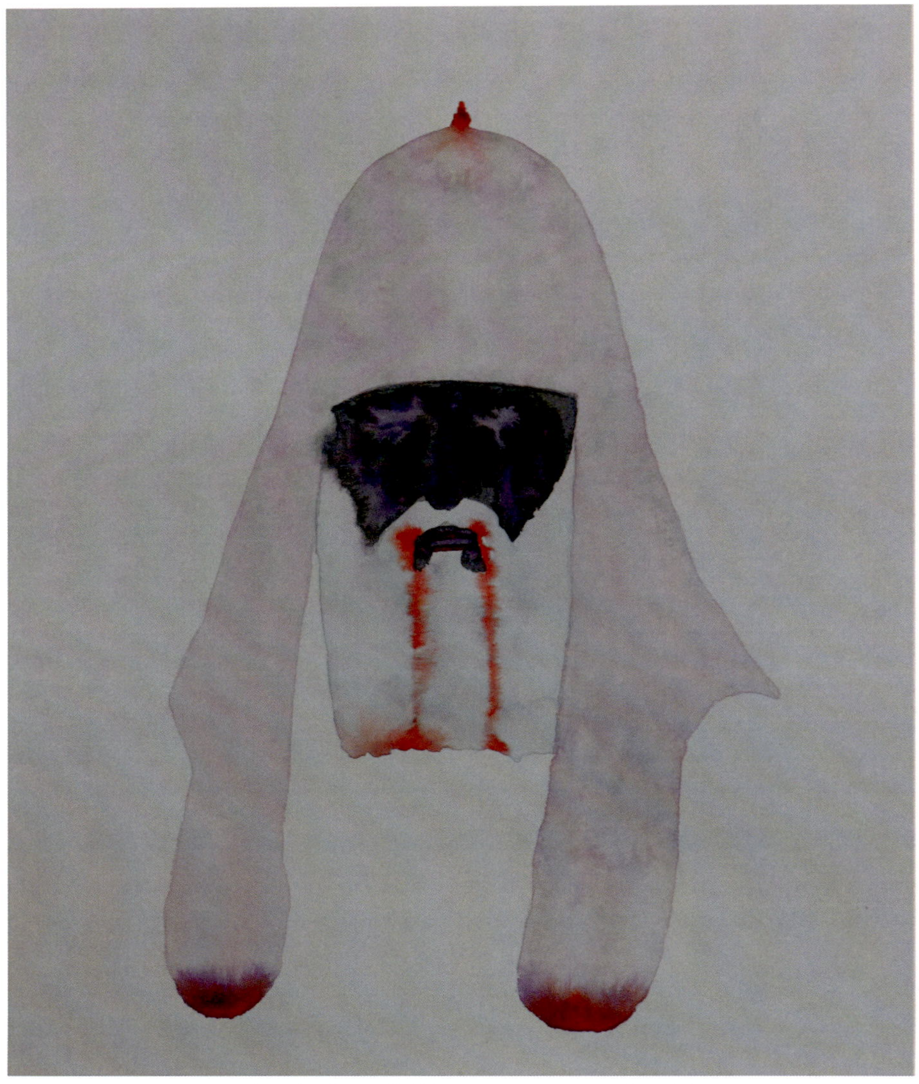

Patriarch Cyril. Watercolor on paper, 35 x 30 cm

Are you referring to yourself?

Yes, it's a self-portrait of me painting Christ while our entire country is under attack. I wanted to show how I understand my work today so that the world learns about what is happening in our country and doesn't forget it.

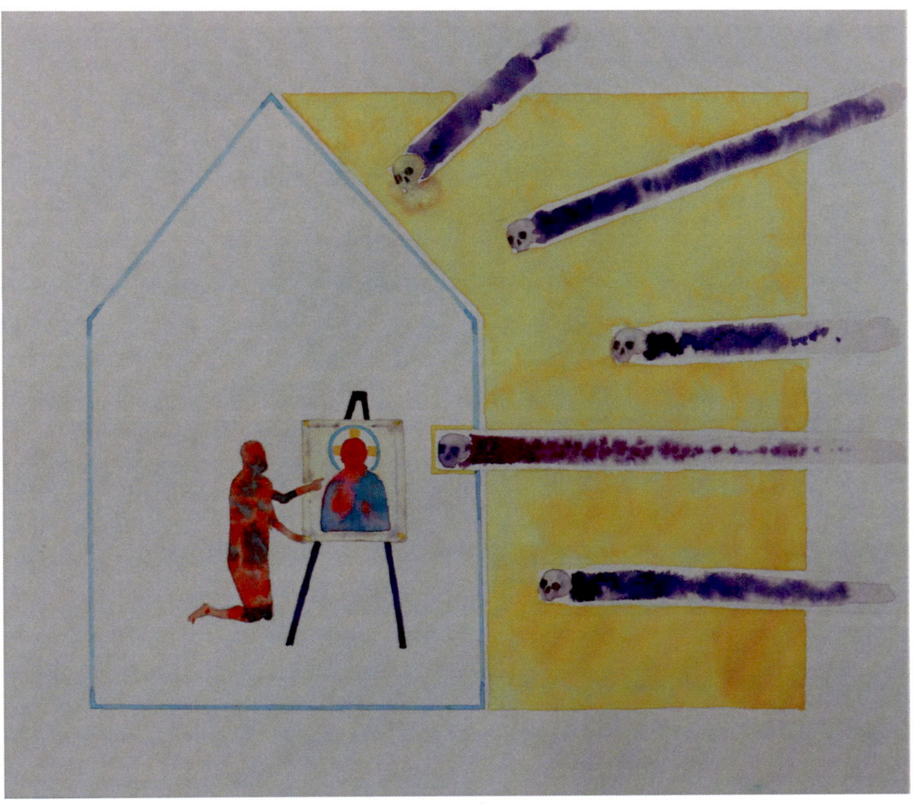

Self-Portrait. Watercolor on paper, 30 x 35 cm

The theme once again is the special connection between Christ and Ukraine.

Here, I wanted to demonstrate how Christ is united with the blood shed for us today through his own blood, which was shed for us. He is united with our suffering through his own. This is about the fact that everyone feels pain and that we are not painless beings. Each of us carries this feeling within us, and every pain flows through us like blood.

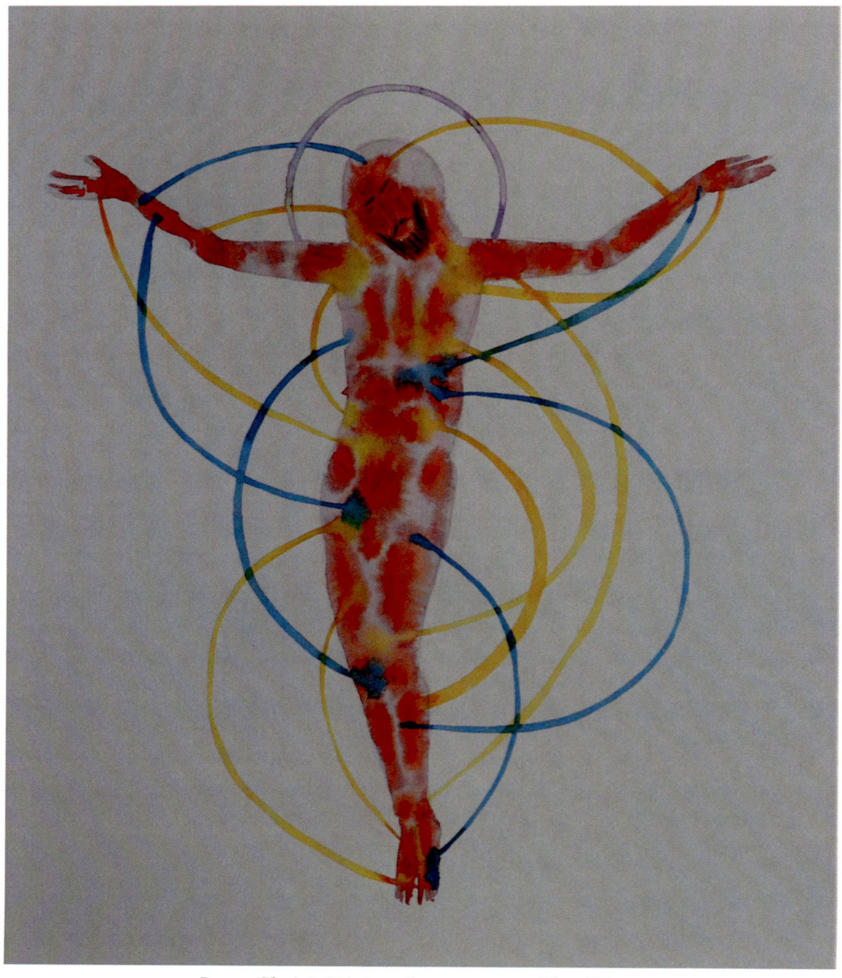

Jesus Christ. Watercolor on paper, 40 x 35 cm

That reminds me of a highly dangerous job. Is it related to Chornobyl?

Yes; many Russian soldiers were forced to work there and exposed to harmful radiation without protection.

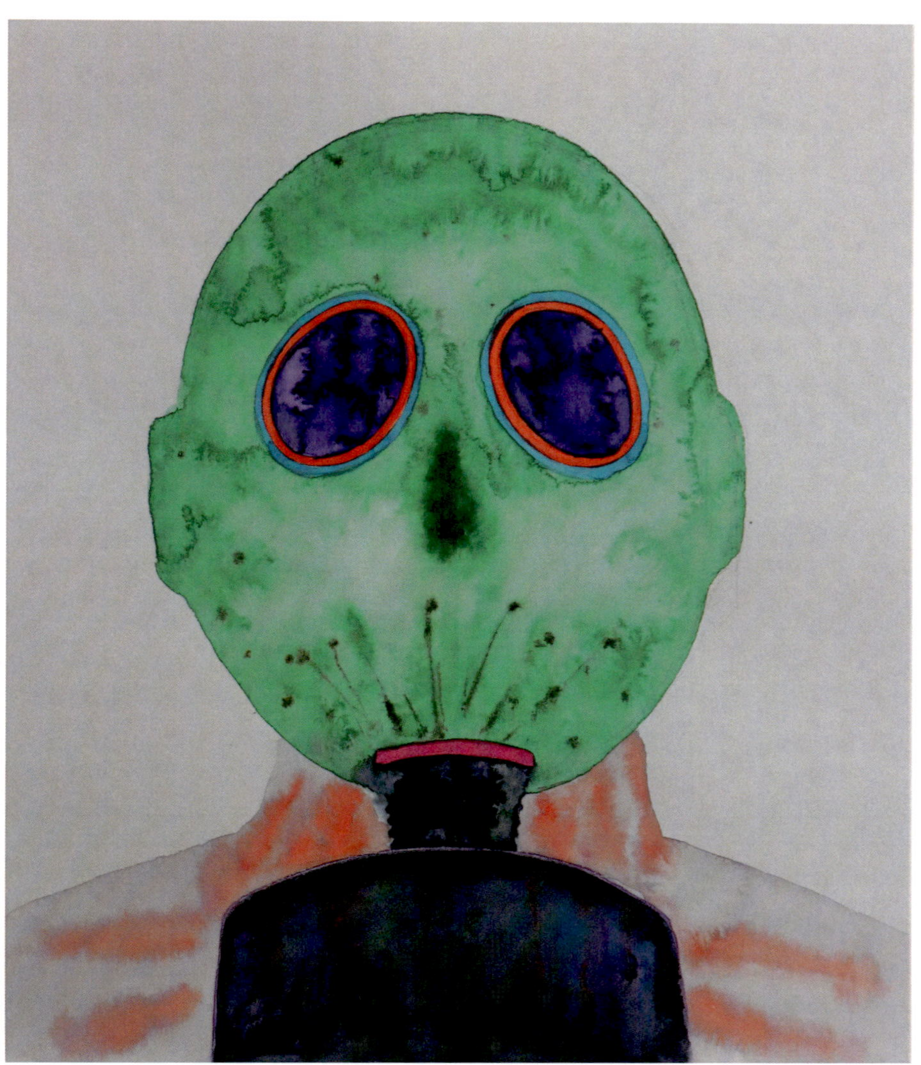

Danger. Watercolor on paper, 40 x 35 cm

"Help."

It's about mutual support and being ready to assist each other when needed.

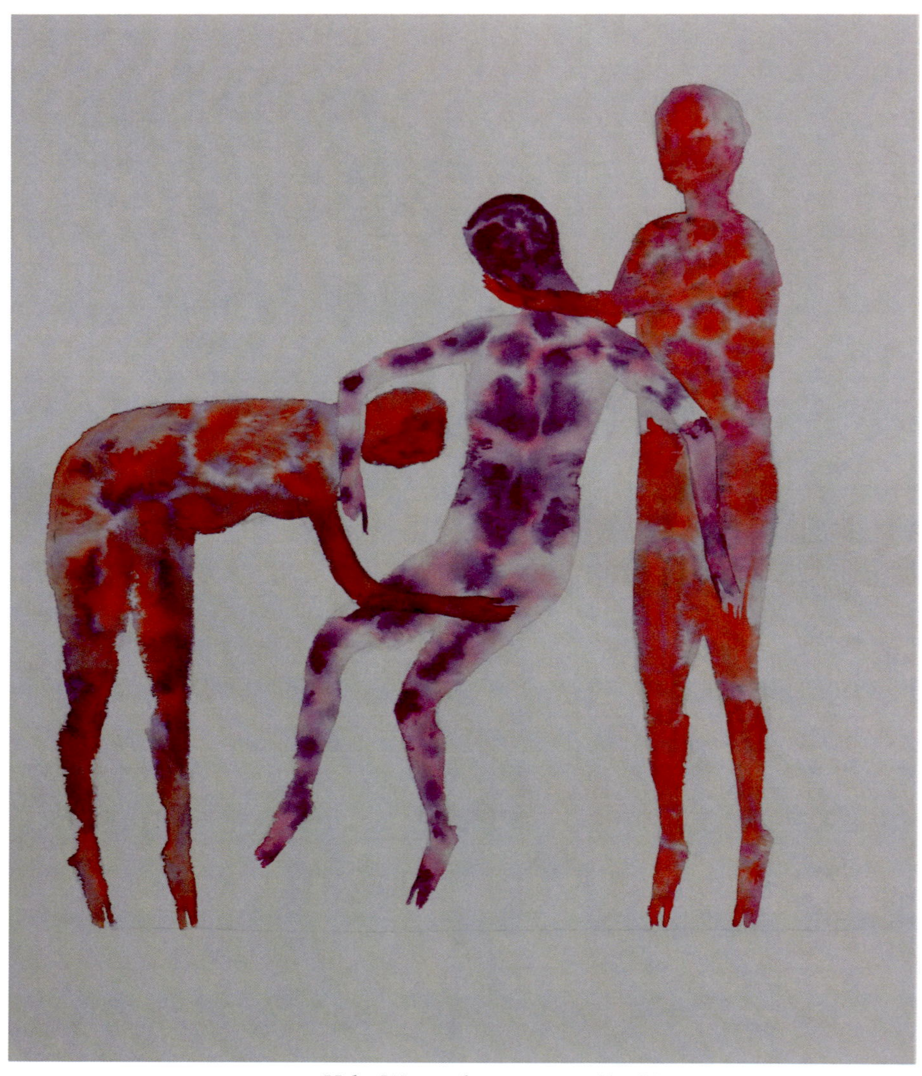

Help. Watercolor on paper, 40 x 35

Another explosion. Someone tries to stop it by pushing it away but fails. Is that right?

Yes, that's correct. We're completely helpless.

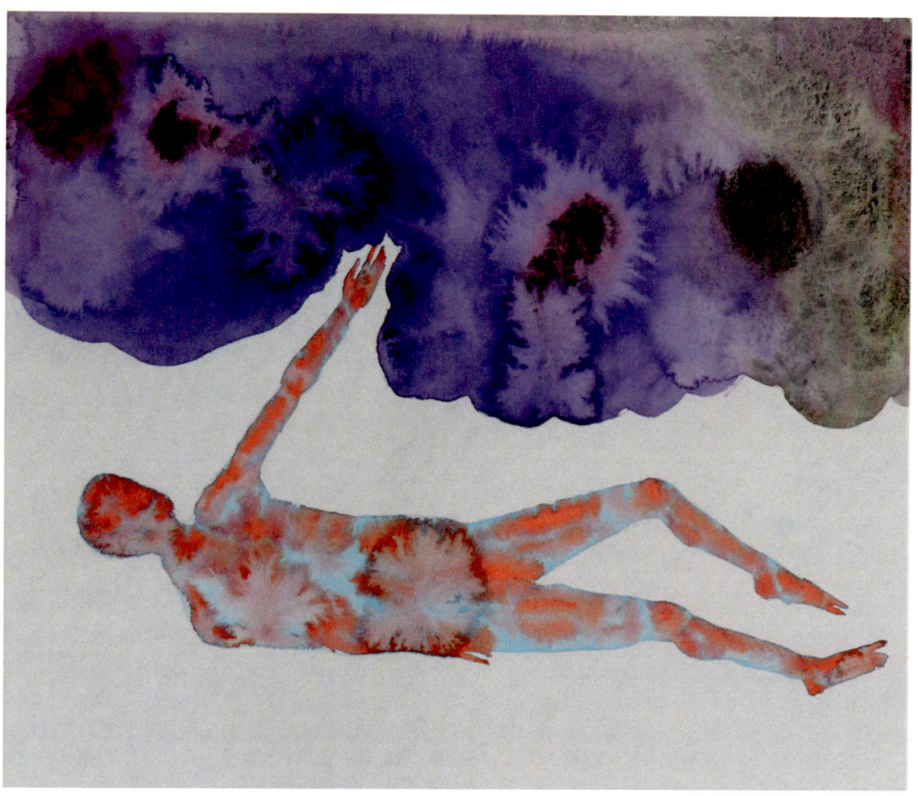

Explosion. Watercolor on paper, 30 x 35 cm

It's probably about a woman who has just become the welcome prey of a Russian occupier who can do whatever he wants to her.

It's also about the news we received about the many people tortured by the Russian occupying forces.

How did you come up with the idea to show us this using what we consider to be a medieval motif?

This work addresses the longstanding theme of martyrdom. Do we still face similar suffering today?

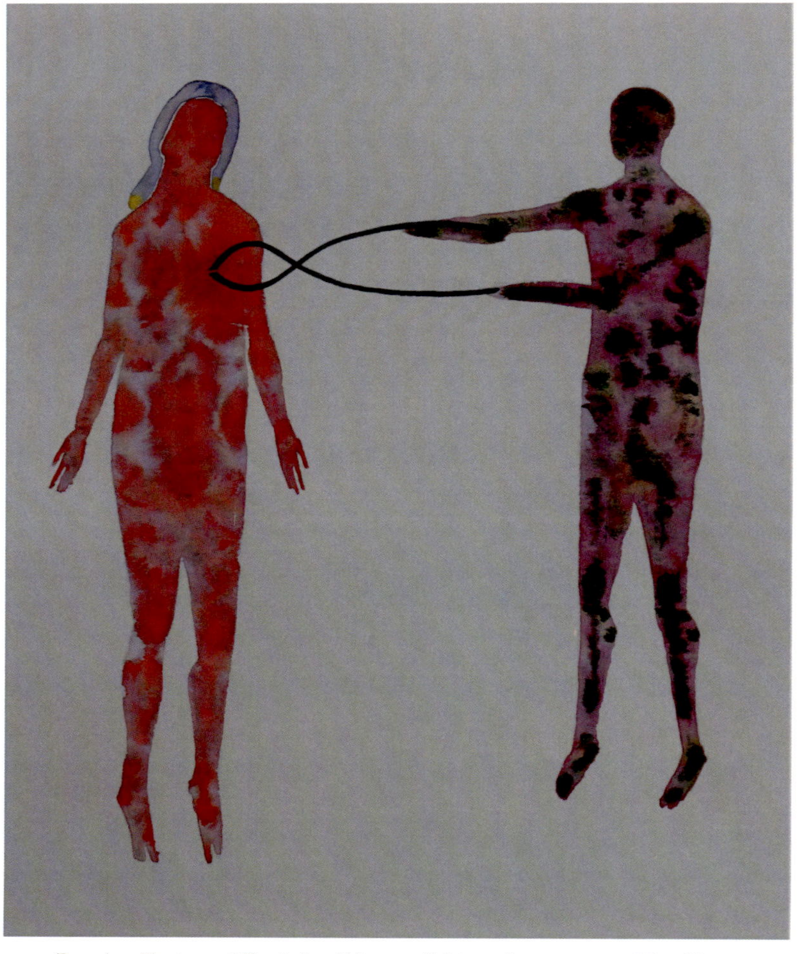

Russian Tortures Ukrainian Woman. Watercolor on paper, 35 x 30 cm

This work stands out as especially emotional to me. The family's grief, observing tragedy with a cross in view, possibly alludes to Christ's crucifixion.

Still, my focus is on today's burdens—do we help each other or remain indifferent?

This piece features symbolic elements but isn't considered sacred art, unlike much of your other work. Do you believe sacred art can be viewed through a contemporary lens?

Yes, because sacred art should be able to evolve and respond to our current situation.

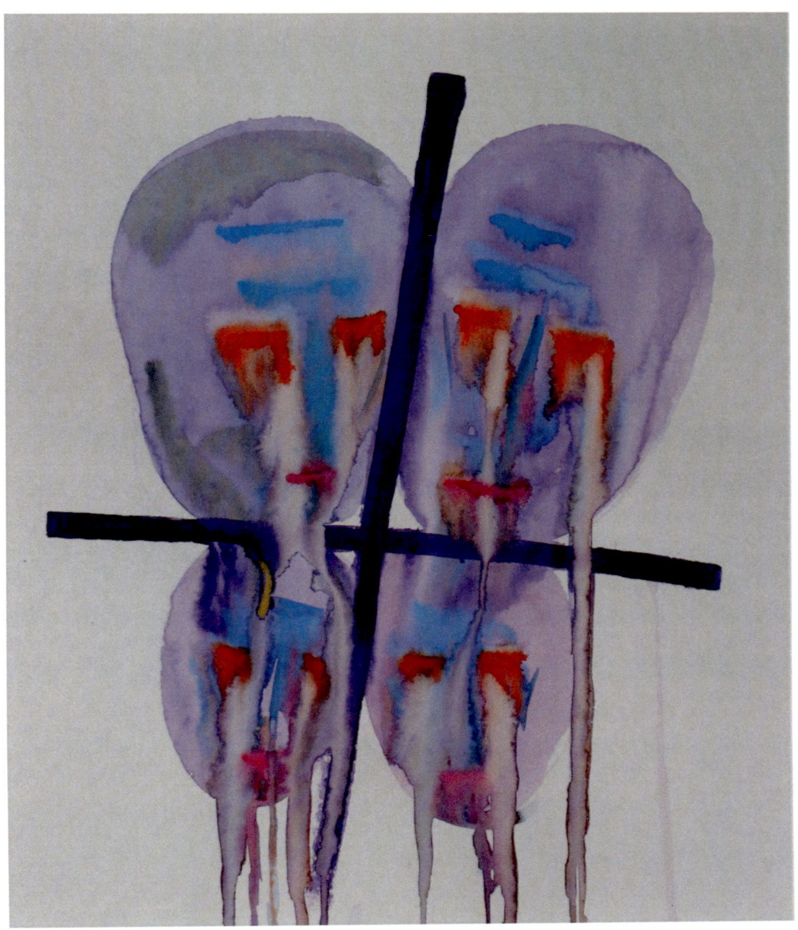

Family. Watercolor on paper, 40 x 35 cm

This extends to your "defense" theme, depicting peaceful self-protection from tattooed killers with unchecked authority

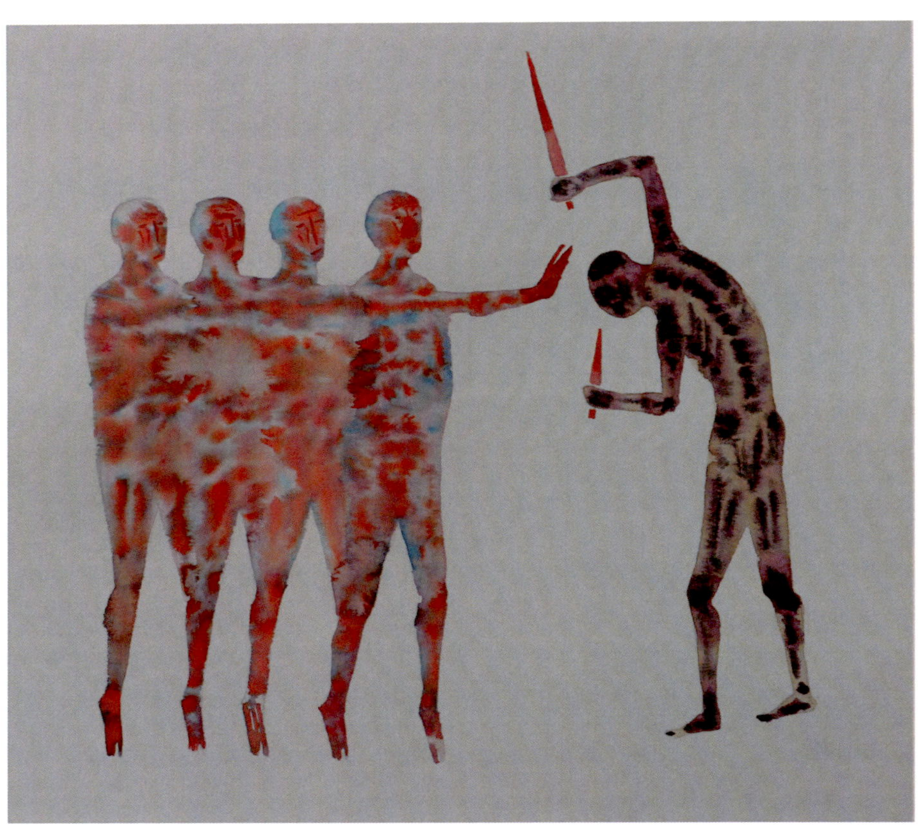

Resistance. Watercolor on paper, 35 x 40 cm

A recurring motif is the crucified Christ depicted above.

This addresses reports of Russian attacks on architecturally significant churches and people seeking sanctuary. The image depicts two soldiers mocking Christ before his crucifixion, focusing on his injuries.

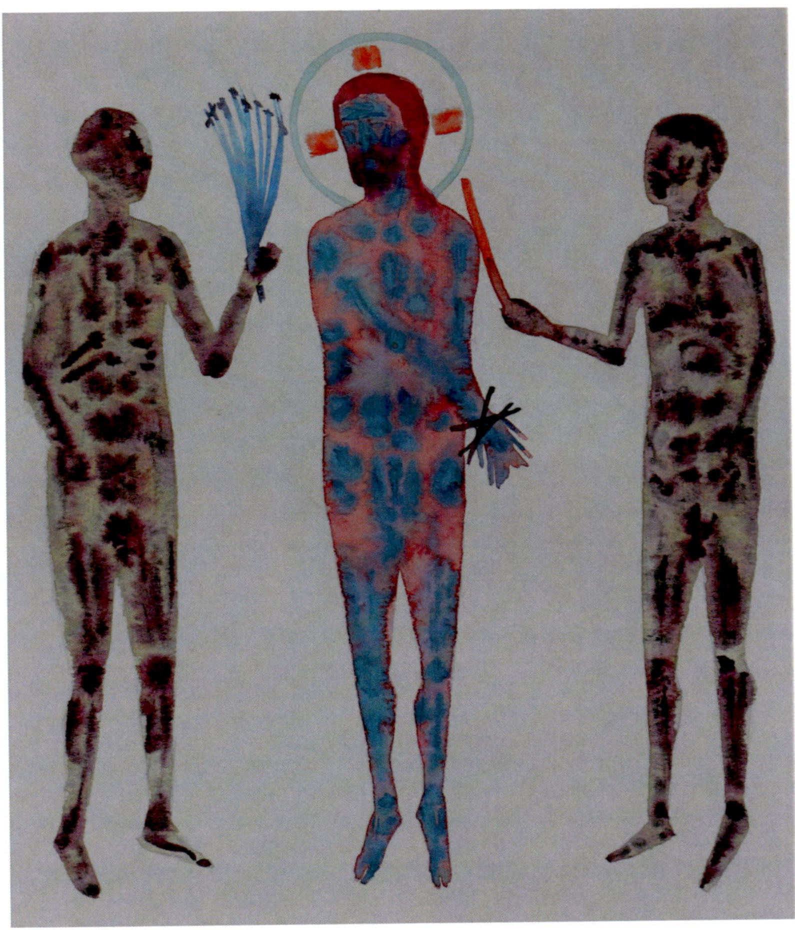

Russians Torturing Jesus Christ. Watercolor on paper. 35 x 30 cm

Your initial piece featuring a skull became part of a series suitable for a diptych, consistently using Ukraine's two colors. Can you share your thoughts on skulls and their appeal to artists and students? Is it the underlying concept that interests you?

The skull and crossbones motif frequently appear in medieval art. For instance, it is present in several prints by Albrecht Dürer. This renowned artist often employed such imagery to convey themes related to the inevitability of death. The symbol reflects the concept of human mortality and serves as a reminder of the transient nature of life.

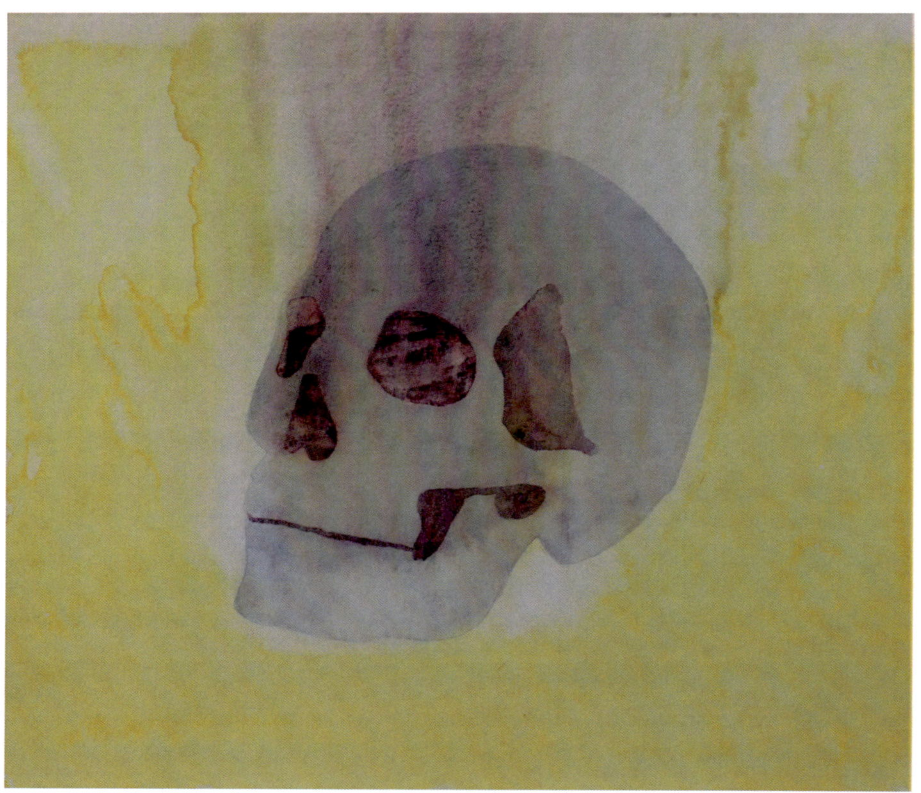

Death in the Yellow of our Fields. Watercolor on paper. 30 x 35 cm

It serves as a reminder of mortality. What meaning did he assign to it? Some medieval ideas, such as public self-scourging by flagellants for purification, are rare today.

We are all mortal. We should always be aware of this while appreciating our lives. Today, science teaches us that the human body is an interconnected system and that the brain can transmit pain throughout it. It's an escape, perhaps, but also a way of finding a language in my art for everyone, these feelings that are inside me.

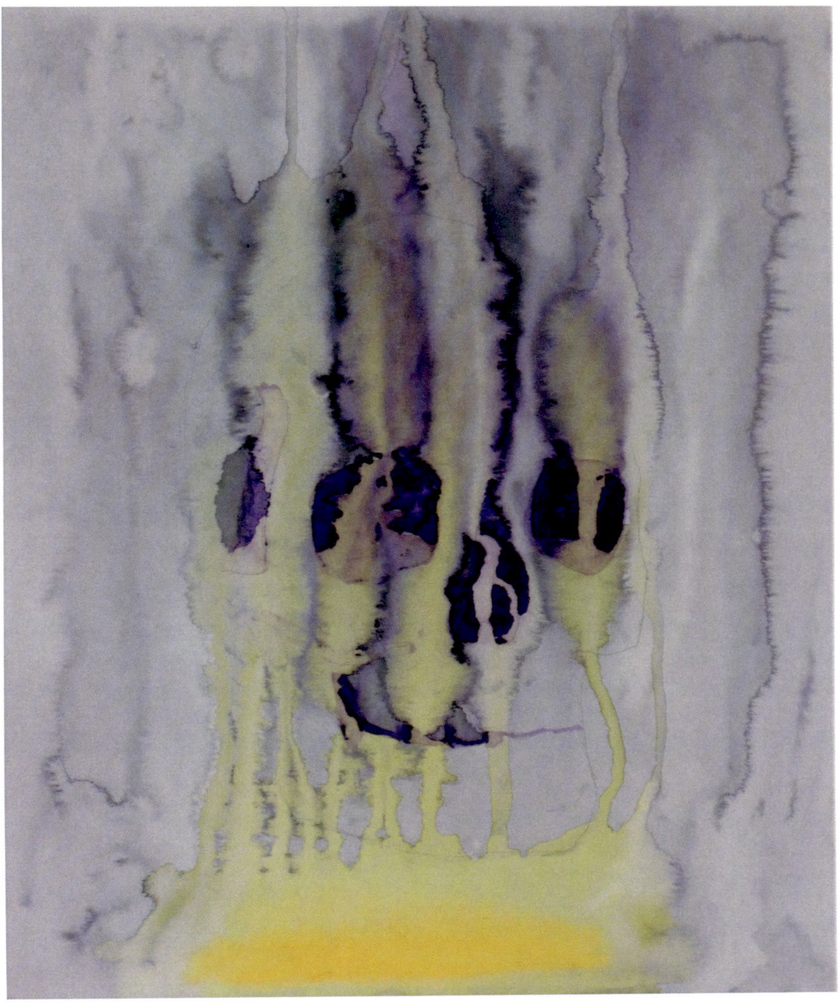

Smoke. Watercolor on paper. 35 x 30 cm

The theme of mutual assistance is depicted. A woman is shown carrying an injured man to a safe location.

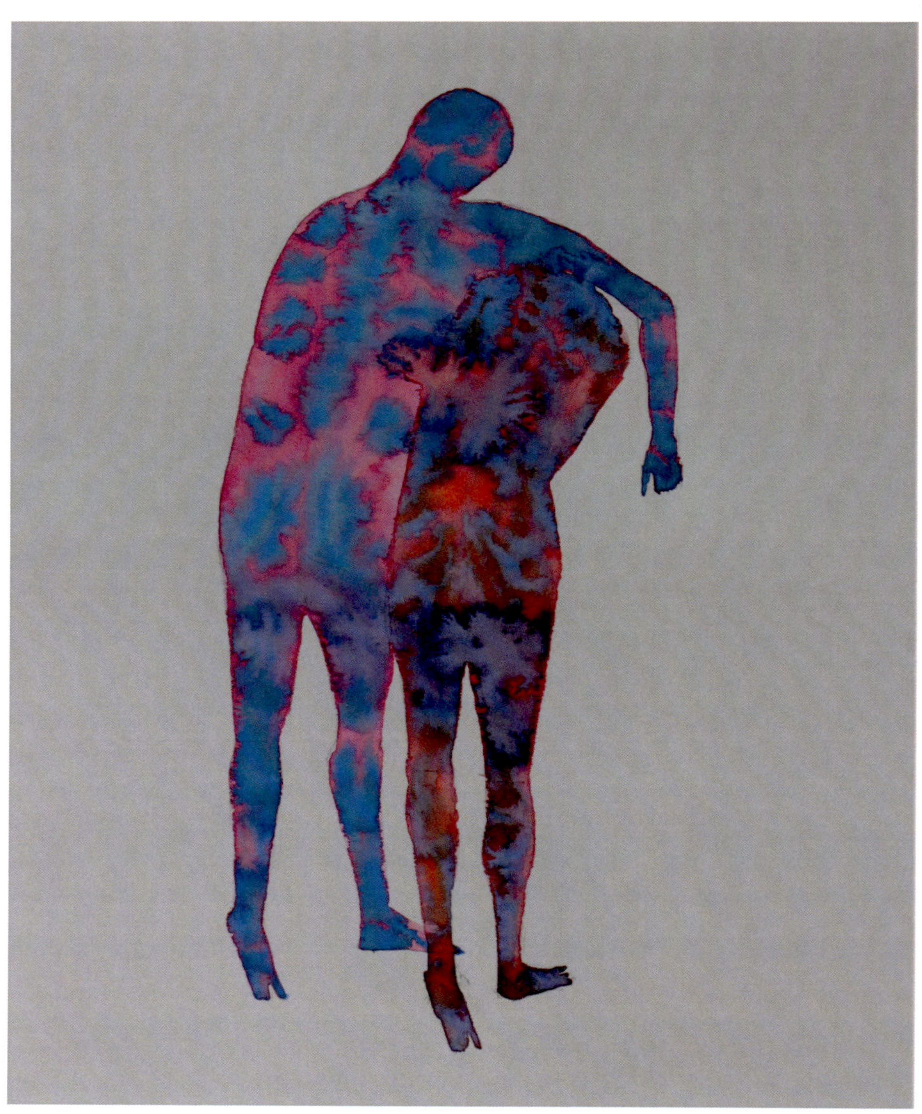

Escape. Watercolor on paper. 35 x 30 cm

Sharing art with an audience fosters wider appreciation and understanding. This work documents significant events from the conflict and provides records for future reference. What kind of feedback have you received from your colleagues? How do they view your work?

As I am neither an art scholar nor an art critic, I will leave the analysis to those with relevant expertise. Today, I decided to join this committee, which will evaluate all art produced during the conflict. Have there been any requests for exhibitions in Western regions? If so, they should be considered for acceptance.

I've already received some requests. One person from the West wrote to say that my work revealed a deeper meaning of these events than what is shown in their media. I've contacted several artists, including Dariusz Pado from Poland. Pado, who is both a poet and a colleague, informed me that my work made him aware of events in Ukraine. He expressed interest in collaborating and wrote some poems.

Are there any actual performances, rather than just images posted on Facebook? Have you read his poems?

No, I haven't had the opportunity to do so yet.

I also saw online that your photos were displayed at a conference in Finland.

It was a fundraising concert for Ukraine, not a conference. My photos were displayed on the background screen.

Apart from some exhibitions, do you have any plans to raise awareness of your work and convey your message?

There have been requests for exhibitions at locations such as the Royal Castle in Warsaw and a venue in Zurich. There is also consideration of publishing printed materials, such as a book combining my photographs with poems by another author.

How are you today? I see that you have started a support program.

I continue to try to understand my situation since the war began, but even after 40 days, it remains unclear to me. I tend to focus on work, although it is difficult to fully convey the current circumstances we are experiencing.

I acknowledge the challenges faced by all involved. Your ongoing work serves as a continuous record that will document these events for future reference. I sincerely appreciate your efforts. I hope that you are shielded from harm in your personal life, that this situation does not adversely impact you, and that you continue to find optimism moving forward.

The phrase "Ars longa, vita brevis" indicates that art lasts beyond the span of a human life. This viewpoint highlights the significance of continuous effort and future planning.

Dariusz Pago: Ra

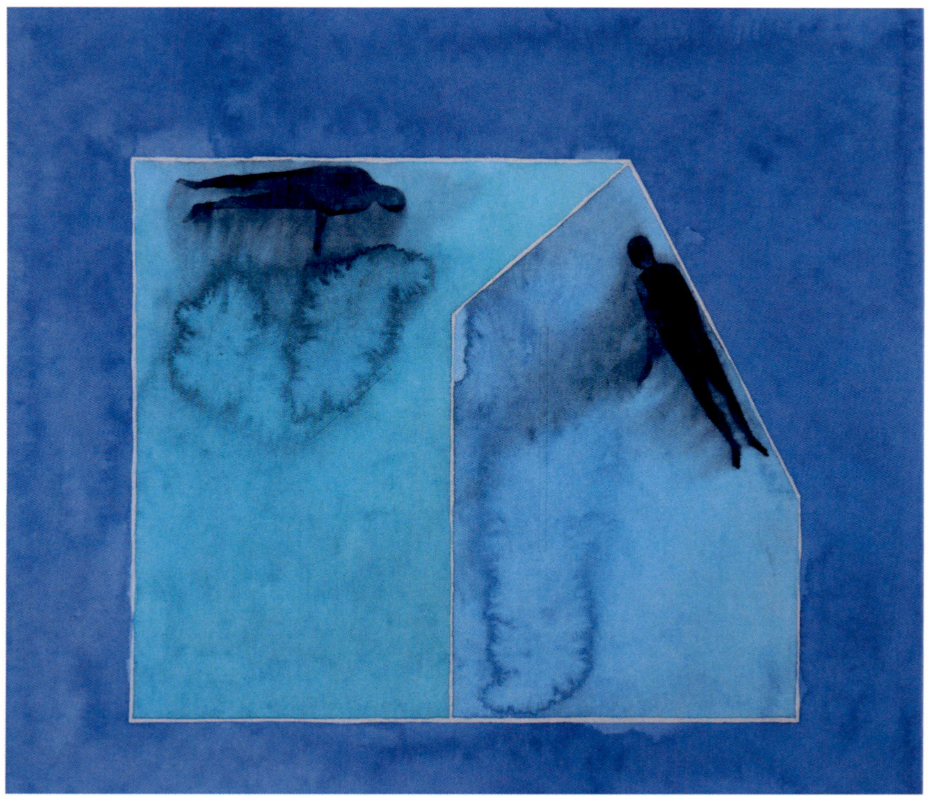

Disappearance. Watercolor on paper, 30 x 35 cm

Rain fell quietly I slept unnoticed
The well filled, mountains grew
rainwater drifted toward her

Ants from the east hid in the girl's bag
while she lay nearby
Stars dropped, their light dimming

I watched the fire, caught a bullet
and though I could do more
moved on – unable to hear anything
when the rain returned

Image Selection 2023

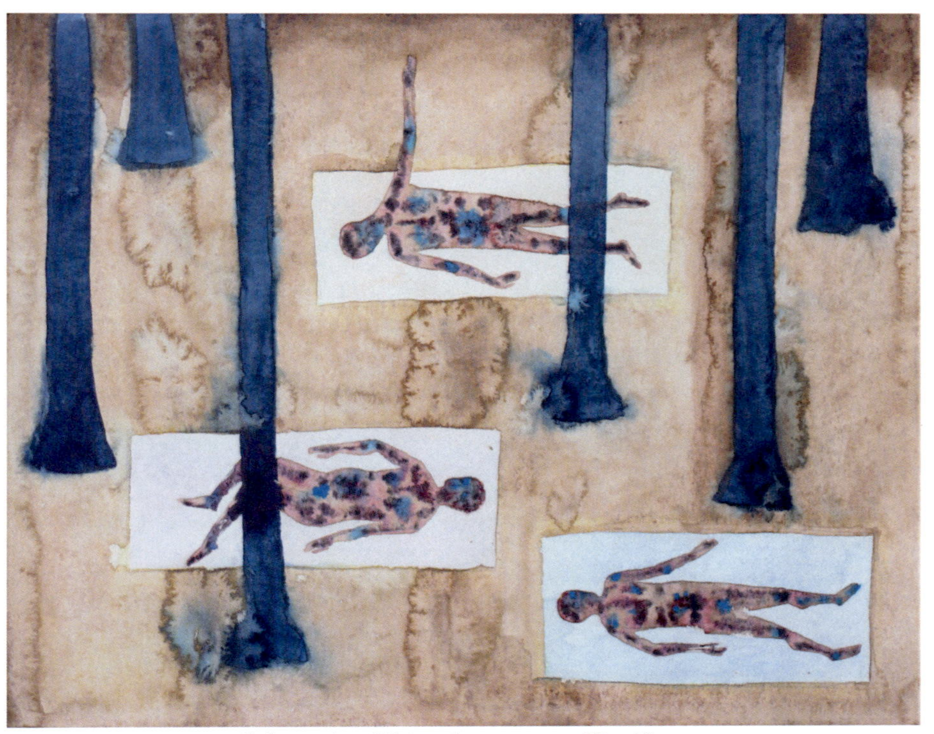

Exhumation. Watercolor on paper, 35 x 40 cm

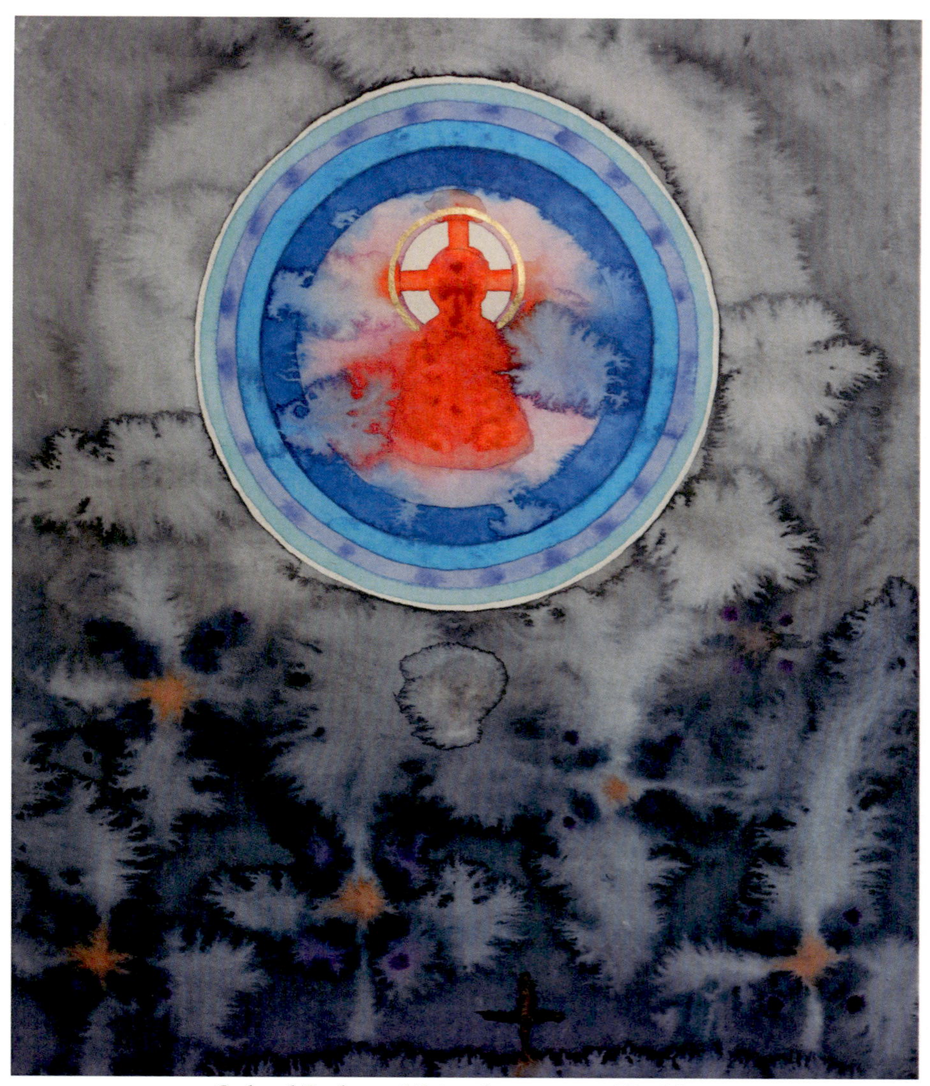

God and Darkness. Watercolor on paper, 25 x 30 cm

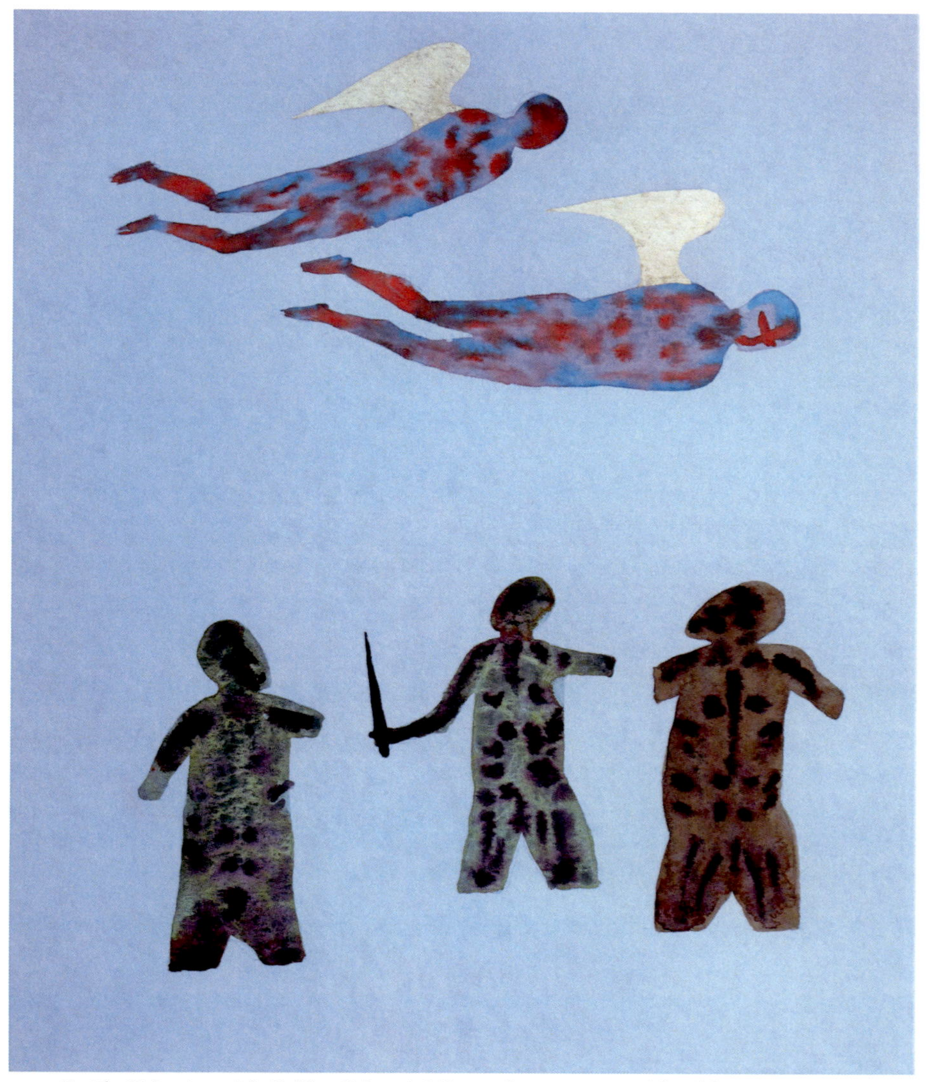

Battle (Warrior with Golden Wings). Watercolor on paper with gilding, 35 x 30 cm

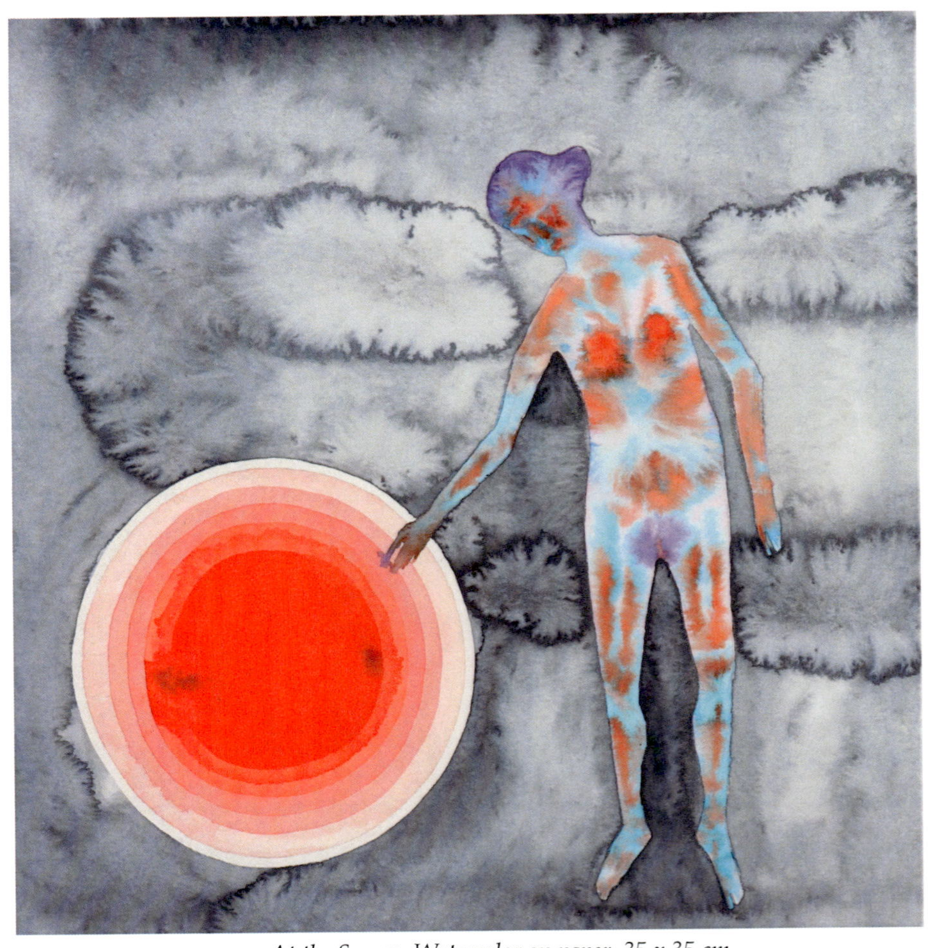

At the Source. Watercolor on paper, 35 x 35 cm

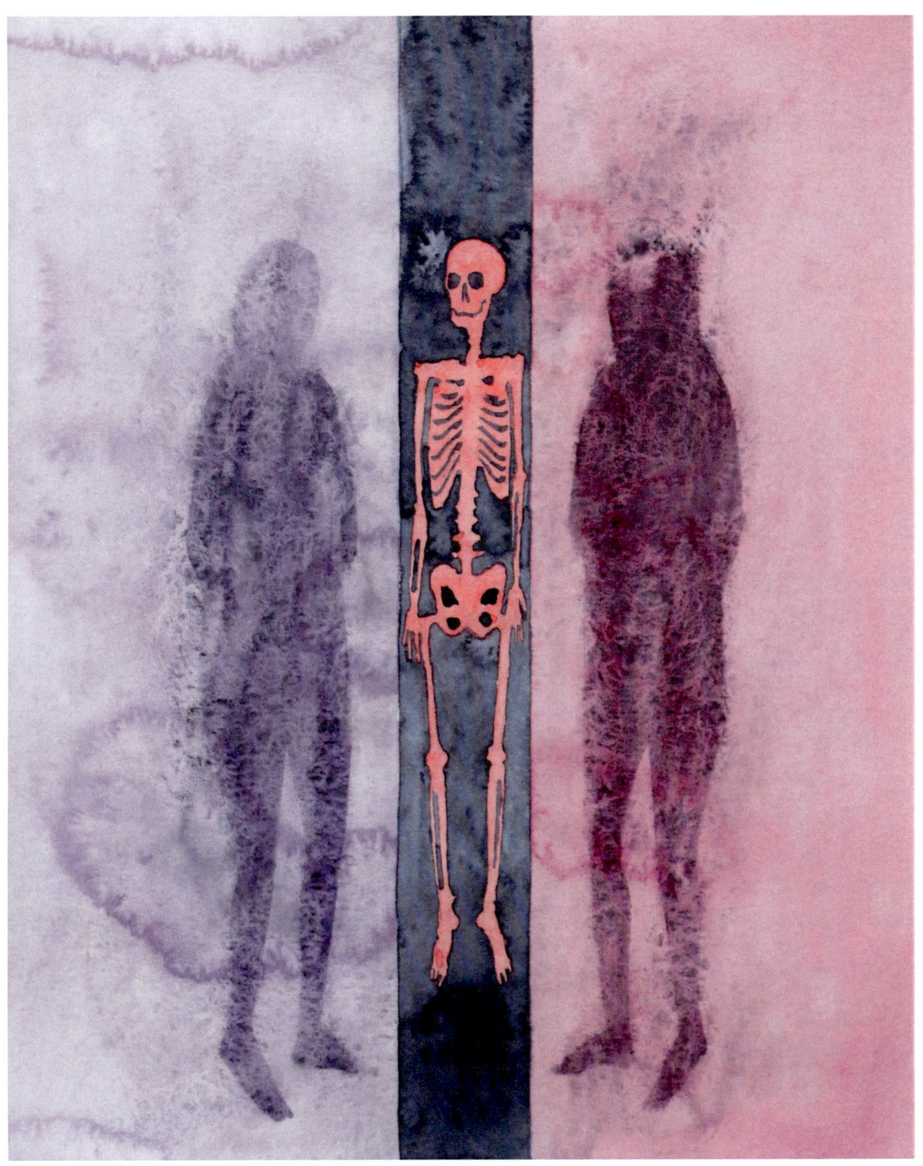

At the Edge of the Death. Watercolor on paper, 35 x 35 cm

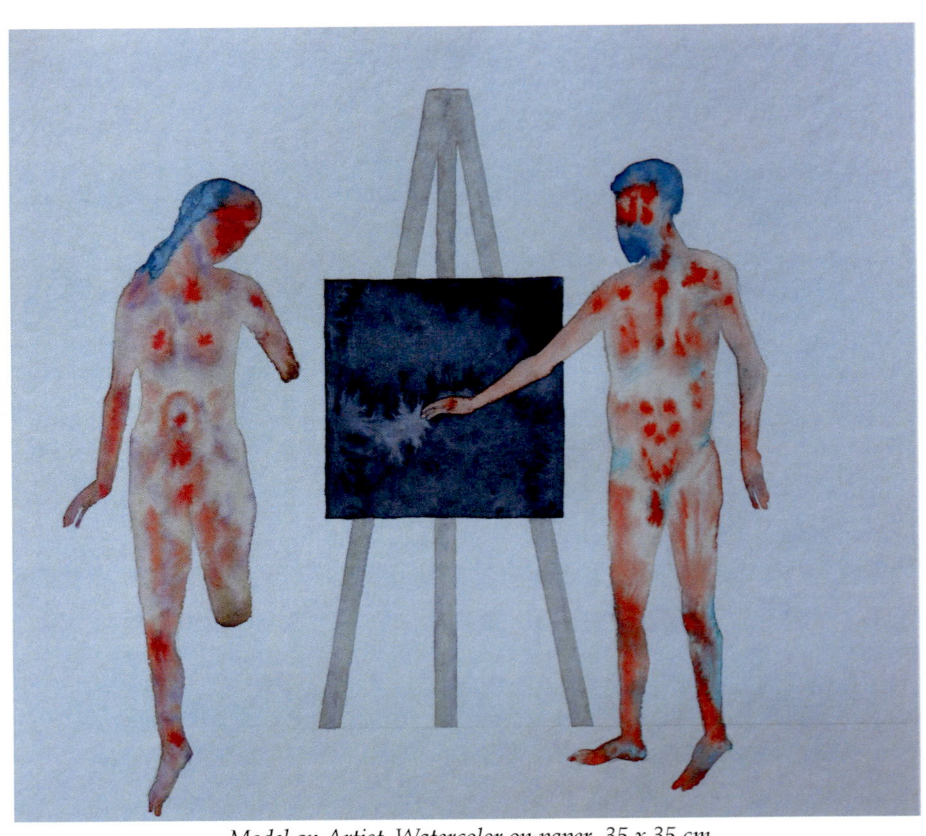

Model an Artist. Watercolor on paper, 35 x 35 cm

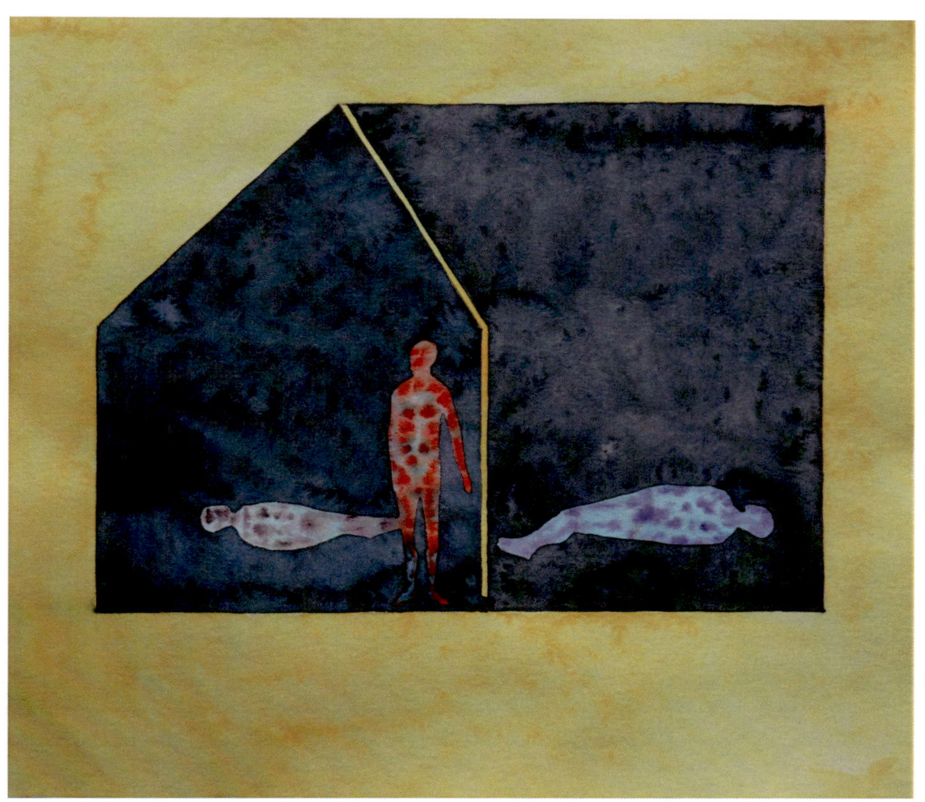

Memory of the Holodomor. Watercolor on paper, 35 x 35 cm

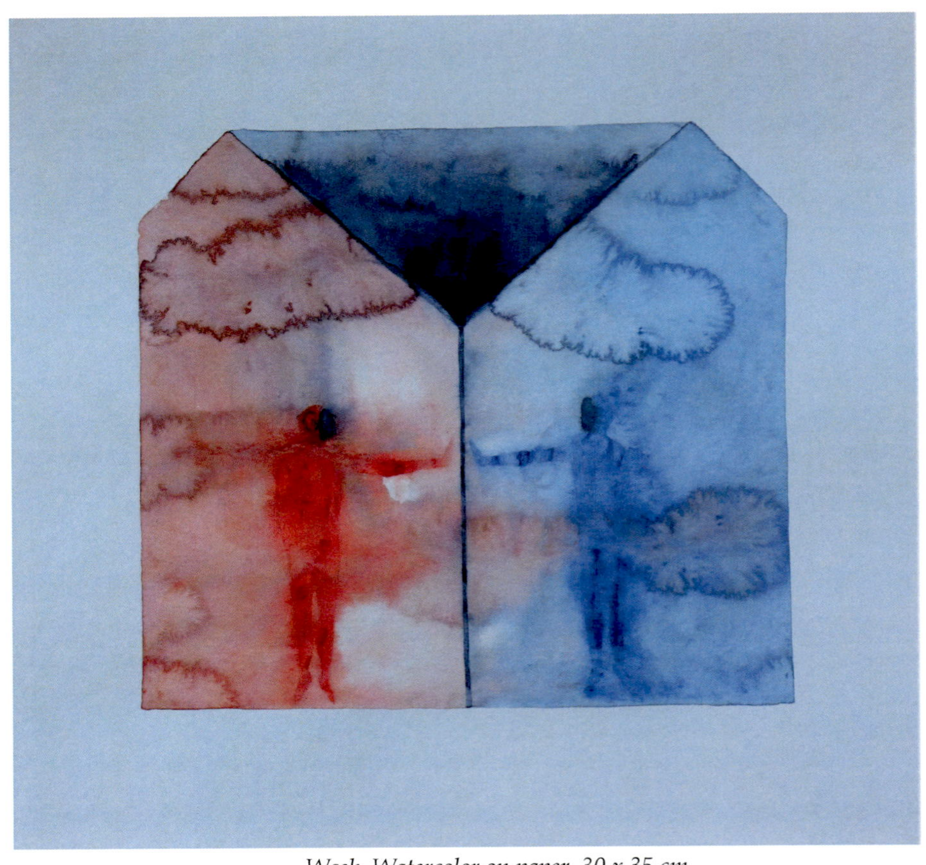

Wash. Watercolor on paper, 30 x 35 cm

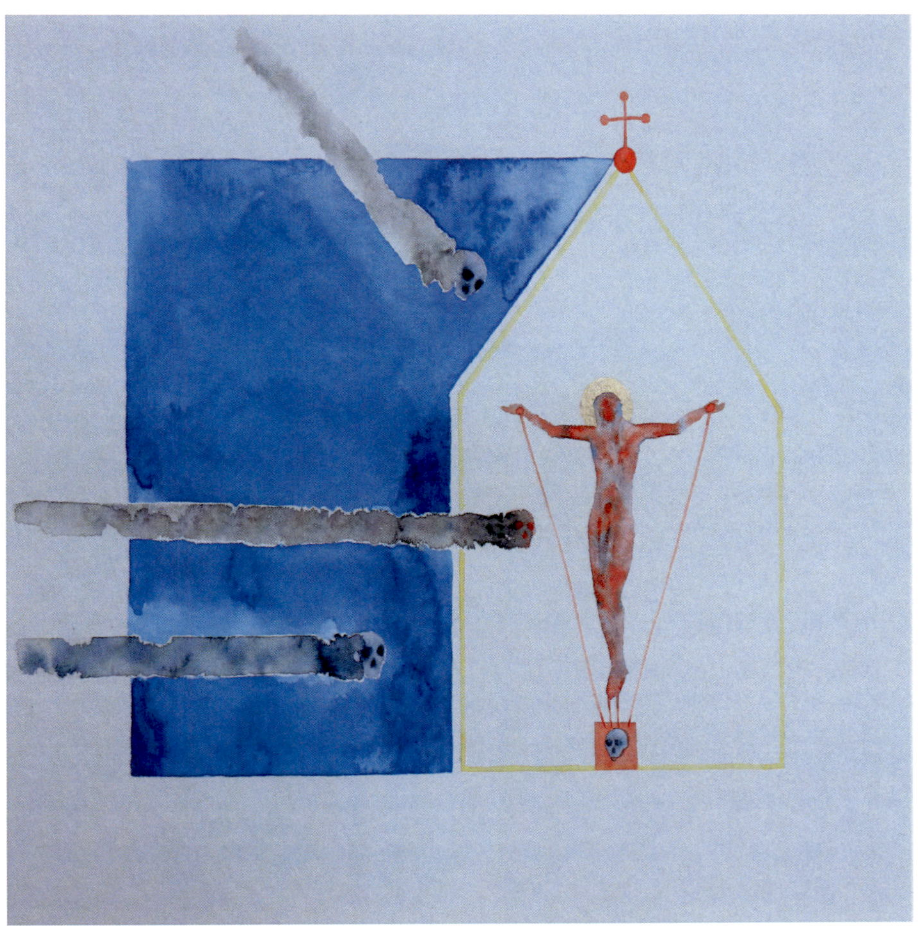

Russians Destroy the Crucifixion. Watercolor on paper, 30 x 35 cm

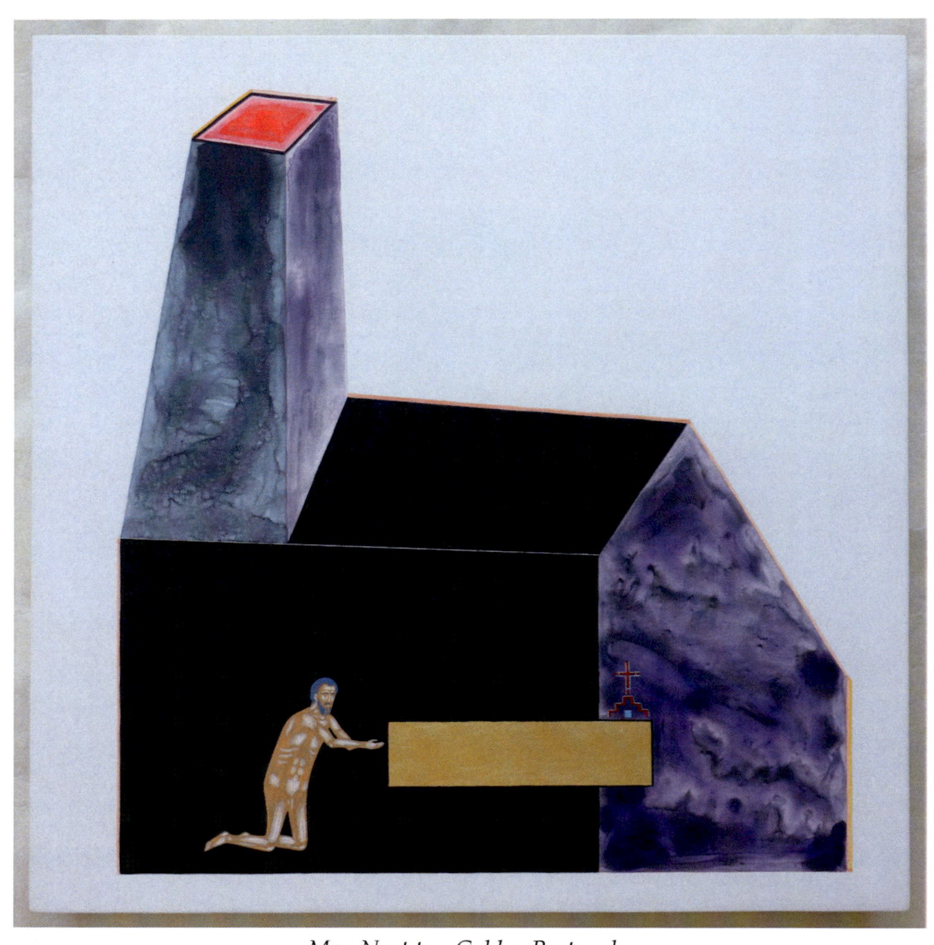

Man Next to a Golden Rectangle.
Wood with primer, tempera and gilding, 40 x 40 cm

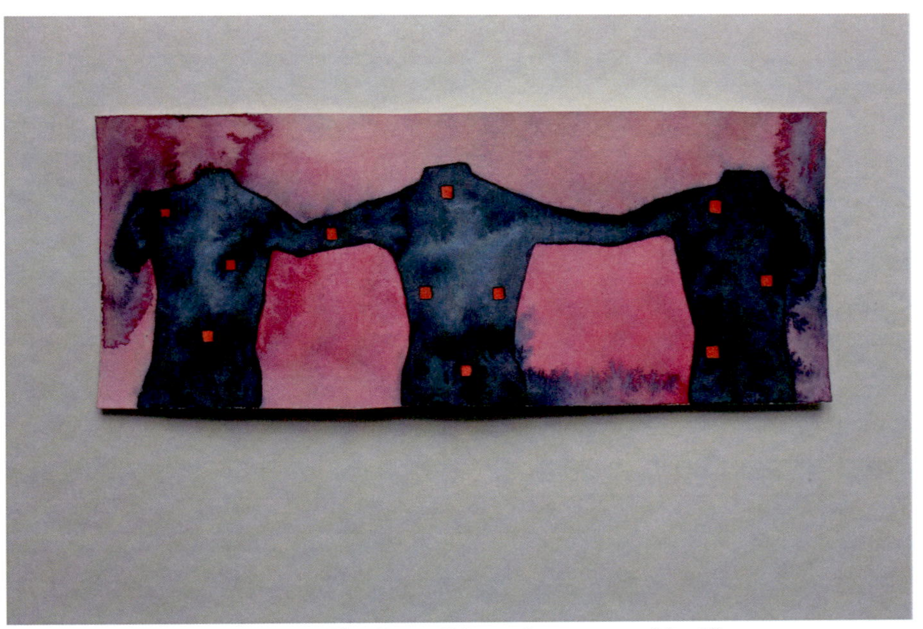

Three Torsos on Blue Paper. Watercolor on paper, 20 x 50 cm

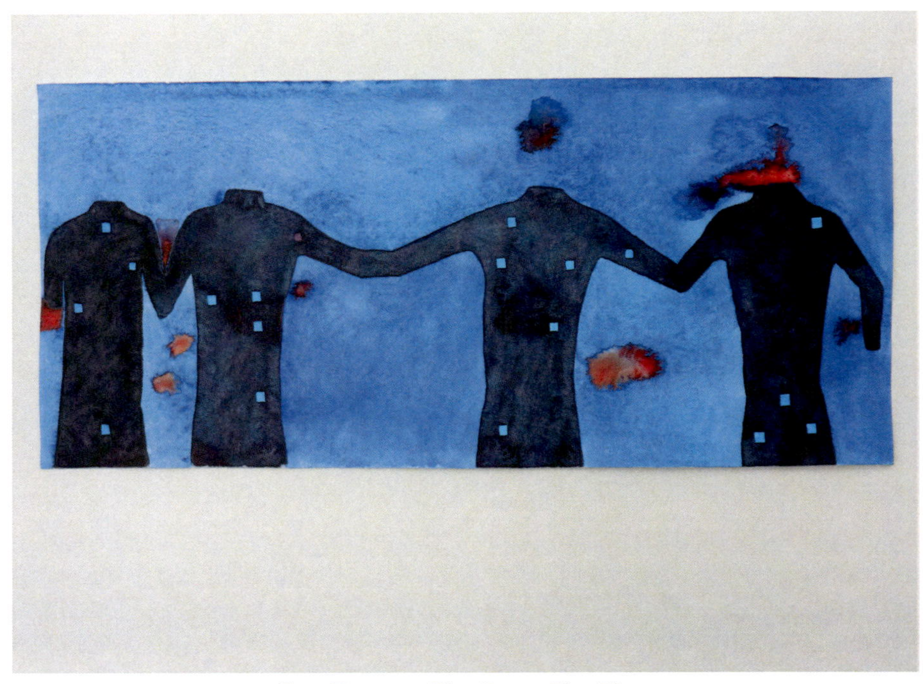

Four Torsos on Blue Paper, 20 x 50 cm

Interview with Julian Chaplinsky[13]

To the Person

In a recent interview, you mentioned having met the renowned Swiss architect, Mario Botta.[14]

As the head of an architectural firm in Lviv, I sought his advice when planning the new Church of the Orphanage Fathers.[15] During his visit, he also delivered several lectures at the Faculty of Architecture at Lviv Polytechnic University. I greatly admire Botta's churches due to their impressive construction and contemporary design, which foster a distinctive spiritual ambience. — Why are you interested in Ukrainians?

Certainly, but before that, may I ask what your task is today?

It's a significant responsibility. You can find information about it in public sources. I work in urban planning for the Lviv city administration. I heard that you received a great offer from Stuttgart but chose to stay. After the war started, I received an offer from Stuttgart too. My colleague, the architect Stefan Behnisch, invited me to join him. He is open-minded and has a solid grasp of the German language. He offered me an apartment in his residence, which is in a central area of Stuttgart and would keep my family safe. In my opinion, Stuttgart is a vibrant city, distinguished by its dynamic

13 https://tvoemisto.tv/exclusive/lyudy_tvogo_mista_yulian_chaplinskyy_pro_ruynuvannya_y_budivnytstvo_lvova_chastyna_persha_89699.html#goog_rewarded

14 Roman Catholic religious order that goes back to the Italian priest Luigi Orione, a disciple of Don Bosco. It is particularly well known for its commitment to victims of war.

15 Benisch Architekten is a global architectural firm offering a wide range of services. It was founded in 1989 by Stefan Benisch, born in 1957. In addition to Stuttgart, the company has offices in Boston and Munich: https://en.wikipedia.org/wiki/Behnisch_Architekten. In addition the following interview provides a good insight into Stefan Benisch's views: Live interview with Stefan Behnisch | Virtual Design Festival | Dezeen

cultural scene and notable architectural landmarks. It is also renowned for being home to globally recognized automotive brands such as Mercedes and Porsche. — Are you from Zurich?

I live in Zofingen, a small town with a historic city center located between Basel and Lucerne. I was a pastor in a Reformed congregation for 35 years. Since retiring, I have had more free time. After the war began, I read the English translation of the memoirs The Universe Behind the Barbed Wire by Miroslav Marinovich, whom you may know. He co-founded the Ukrainian Helsinki Group for Human Rights and spent seven years in a penal camp with dangerous criminals. This was followed by three years in exile in Kazakhstan. I was able to publish his memoirs in a revised edition of an existing German translation, and they reveal the problems that contributed to the current war.

In 2017, I visited Lviv for the first time and was immediately fascinated by the city. During my stay, I saw reminders of the 2014 war everywhere, such as photos of fallen soldiers and appeals for army donations. During my visit, I bought a new type of icon. I later learned more about this art form and contacted Danylo via Facebook.

After the Russian invasion began, I noticed that he had started painting watercolors depicting current events. I expressed my admiration for his work and suggested that we publish a book together.

Thank you for your interest in Ukraine and for the significant contributions you have made on our behalf.

I read that you wanted to be an artist.

My older brother is a percussionist who used to play in a symphony orchestra. Our mother is also a musician. She worked as a musicologist and music theorist until she retired. She was a real pioneer in these fields. I wanted to continue our family's musical legacy, but I clearly remember my father telling me that he never wanted anyone in his family to doubt their ability to earn a living. This is why he strongly advised me against becoming a professional musician. I still love music very much, though, and I play by myself. I like to get my bass guitar out from time to time and play a few chords. Later, when I wanted to study art, I unfortunately could not pass the entrance exams because I fell ill on the way there. Near our house was our neighbor's workshop. He was a sculptor. When he visited us, he told my father that he would advise his son to become an architect. However, if his son wanted to become an artist, that would be fine too.

Ultimately, I chose to attend a technical college and became an architect. In my current job, I always have something to draw, such as sketches for urban development projects or façade designs. However, I love music more because it touches my emotions and is more in tune with my inner self. In my spare time, I enjoy playing the bass guitar and listening to music. Unfortunately, I don't do any sketching at this time.

Do you ever collaborate with others to perform music?

I usually compose music for personal fulfilment. Nonetheless, I once considered inviting fellow artists to my holiday home, which has an exceptional view of the mountains. When a friend visited, I mentioned my idea of organizing outdoor art sessions. He responded enthusiastically, suggesting that we collaborate and noting that the location was ideal for such activities. Observing artist friends, particularly painters, allows you to see their different approaches and techniques. I intend to resume organizing these plein air sessions once circumstances permit after the war concludes.

The General Mood in the West

What is the general public's perspective on this issue in Switzerland, beyond the views of politicians? Are there widespread concerns among the population? What are the most common positions? I have visited Switzerland approximately six times and have gained a general understanding of the country. It is known for its prosperity, cultural events, political stability, and attention to environmental issues. While these factors may be of significant interest within the country, I have not conducted extensive research on this topic.

Three types of reactions have been observed. Some individuals have expressed support for Ukraine for an extended period. Their support has taken various forms, including actions through governmental channels, as well as personal efforts, such as helping refugees or providing aid. Following the onset of the war, a weekly peace gathering was established in our town. However, many people in our country are unaware of Ukraine's history and its interactions with Russia. We also face Russian cyberattacks, which demand vigilance and significant resources.

Some people avoid mainstream media, believing it to be biased or deceptive. They turn to sites they consider more trustworthy, but these sites often spread Russian propaganda. For this reason, some argue that Western nations should seek a deeper understanding of Russia. During the pandemic, conspiracy theories spread, and some people accused the government of committing crimes against citizens. Disagreements over the virus have led to ongoing divisions.

More people also ignore the news and show little interest in global events. They prefer to focus on their own well-being, believing that world events will occur regardless of their involvement. Regarding our government, it is currently organizing an international peace conference that could potentially result in a "cold war."

Challenges to the Core Principles of Western Societies

I attended a seminar led by Professor Mikhailo Hrushevsky in which we studied the foundations of philosophy. Our group read texts by significant figures in the Enlightenment, such as Plato, Voltaire, and John Locke. We analyzed Locke's concepts of human liberty and his framework for effective governance, both of which informed the foundation of modern liberal democracy. These accomplishments are often overlooked and are currently at significant risk due to ongoing conflict.

The ideas of these philosophers offer relevant perspectives in challenging times. The insights contained in these books remain significant in contemporary discussions. During the Enlightenment, distinguished intellectuals promoted liberalism and democracy within their nations, contributing to Europe's and the United States' independence. There was widespread optimism during that time that international conflicts and disagreements could be resolved through peaceful means rather than warfare.

John Locke stated: "There is one thing we should never forget in our lives: It is freedom." Our professor frequently emphasized this idea. Today, this idea is less commonly mentioned to children. European concepts of freedom and democracy are historically connected to Christianity, which played a role in developing democratic ideas.

Currently, the emphasis is on individual self-improvement, which has contributed to a diminished sense of collective responsibility for the well-being of all. I have observed little variation among your governments' responses. The prevailing sentiment appears consistent: "This conflict is not our concern. We should refrain from involvement because we understand that this war centers around Putin." This raises the question: Is there truly a need to defend our values right now?

During President Reagan's administration, certain U.S. government officials were expected to advocate for the Soviet Union to adhere to principles such as free and fair elections, freedom of expression, and other international human rights standards. John F. Kennedy, a well-known Democratic president, was Catholic, while Ronald Reagan was Protestant. The influence of Protestantism remains apparent in Scandinavian countries today. However, there are still concerns that the Western world has yet to fully acknowledge the gravity of the present circumstances. The principle of global freedom may be at risk due to the influence of regimes such as those in Iran, China, and Russia, which do not prioritize individual liberties. These regimes maintain the concept of a "sacred alliance" between power and religion as it was understood prior to the Enlightenment in the 18th century. This "unholy coalition" contradicts the modern concept of a liberal state, in which religion can play a positive societal role independently.

In my view, the West's lack of awareness of the seriousness of our global situation is dangerous. I am convinced that, because of this war, a new ideology will emerge that will one day rule us all. Conversely, some analysts have noted that the Western world has moved away from emphasizing its Christian heritage, which has been linked to the development of liberal and democratic states. Currently, these historical influences are less recognized.

Eighteenth-century intellectuals, however, demonstrated a keen awareness of these concepts. For instance, Isaac Newton had strong religious beliefs and claimed that divine laws governed the natural world. He viewed the study of physics as an exploration of God's actions. Similarly, John Locke expressed his spirituality through his unique perspective. He discussed the concept of human freedom with his peers and supported his views with references to the Holy Scriptures. All participants shared a belief in God, so their ethical perspectives were closely connected to their religious beliefs, whether Catholic or Protestant.

Kennedy and Reagan's faith influenced their presidential decisions. Both opposed the risk of a third world war, with Reagan acknowledging the disastrous effects of the Vietnam War. The Vietnam War ended during Nixon's presidency. Some analysts have suggested that the continuation of the conflict might have impacted Nixon's reelection campaign. Historically, candidates for major government positions have told voters that communism poses a significant threat to the United States and the Western world. Many initially supported the prospect of war, but public opinion shifted after casualties became apparent. Reagan's Christian beliefs prevented him from prolonging the war.

For this reason, President Kennedy selected the Vatican as a trusted intermediary in negotiations with Khrushchev during the Cuban Missile Crisis. Additionally, Pope John Paul II of Poland played a significant role in facilitating the peaceful dissolution of the Soviet bloc. The consensus reached was, "Let us establish peace." Although the Catholic Church held significant authority at that time, it no longer possesses such influence in contemporary society.

I agree with your analysis. As a pastor, I have observed the church's declining influence, partly due to concerns about the credibility of its representatives. My own Reformed church has yet to recognize that the alliance between church and state is outdated. As you said, it's important for the church to play a positive role in society. I have also noticed a general lack of awareness of the Christian origins of many Western values.

For many people, the concept of universal truth has diminished as perspectives have become more individualized. Today, anything can be said, including harmful ideas. The Kremlin has exploited this tendency, and its actions may ultimately harm us.

Rise of Modern Totalitarianism

How will this war end?

We cannot be sure. Based on recent experience, it's clear that Putin refuses to negotiate and does not seek peace with us. His ambitions extend beyond Donbas and Crimea. He intends to spread his ideology worldwide. Putin is obsessed with the idea of reviving the great Russian empire of the 19th century.

His former KGB colleague from St. Petersburg, who assisted him during his time there, is currently the metropolitan of the Russian Orthodox state church and supports this idea. The church has always wanted to share power with the state.

Kirill's statements in documents and sermons justifying this genocide against Ukrainians are criminal. They also constitute a "holy campaign" against the entire Western world and NATO.

Putin is obsessed with the insane idea that Ukraine and Ukrainians don't exist. He undoubtedly wants to overthrow the government in Kyiv and annex Ukraine to his "Great Russian Empire." This war marks the beginning of this plan. Next will be the reintegration of states formerly behind the Iron Curtain, including Poland, the Baltic countries, Romania, Bulgaria, the Czech Republic, and former Yugoslavia, especially Serbia.

One of Putin's favorite philosophers, Vladimir Ilyin, opposed Bolshevism, supported monarchy, was a Slavophile, and sympathized with fascism. Initially buried near Zurich, Ilyin's remains were moved to Moscow's Donskoy Monastery cemetery in 2005. President Putin attended the reburial ceremony, and Ilyin's grave is now located near those of Pushkin and Solzhenitsyn. The event was organized and sponsored by Viktor Vekselberg, an oligarch. Alexander Dugin is another one of Putin's masterminds and is even more aggressive than Ilyin. He constantly smears the

West in his work and public appearances and maintains good relations with the Western far-right.

Today, communists claim to be the holiest Christians in the world. At the same time, they tell people: "Stalin was a very good leader." Yet Stalin had thousands of priests killed. Despite these unbelievable crimes, they still worship him today.

The Russian Orthodox Church is collaborating with these people again, just as it did before. No normal person could begin to understand something like this, let alone its horrific extent.

Some of these people claim, "Stalin was a very good leader." However, it should be remembered that Stalin was responsible for the execution of thousands of priests. Despite these atrocities, many still revere him. The Russian Orthodox Church is aligning itself with these individuals once again, just as it has done before. Such actions are difficult for any reasonable person to comprehend, let alone grasp the full horror of.

If asked which countries are members of NATO, many Russians might primarily mention the United States. Awareness of NATO among the general population is often shaped by television media. The same ignorance exists in the West, particularly among supporters of the Alternative for Germany (AfD) party. Unfortunately, this is nothing new in Germany.

Currently, right-wing extremists are promoting new Russian propaganda while some old left-wing extremists are still arguing for the abolition of capitalism despite changing times.

Today, I see the extreme rights' total opposition to America as a new religious phenomenon. In my opinion, a unified and self-aware West is a thing of the past. This is not consistent throughout Europe yet. Some regions, such as Scandinavia, the Netherlands, parts of Germany, and parts of Great Britain, remain exceptions. These areas have historically had a Protestant majority. Today, Europe is noticeably divided and disunited.

If you travel south, for example, to Spain or Italy... After repeatedly visiting Italy and hearing what people say, I simply consider them hopeless cases. It no longer has anything important to contribute to the world except in the areas of design and architecture. This great, ancient country, once home to some of Europe's greatest philosophers, can no longer boast that. Most Italians are only interested in nice furniture, beautiful bags, and expensive fashion. They are more concerned with opening more stores in Moscow that sell their products at high prices. These things are the real philosophy in today's Italy.

In advanced northern countries like the Netherlands and Denmark, significant attention is devoted to combating climate change through sustained efforts to develop innovative environmental technologies. They are considering involving other countries in their environmental plans. They also live in countries that take these concerns seriously. However, it seems that consumerism and material pursuits have replaced the intellectual and philosophical traditions that once defined Italy's cultural legacy. The current focus on luxury goods and fashion overshadows deeper societal contributions, prompting many to question whether Italy can regain its position as a beacon of thought and creativity in Europe.

The Desperate Situation in Ukraine

That is the situation here today. We are worse off now than we were two years ago.

Why is this the case?

I no longer see much enthusiasm in the West to support us. There may be negotiations going on behind the scenes that we know nothing about, but I no longer have much hope for them. It is disheartening to realize that we Ukrainians cannot rely on anything. We are completely powerless.

What will happen if Russia soon has more weapons and, therefore, more power? They are constantly producing new missiles and tanks. They still have a lot of money from their gas and oil. Ukraine doesn't have anything like that. This is why we consistently request assistance from other countries regarding access to their weaponry. A few more would help us defend our borders.

Currently, we don't even dare ask Russia to return the territory we've lost to maintain peace. One day, Europe will probably send us soldiers. However, the arguments in these discussions are always the same, and they're demoralizing. That is the worst part for me. We used to believe in beautiful European values, but today, they have somehow fallen by the wayside for everyone.

In the US, we've been told the same thing for a long time: "No, no, and no again." Once again, you must understand that we really can't give you anything more. We must also be able to defend ourselves against all the people coming from Latin America and flooding our country." I hear similar words in Europe, which to me means nothing other than that today, we can only invest in arming our armies.

These statements are also made in Switzerland. However, due to the country's neutral status, providing military support is prohibited, and increasing non-military aid is limited by Switzerland's need to maintain its own military readiness.

I remember what Macron, the French president, said in the first months of the war. He was tired of repeatedly trying to talk to Putin. How many hours had he spent trying, only to be unsuccessful? It was all just empty talk. He decided it would be best to fly to Moscow and tell Putin once again: "Let's resolve this peacefully. Okay, Crimea is yours now, but let's get back to normal." Today, he finally tells us, "We are considering deploying some of our soldiers to Ukraine. It may be possible."

We have been at war for two years. Two extremely long years. Probably 200,000 people have already died in our country as a result of this war. How many more must die just for you? When will the French or NATO soldiers come to save us?

Scholz keeps telling us the same thing: "No, that's not possible. We are not supplying German missiles to Ukraine!" Please understand: We cannot unilaterally take sides with you. We don't want to become another theater of this war. However, Scholz, you have supported us for a long time and been on our side. It's a gift to Putin that we can rely on people in the West. There are even parties in Germany that openly oppose us. I have no illusions about that. At some point, Europe may provide us with a contingent of soldiers. Unfortunately, these discussions repeat the same discouraging arguments, which is disheartening. The European values we once believed in seem absent today.

Challenging Outlook for Europe

Ukraine has demonstrated a strong commitment to its relationship with Europe. The nation has consciously chosen liberal democracy and alignment with the European community, viewing this decision as both natural and an exercise of sovereignty.

However, it may be many years before Ukraine joins the European Union. Perhaps Ukraine will join NATO one day—but then again, maybe not. It's a tricky game. Europe does not understand us. If Putin conquers Ukraine in five or seven years, Ukrainians may become Russian soldiers and one day conquer Poland and the Baltic countries.

This is not unrealistic; it happened before in our history when Ukrainians fought for Russia in World War I and killed Poles. The same was true in World War II. Ukrainians were always part of the Russian or Soviet army.

However, the Finns have never forgotten the Russian invasion. The Finns remember everything. They also empathize with the Baltic countries. They know that if they don't support Ukraine today, their nation will face the same fate tomorrow. It won't happen tomorrow, but maybe in ten to twelve years, we'll be ready. Okay, by then I'll be an old man. But everyone dealing with these issues today understands tomorrow's perspective.

The Power of Artificial Intelligence

In twenty years, there won't be anyone left to fight with outdated equipment when we consider how efficiently AI is used in warfare today. What does war look like today? It is already characterized by drones and missiles equipped with artificial intelligence and deployed accordingly.

It has also become easier to kill an enemy because it's easier to hit the target. Even now, a bullet could hit you in the face if someone wanted it to. War today resembles a computer game, the objective of which is to kill as many enemies as possible.

I realize this when I see how the war in Ukraine is being fought. However, NATO still does not have drones. Drones are already being used very efficiently in warfare. We use them in countless underground basements and kitchens at home, yet NATO does not even have a standard for these FPV drones.

They are still debating whether to use AI at all. Meanwhile, tanks are becoming obsolete. You don't gain much by destroying a tank. With drones, though, you can destroy a tank or at least stop it. The enemy is finished. We are also seeing satisfactory results from the American Patriot system. There is already highly successful modern technology. We have upgraded our outdated technology from the 1960s and 1970s, and it is still useful.

However, today, war is waged differently. We experience war in new ways, such as through fake news on the internet and cyberattacks. For a long time, we have all had to protect ourselves from these threats. During World War II, it was difficult for Hitler to spread his propaganda because it could not easily be translated from German into other languages. He could hardly influence the Slavic peoples. Today, you can simply tell your cell phone: "Translate what I say into another language." Unfortunately, new media has a problematic side. People often tell me that there is no way of knowing whether everything the media spreads is true.

However, we should have considered the ethical implications of our actions long ago. AI. No EU government has seriously considered this, let alone established where the red lines should be when using it. Many of us have been using AI at home for a long time. Today, you can use your cell phone to tell it: "Make a video of Zelensky saying something like: We're going to kill you all!" The video immediately goes viral, and many people who see it—not just a few old women from the countryside—believe that Zelensky said it. They don't believe the real Zelensky said it; they think it's something crazy Trump would say.

The Mendacity of Trump's Ideology

Trump can tell his supporters anything and they will believe him. He knows this very well, which is why he says, "I just tell people what they want to hear." If an evangelical called Trump and asked if he were also a devout Christian, Trump would respond, "Great that you're born again. I believe in God like you do." Then he would say, "I'm glad you're Ukrainian. I love you all, so vote for me." To the Latin Americans: "You are all so beautiful on this planet Earth." And that is it. Trump also makes good use of his relationships with the powerful people who own his favorite media outlets.

However, all of these wealthy individuals are still afraid of the man in the Kremlin who threatens us with nuclear weapons. You don't have to be afraid of his nukes anymore, though. Nowadays, you can easily use AI to send extremely dangerous messages and make them afraid of you. This has been happening for a long time. We all witnessed it when calls to storm the Capitol suddenly appeared online. I can see what Trump is up to on his Instagram page. You can really see what he's like there. I'm shocked by how primitive his paintings are!

This is the level of the once-great European culture! He gets up to 400,000 likes for them. His behavior is unethical and uninhibited. Trump knows how to use the media to his advantage, and the media is happy to help him win the election.

Many Americans see Trump's public appearances as entertaining. However, presidents in any country should be serious leaders, not individuals with pending criminal charges. Trump's impact has contributed to increased polarization in Western society, which is concerning. In times like these, Martin Luther's advice is relevant: "If you know that tomorrow this world will end, then today, plant a new tree." If we give up all hope for ourselves and this world, we might as well lie in our coffins today.

The Unpredictability of Future Developments, Including from an Economic Standpoint

The number of people who have already fled Ukraine, as well as those likely to do so, worries me greatly about our future. After the war, Ukraine's population will be just over thirty million. I doubt most of them will return. We will miss them during the reconstruction process and in the future of our economy.

Putin will never return what he has taken since 2014, especially now that the war has begun. The strongest sectors of our economy are at stake in these regions. Consider the industry and natural resources in the Donbas, the thriving tourism in Crimea, the beautiful beaches in southern Ukraine, Mariupol's largest steelworks in Europe, and Zaporizhzhia's largest nuclear power plants. Europe's largest hydropower plant, located in Kakhovka, has already been destroyed. All of this has taken an enormous toll on our economy.

I was previously unaware of this. Very little information about it is available in the media. These losses are especially consequential.

Ukraine's Prospects in Western Partnerships

Based on your experience in Europe, what influence do you think Ukraine could have on the continent? There are already around five million Ukrainians in Europe, and this number is expected to increase. Sometimes it seems like Ukrainians will end up like Jews. We could become a nation without our own state. To me, that seems like a very realistic scenario. Can we achieve anything at all in Europe? You know about Myroslav Marinovich's optimism regarding the potential for a different Ukraine. What mental or psychological prerequisites do you think are essential for us as Europeans?

In the interview, you mentioned the environment in Silicon Valley and noted that skilled people, including Ukrainians, are eager to prove themselves. Support their progress. Additionally, due to security concerns and ongoing global uncertainties, Europe should consider resuming production of goods currently manufactured in China or India. The shortage of essential medicines, for example, shows the consequences of depending on other countries for production.

Ukraine has achieved significant recognition in multiple artistic fields. At a recent exhibition in Lviv showcasing modern Ukrainian art from the Soviet era to the present, the extensive range and quality of the artworks were evident. Despite operating under the constraints of Soviet repression, when creative expression was forbidden and artists were persecuted, many of the works demonstrate substantial depth and a distinctive expressive quality.

Zelenskyi's demeanor reflects bravery, commitment, perseverance, and authenticity, as seen in his vulnerability and his unique presidential appearance. Since the start of the war, his choice of attire has indicated his focus on Ukraine's survival, and he has stated his willingness to risk his own life for this goal.

The younger, educated generation can contribute to development by taking initiative and showcasing their skills. This helps them demonstrate their abilities to domestic and international audiences. The new "Made in Ukraine" stores in Lviv sell a variety of locally produced goods. Opening similar stores in other locations could increase accessibility for more consumers because purchasing these products means not choosing imported European designs. These products can also be purchased online.

Just look at my cufflinks, which come from China. What doesn't come from Asia these days?

Poland as Part of the EU

Has your view of Poland changed since it joined the EU? At the time, some Poles expressed disappointment with Europe. However, the current government supports European integration. There is also interest in Ukraine's potential to join the EU in the future.

Although Poland and Switzerland have robust economic relations, Poland is sometimes perceived as less developed in Switzerland. Many companies have successful operations in Poland, and Swiss imports of Polish products exceed what is commonly known. Poland attracts many European and international tourists, but relatively few from Switzerland. Right-wing groups recognized the previous government for its stance on the European Union and emphasis on national independence.

In recent years, Poland has undergone changes, allocating EU funds to various projects. The arts sector, including painting, music, and film, remains active. Infrastructure, such as roads and public transportation, has been modernized. Digital services are available and comparable to those in other European countries. The restaurant and hotel sectors offer a variety of options and maintain high service standards. English is commonly used for communication, particularly among younger people.

However, Poland is divided between modern, cosmopolitan cities like Warsaw and more traditional regions where conservative Catholic values remain influential.

Recognizing the threat posed by Russia from its own history, Poland supports an increased NATO presence in Ukraine. Some Poles are concerned about competition from Ukrainian imports, especially agricultural imports, and historical ties still affect current relations. Addressing these challenges requires ongoing effort. Ultra-conservative politicians preach the same nonsense to Poles as they do to Russians. They claim that things should be as they were when there was a "holy alliance" between church and state.

We can see where that can lead, as evidenced by Russia's current war against Ukraine. The way Poles have been treated in Europe throughout history is a recurring topic. This historical experience is often referenced as a factor influencing decisions on domestic issues.

Like Ukraine, Poland has faced repeated division throughout its history. After being ruled by Russia, Germany, and Austria, both countries reemerged on the world stage. The memory of those difficult periods remains present among individuals in both countries and contributes to ongoing concerns that similar events could recur. For this reason, we consistently emphasize to the Russian government that both countries are now sovereign states recognized globally as independent entities.

Other European countries that have not had similar experiences may find it challenging to fully comprehend this perspective. For instance, it is worth considering whether Switzerland can truly relate to these circumstances.

Switzerland's View on Ukraine

Switzerland gained its independence as early as 1291, when the first cantons freed themselves from foreign rule. An important part of Swiss tradition is the legend of William Tell, who killed the bailiff Gessler. Although

Switzerland officially remained part of the Holy Roman Empire for a long time, its autonomy was generally recognized.

Switzerland has always maintained peaceful international relations and has never waged war against other countries. It is perfectly clear to all of us that German-speaking Swiss are not Germans. The same applies to French- and Italian-speaking Swiss. None of us wants to belong to Germany, France, or Italy because of our language. Our identity is Switzerland.

When a representative from a Viennese social research institute asked me if I was concerned about politics in Russia, he said he was more worried about Ukraine shifting rightward. I replied that, with war ongoing and hundreds of thousands of deaths, our immediate concern is survival, not future nationalism. He expressed his view that we might eventually face serious difficulties in the context of our present challenging circumstances.

For example, he said, imagine a scenario in which Italy elects a leader like Mussolini who claims that the Italian-speaking region of Switzerland should be part of Italy. I think all Swiss people would quickly become nationalists if faced with such a prospect.

Religious Freedom within the Occupied Territories[16]

Another concern is the situation facing individuals in southern Ukraine, a region that receives limited media attention.[17] Although recent reports indicate considerable local opposition to Russia, resistance appears unfeasible given the current circumstances. This leaves the population with few viable options.

One form of protest is to choose not to attend church. She also discusses issues related to religious freedom in Ukraine and communicates with Western Christian groups that share her views. In the United States, this is observed among certain evangelical and other conservative communities.

---

16 Written after the interview to address an important development that has occurred since them

17 https://www.youtube.com/ watch?v=EpE8czL_JIM. The extent of state persecution is comparable to the atheist repression in the Soviet Union. An important NZZ article on this: https://www.nzz.ch/international/ukraine-krieg-russische-besatzer-schaffen-im-donbass-fakten-ld.1829078

The Russian Orthodox Church blames Western influence for the rise in atheism. The church now wants to send missionary groups to Ukraine to bring people back to its nationalistic interpretation of Christianity, which it considers the only true faith.

The ban on the Russian Orthodox Church in Ukraine is an important factor here. Christianity, which it considers to be the only true faith. The ban on the Russian Orthodox Church in Ukraine is an important factor here. When it promotes the ideology of the "Russian world" with its imperialism, it becomes a sect that even wages war against other Christians.[18] It has been documented that freedom of religion is generally observed across Ukraine. In territories currently under Russian control, however, Western Christian groups have encountered increasing limitations, including prohibitions on certain churches. Furthermore, several independent churches have been destroyed amid the conflict, and some pastors have lost their lives, according to reports. Existing policies in these areas also prohibit the reconstruction of affected religious institutions.

18 The first part of the appendix contains Miroslav Marinovych's statement, which I am permitted to share.

Darius Pado: Watercolor Karabele

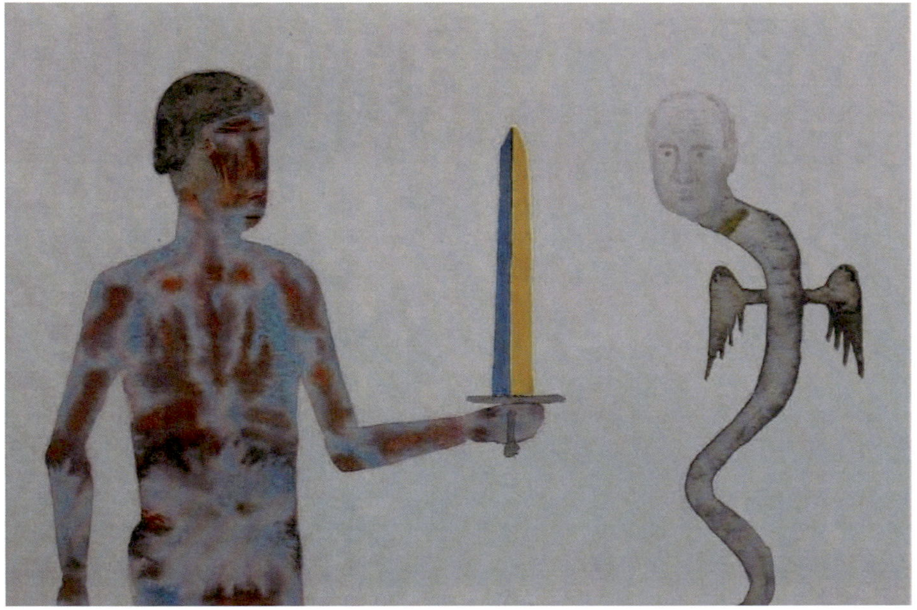

Fight against Snake. Watercolor on paper, 35 x 40 cm

You wrote "We are going to Odesa!"
and pack watercolors
into boats like carabiners
touching the front line

As soon as the horizon of sweat
is gone the corrugated screen
of a summer movie theater is dark
an orchestra plays for a silent moment

Today I wonder if the plane tree avenue
will be as safe as it was on Babel's birthday
when pomegranate wine
colored our lips

Image Selection 2024

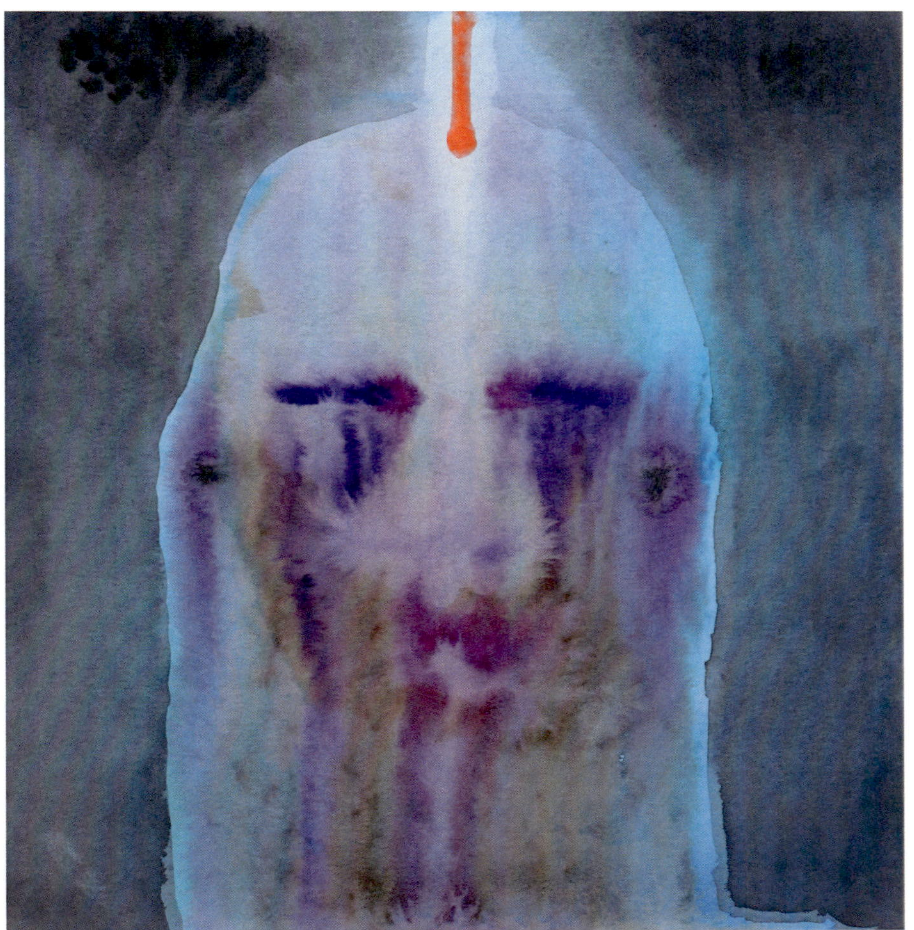

Fire of the Russian-Orthodox Spirit. Watercolor on paper, 35 x 35 cm

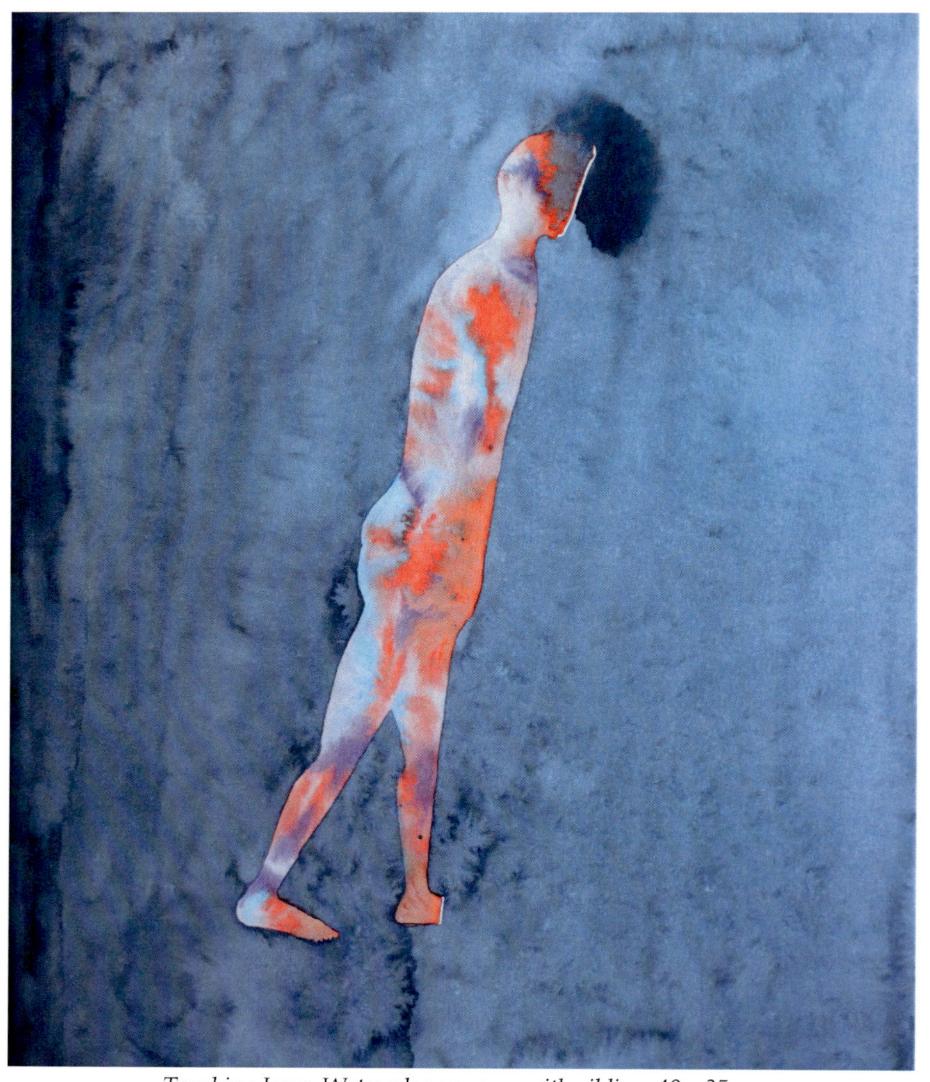

Touching Jesus. Watercolor on paper with gilding, 40 x 35 cm

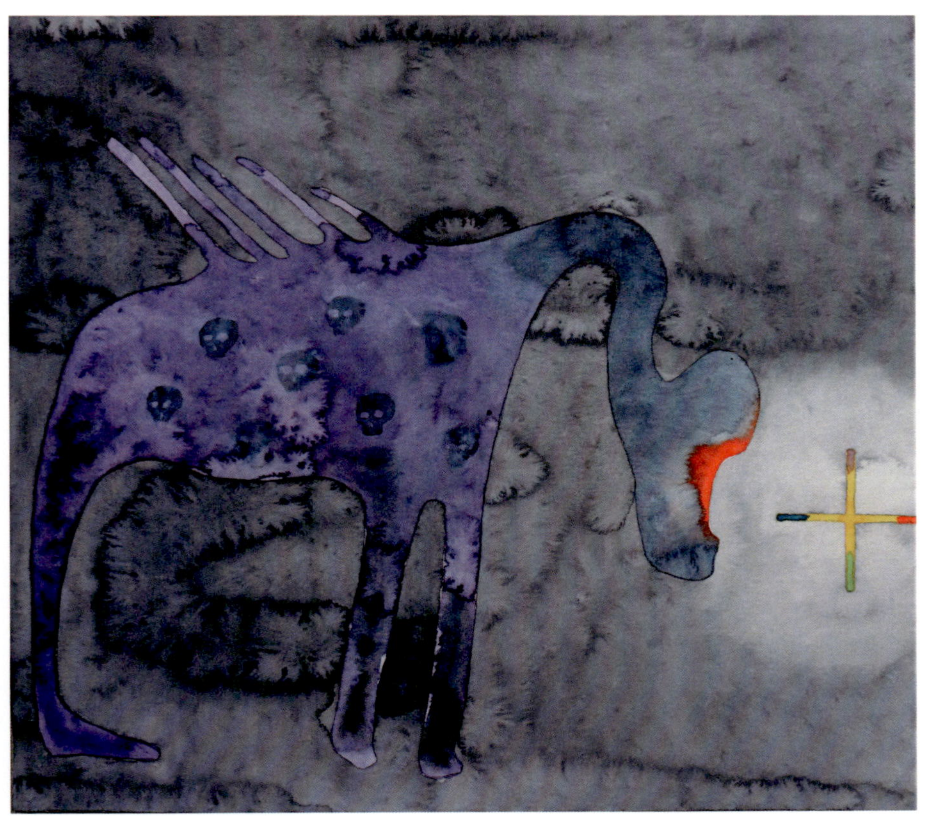

Animal Trying to Eat a Cross. Watercolor on paper, 40 x 35 cm

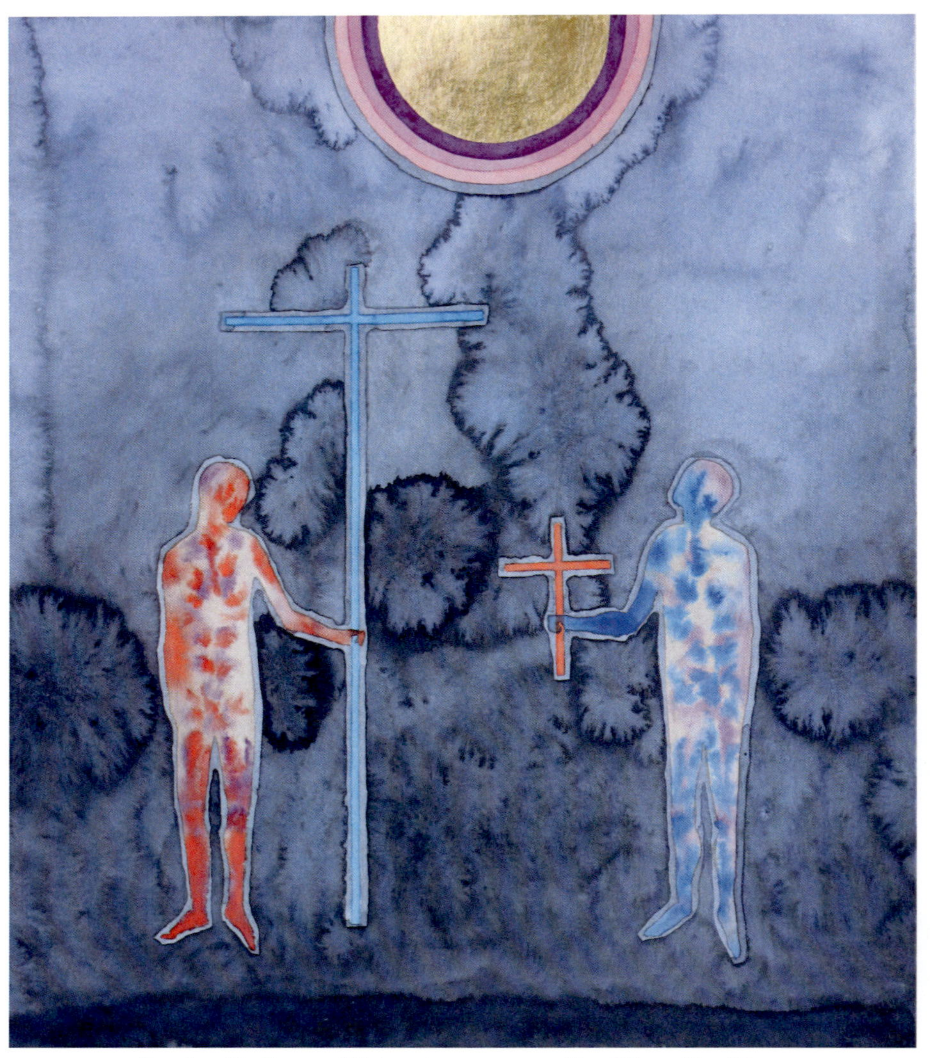

People with Crosses. Watercolor on paper with gilding, 40 x 35 cm

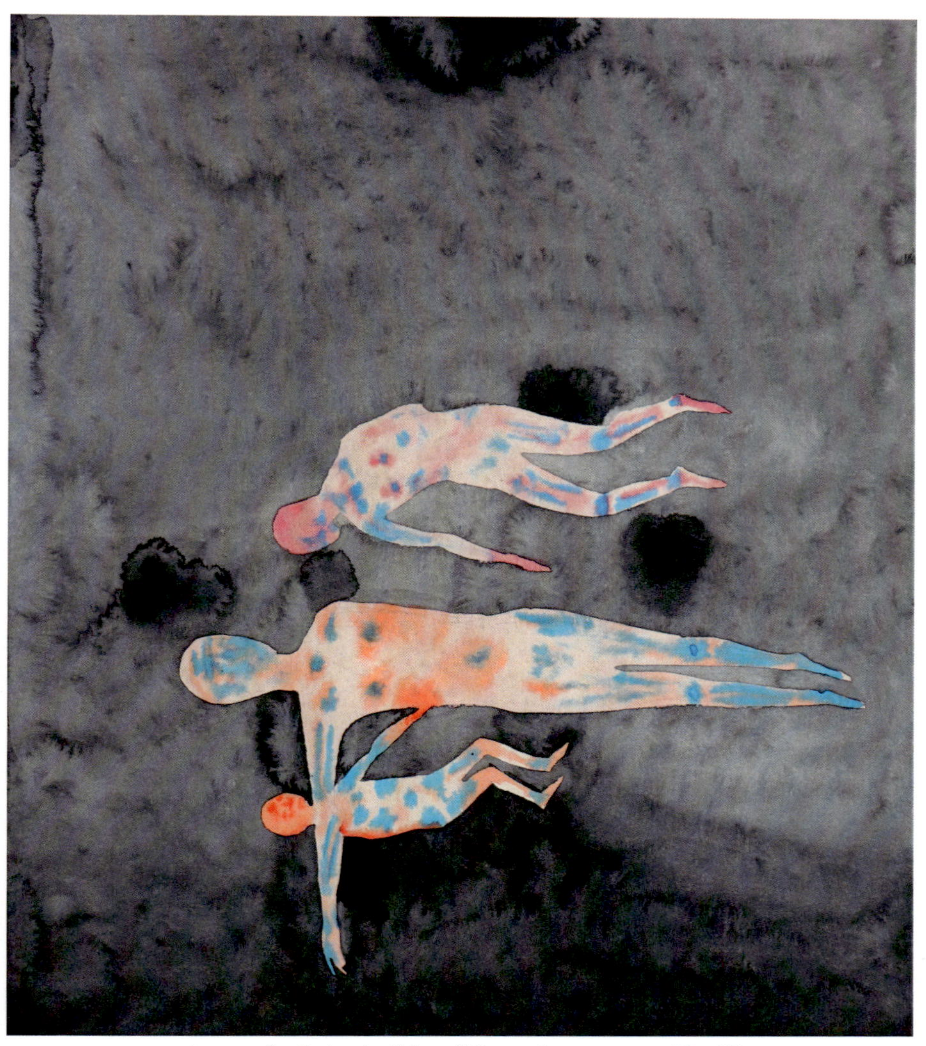

Among the Ruins in Odesa. Watercolor on paper, 40 x 35

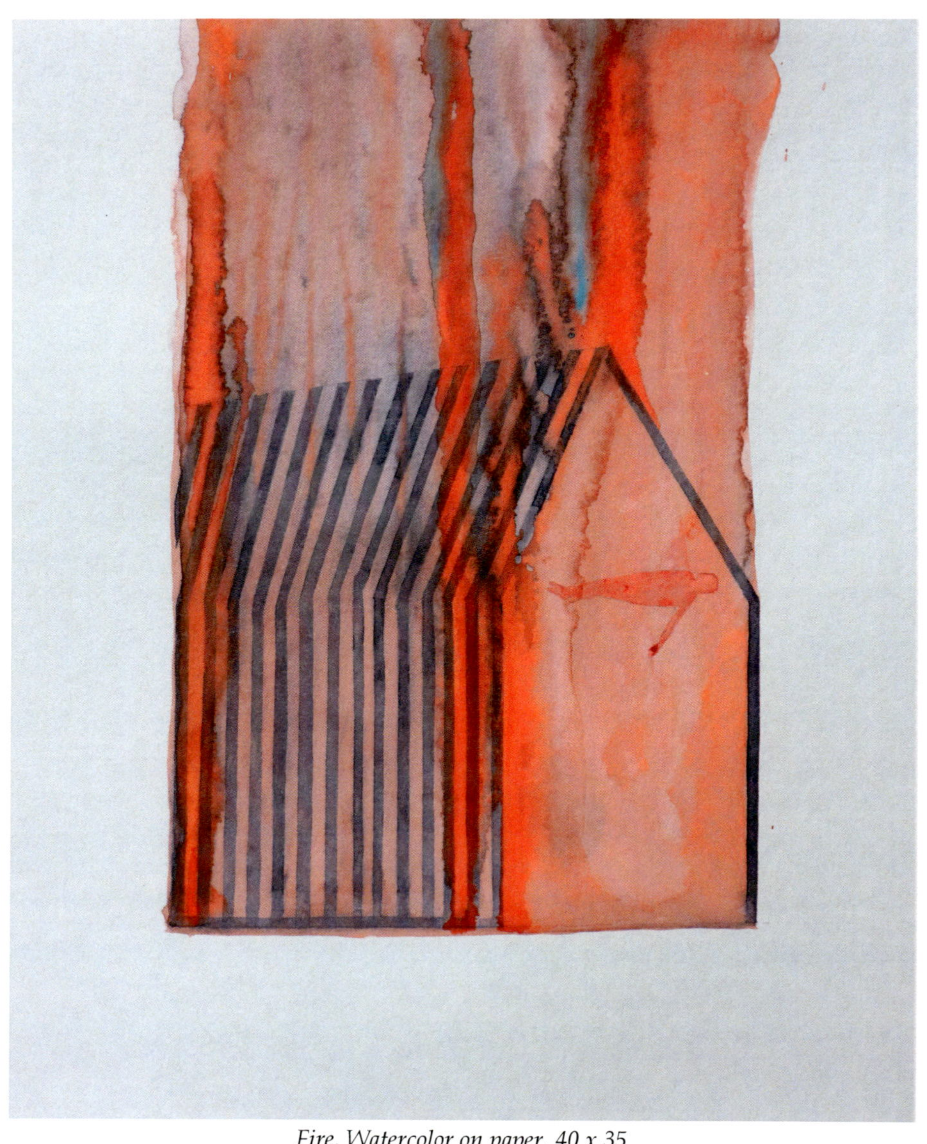

Fire. Watercolor on paper, 40 x 35

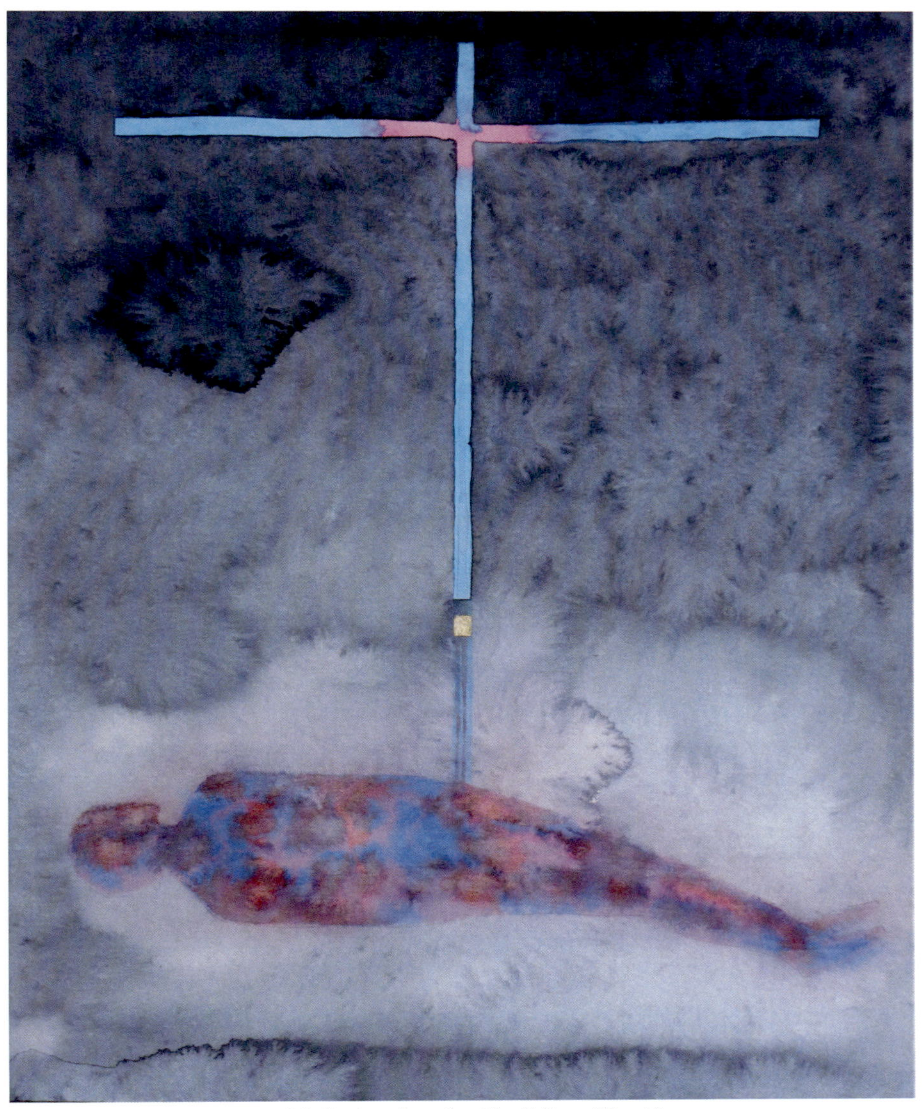

Mediation. Board with gilding, 35 x 40 cm

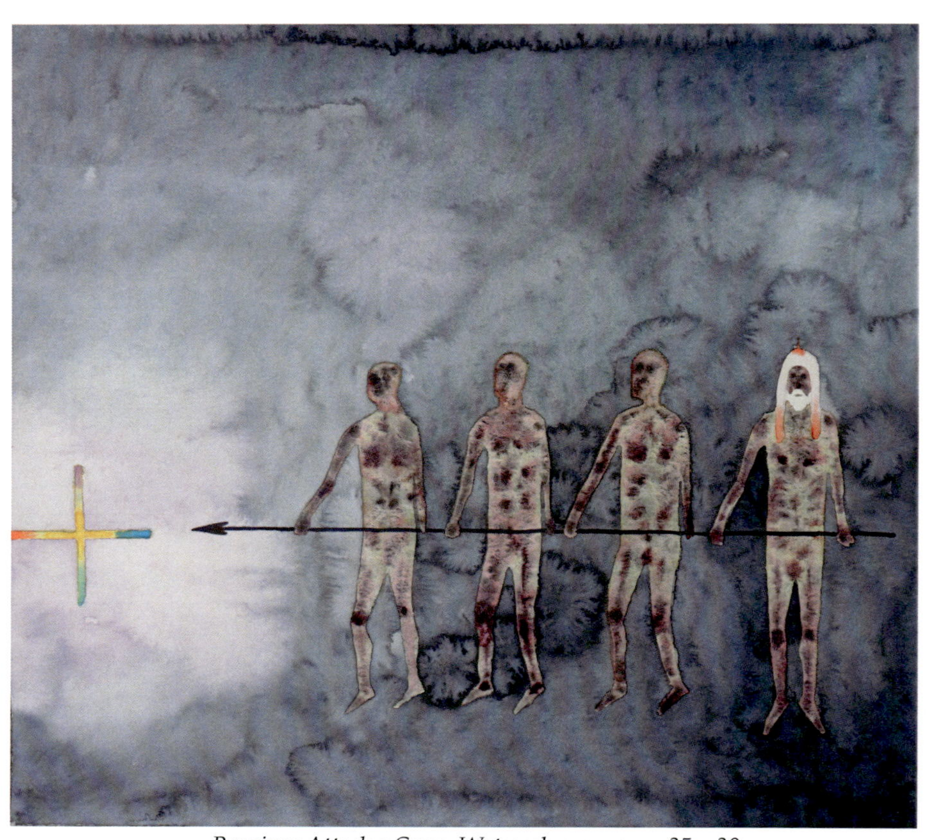

Russians Attack a Cross. Watercolor on paper, 35 x 30 cm

In Memoriam Mikhailo Movchan

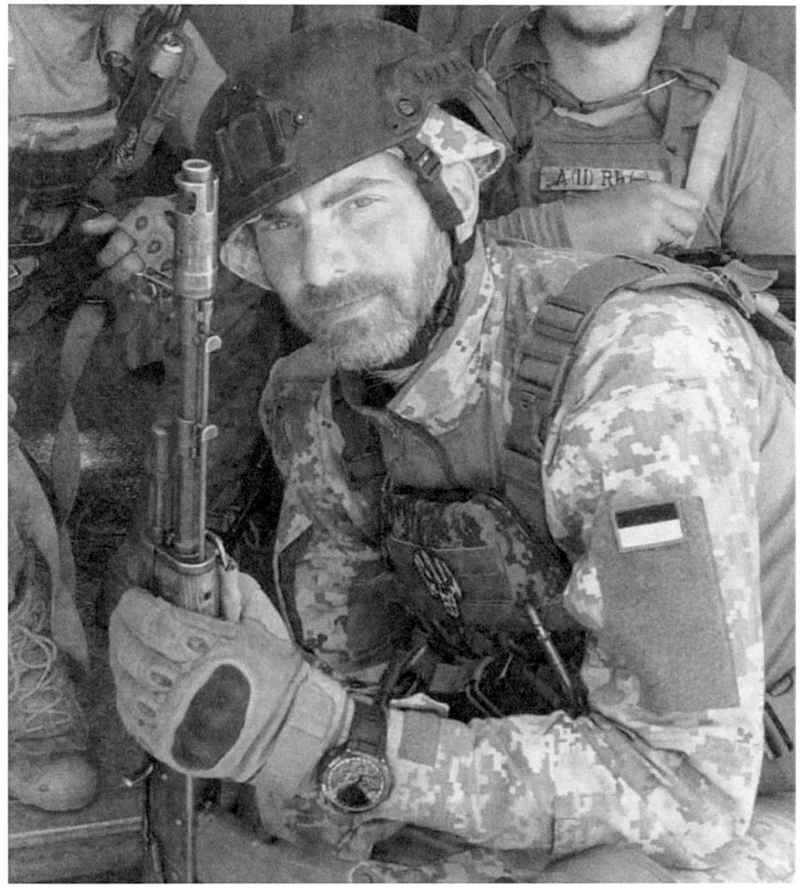

Mykhailo Movchan, born on June 2, 1981, in Lviv, graduated from business school and was drafted into the Ukrainian Armed Forces in spring 2022. He served in eastern Ukraine and died near Bakhmut on July 14, 2023. He was buried in Lviv.

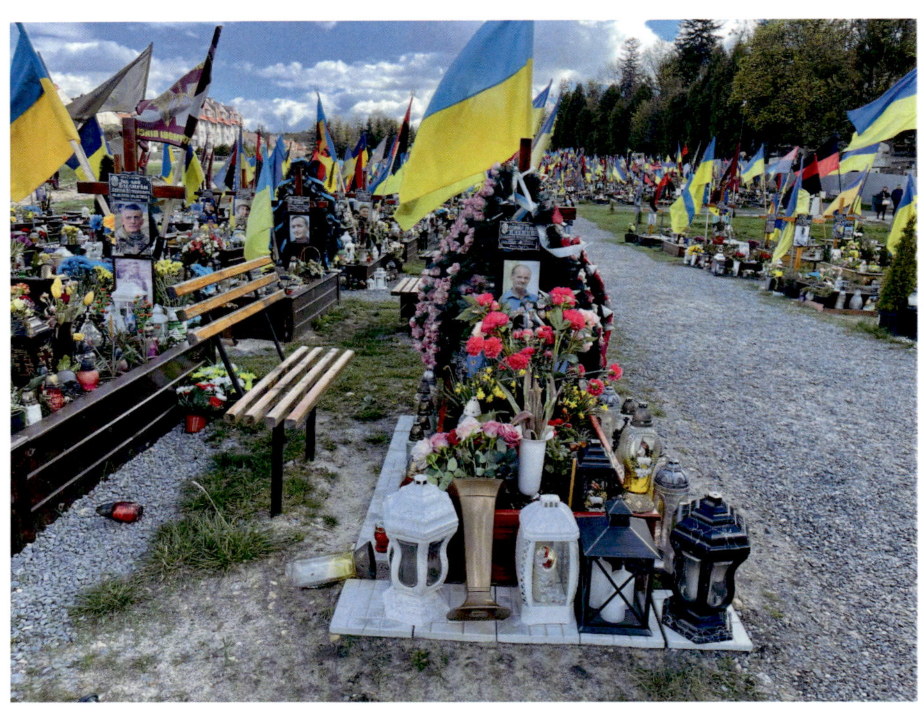

Military Cemetery Lviv, 03.04.2024. Foto Max Hartmann

Appendix

To the Ban on Russian Orthodox Church in Ukraine

Myroslav Marynovych

During the thirty years of Ukrainian independence, a significant part of the clergy of the Ukrainian Orthodox Church, in unity with the Moscow Patriarchate, has always supported the restoration of the USSR and the independence of Ukraine as an independent state. The "tragic mistake" in doing so, the hierarchy of this church fully solidarized with Moscow's desperate belief that it is possible to put an end to this unloved independence of Ukraine and return it to the coveted "union of brotherly Slavic peoples", in which the firm hand of the "big brother" will immediately put an end to the "heretical nationalist split" and restore the unchallenged supremacy of the Moscow Patriarchate. The UOC-affiliated press has been constantly promoting the termination of Ukraine's partnership with the West, NATO, and the European Union. In short, the Ukrainian Orthodox Church was completely subordinated not only to the church doctrine of Russian Orthodoxy, but also to the political and ideological orientation of the Third Rome.

But what was a "nostalgia for Moscow's Egypt" in peacetime became a full-fledged criminal offense with the beginning of Russian aggression. In some places the situation has turned into a scandal. The Security Service of Ukraine discovered facts of direct cooperation between the clergy of this church and the Russian occupation forces.

The situation has besom increasingly intolerable, and according to a survey[19] conducted by the Kyiv International Institute of Sociology from May 26 to June 5, 2023, 66% of Ukrainians believe

19 https://ukrainian-studies.ca/2023/11/28/revolution-of-dignity-in-ukrainecasts-off-once-dominant-russian-orthodox-church/

that the activities of the Ukrainian Orthodox Church, which is in unity with the Moscow Patriarchate, should be banned for reasons of national security. The current decision by the Verkhovna Rada of Ukraine is an attempt to respond to this public demand.

I have not yet had time to familiarize myself with the adopted law in detail. However, I would like to emphasize that it is not the church that is being banned, but its connection with the aggressor state. Unfortunately, the term "banning the church" appears in all Western media.

However, I would like to draw attention to another very important point. The Russian Orthodox Church has developed the doctrine of the "Russian world", which is of a hybrid nature. By asserting the spiritual unity of the Russian, Ukrainian and Belarusian peoples, this doctrine leads to the political denial of the identity of the Ukrainian people and their right to state independence. For this reason, Patriarch Kirill of Moscow described Russia's current war against Ukraine as a holy war.[20]

It is the Moscow Patriarchate that makes and spreads the claim that "today there is a war of the Jewish Freemasons to destroy Orthodoxy" and the belief that the Russian soldier is defending Orthodox civilization against the Western "sodomites". It was the Russian Orthodox Church that brought to the earthly Caesar what belonged to God and thus led the faithful into satanic fornication.

The hybridity of this doctrine means that we find ourselves in a typical zugzwang situation: We are defending the faith and ignoring the political aspects of Russian world ideology and the collaboration of the followers of this ideology with the aggressor in times of war. And by fighting propaganda and collaborationism, we hurt religious feelings and risk violating religious freedom, which is a fundamental feature of democracy in general and the most important achievement of Ukrainian democracy in particular. And unfortunately, it is impossible to separate one from the other. And that is the main problem. In the West, the Russian political-spiritual hybrid is perceived as an authentic religious faith, as the Russian

20 https://www.atlanticcouncil.org/blogs/ukrainealert/russian-orthodox-church-declares-holy-war-against-ukraine-and-west/

Orthodox Church propagates it. By dogmatically defending the principle of religious freedom, concerned Western democrats are depriving the

Russian people of their only chance to free themselves from deception. After all, what is religious freedom? It is the right of man to respond freely to the call of the Creator and to protect this right from the pressure of tyranny. Instead, the politicoreligious hybrid of the Russian world makes a terrible substitute: it tempts man to respond uncritically to the calls of the tyrant and to regard them as the will of the Creator. Therefore, Western democracies, unwilling to recognize the hybridity of Russian faith, are not really defending the religious freedom of Russians, but their spiritual captivity to the tyrant. Therefore, the blind absolutization of religious freedom without sanctions for those who abuse it becomes the freedom to assert the spiritual captivity before which society is defenseless.

By refusing to acknowledge this substitution and succumbing to the magic of the word "changer", defenders of religious freedom in the West often run the risk of unwittingly contributing to the punitive freedom of the Russian regime, which has been indiscriminately traumatizing religious freedom for a century.

However, Ukrainian society faces an equally responsible task: it must prevent the defeat of Ukrainian Christian culture. Finally, Ukraine faces a truly epic task in the question of "Ukraine's national security and religious freedom in the context of Russian aggression": how to slip between Scylla and Charybdis, i.e., how to clearly distinguish between the right and the wrong?

The difference between a person's attempts to practice their religion and a person's attempts to collaborate with the enemy—especially in times of war. I believe that Ukraine will master this task.

Job and the Question of God's Justice

Max Hartmann

This challenging subject is the focus of this year's plein air event for icon painters. As the participants work, it will have been a thousand days since the start of Russia's war of aggression. When I was in Lviv this spring, I had the opportunity to meet my friend Julian Chaplinsky, an artist and urban planner, who told me: 'What we are witnessing today is the rebirth of old totalitarianism that will soon dominate our whole world.' This is a very sobering realization that raises many questions. The problem of theodicy also preoccupied the poet Johann Wolfgang von Goethe. The Lisbon earthquake of 1755 killed 100,000 people and shaped faith and thought in Europe more than any other catastrophe before it. The Enlightenment soon led more European thinkers to doubt the existence of God. If He did exist, He would appear to us as a monstrosity—the terror of the world—yet He made it possible.

The age-old theme of God's justice is also central to the biblical Book of Job. A clear, almost artistic order can be recognized in it. This corresponds with the idea of the renowned icon artist Jerzy Nowosielski, who once said, 'A good work of art should show a clear order in its composition.'

Theological research distinguishes between a 'frame story', written in prose, and the extraordinarily long main part, skillfully composed in poetry, in the structure of the Book of Job. It was assumed that the two parts came from different sources representing various views on the question of God's justice. Today, however, the book is increasingly seen as a unit again. This view also aligns with psychological findings in the field of traumatic experiences. If we only considered the frame story, it would have to be judged as psychologically dangerous.

In the Book of Job, we encounter evil in the form of Satan. He appears before God with the realistic assertion that Job only believes in him because he is prospering. If God were to take away all his wealth, Job would blaspheme in his face.

However, because God believes that Job's piety is genuine, he allows Satan to do so. The famous 'tidings of Job' then follow robbers invade the land, steal Job's vast herd of cattle and kill his servants. When Job receives this news, he is then told that his sons were celebrating at a party when a huge storm blew up, destroying their tent and killing them all.

Job's response to all of this is incredibly godly: he simply says, 'The LORD has given, the LORD has taken away, the name of the LORD be praised' (Job 1:21). Satan, on the other hand, does not give up and demands an even tougher test from God: 'Let Job become deathly ill, and he will surely blaspheme in your face.' God allows this to happen, which is completely incomprehensible to us. Job is covered in evil sores from the soles of his feet to the top of his head. They plague him to such an extent that no human could endure them. The situation worsens when Job's wife says to him: 'Are you still convinced that you are blameless for all this? Blaspheme God and die!" Yet Job still answers with conviction: 'Should we accept good from God and not evil?' (Job 2:10).

I feel ashamed when I hear these words today, as very pious people try to comfort those who have experienced misfortune. Their intentions are good, but their words are completely inappropriate. If I were to say something like that to someone in Ukraine in the context of the current war, it would simply be like shooting poisoned arrows and would cause great hurt.

If we could only read the beginning of the Book of Job, the framing story, it would simply be an old tale, as would the stories of certain saints who were prepared to die as martyrs. We might even describe Job's faith in God as morbid. However, in the rest of the book, we also find a different Job who does not simply submit to his fate as God-given, but who resists it.

In my pastoral ministry, I have encountered people who initially reacted like Job. They seemed incredibly relaxed, and many were admired for their resignation to fate. However, I was still very concerned about them. Eventually, they lose their composure and enter a major crisis until they can finally admit their repressed feelings and questions. This requires a lengthy period of medical treatment. People who can admit their feelings and questions at an early stage cause me less concern. Even then, sometimes specialists are needed.

Job's journey back to life is a long one. Helpfully, he learns that some of his friends are coming to visit him soon. They sit with him in silence for seven days. But then Job suddenly begins to speak. The whole thing hits him like an avalanche, and, in his utter despair, he cries out, "The day of my birth has been blotted out, and the night that said, 'A boy has been conceived!' Why was I not allowed to perish in the womb, never to see the light of day? Why did knees receive me? Why did breasts make me drink? I would lie down and rest; I would sleep and be at peace. Why does He give light to the afflicted and life to the embittered? What I feared has come upon me; what I feared has overtaken me. I have not found peace, rest or quietness; only restlessness has come upon me" (Job 3). Now even his friends are no longer silent. Horrified, they try to help him using ideas that are still familiar to us today. Theology calls this approach the 'do-go context'. They believe that nothing happens in this world without reason. Anyone who sins will eventually suffer the consequences. They believe that a harsh fate is deserved.

However, Job contradicts this repeatedly over many chapters. Despite his best efforts, he cannot find anything to justify his suffering. He courageously refuses to feel guilty.

He wants to persuade God. Job questions God, not because he denies his existence, but because he wants an answer from him. This is the context of the famous words that we also hear in some oratorios: 'I know that my Redeemer lives', literally: 'I know that my Advocate lives'. Job is convinced that God will vindicate him.
Job rejects the misguided views of his friends when someone else tries to do the same. His conviction has become proverbial: the Bible (Hebrews 12:6). However, Job also rejects this concept of God.

So, God is all that is left for him. Finally, God begins to speak. However, what God tells him seems very strange to us. He simply talks for a very long time about the many mysteries of creation, reminding us of humans how little we still know today. God gives Job an extensive lesson in zoology. He gives Job a glimpse of his greatness, making him realize how great God must be in relation to humans he had to suffer. He manages to live without a truthful answer. Even great faith in God does not explain everything. We will find out the reason why later, when we meet God himself in eternity. However, by then, we may no longer want to know.

In addition, God calls Job's friends to account: 'You have not spoken the truth about me like my servant Job' (Job 42:7). For me, this is one of the most profound statements about God in the Bible. It shows us that God likes it when we ask questions and don't just accept the first answer we get. We are allowed to ask God questions, just as Job did. God has a thick skin when it comes to us humans. However, he simply does not tolerate any false images of him that limit him to our own understanding.

Returning to the question of why God allows evil, there are no satisfactory answers. However, the Book of Job provides a way forward, which is also confirmed by psychological findings.

Dariusz Pado: What for?

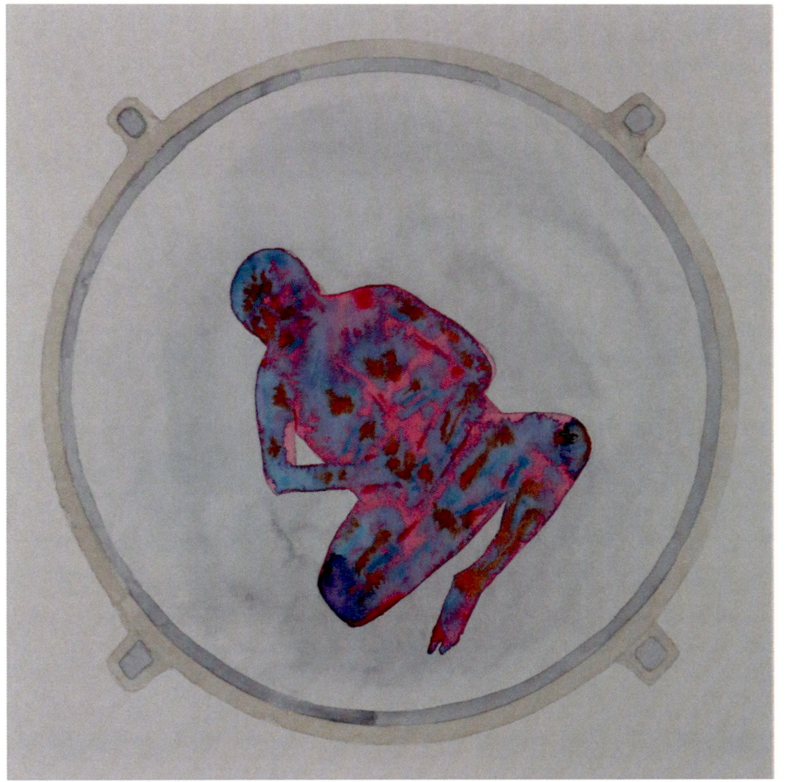

Man in Jackdaw. Watercolor on paper, 30 x 35 cm

Not saved from a cross
but discovered in a shaft—
A mother's son lies in
not with cries
but amid silent tears
in the embrace
of an underground river

Image Selection 2025

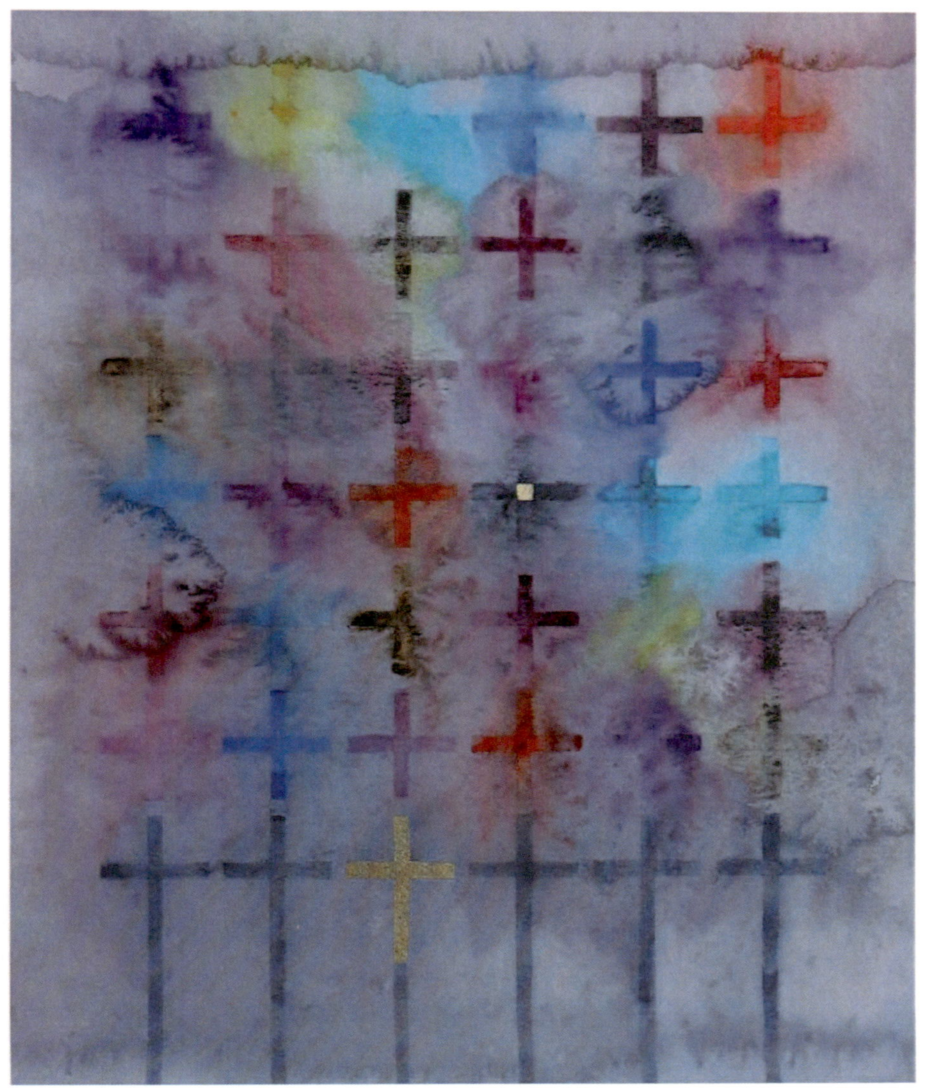

Crosses. Watercolor on paper and gilding. 35 x 30 cm

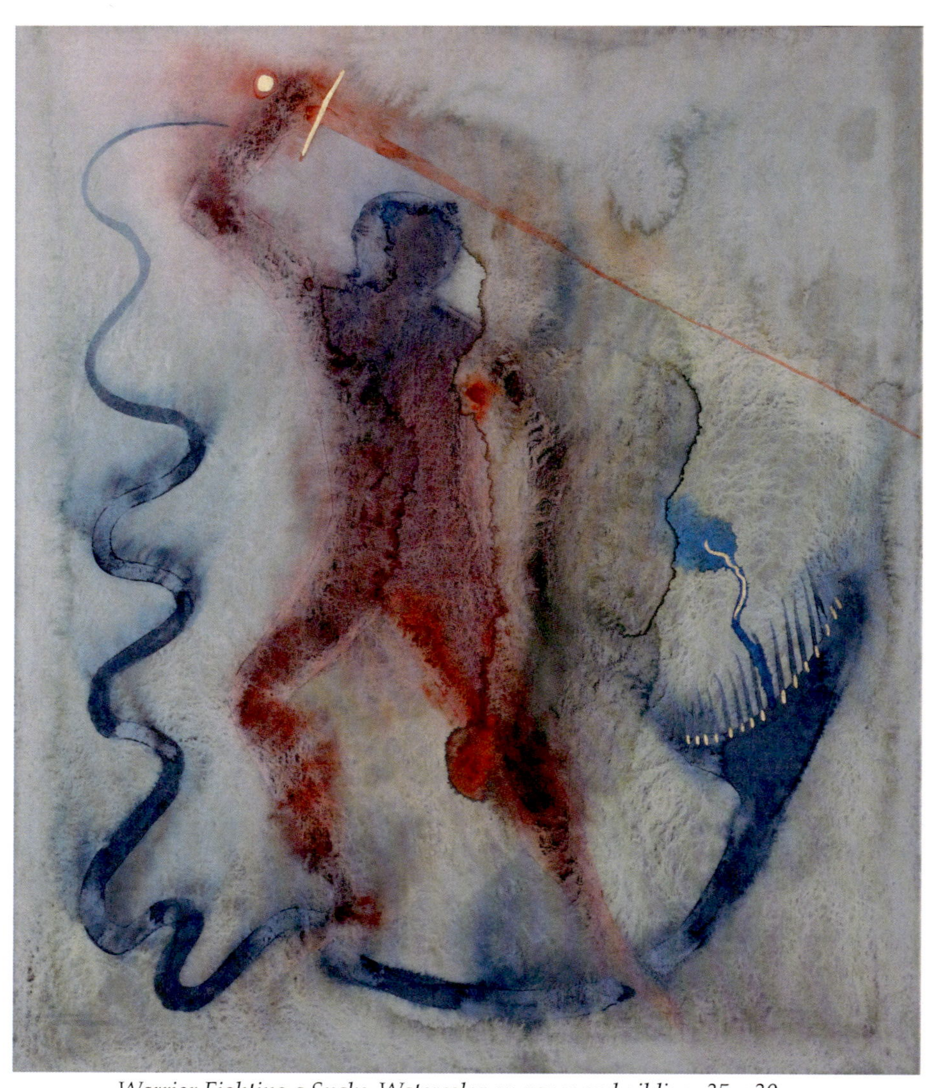

Warrior Fighting a Snake. Watercolor on paper and gilding, 35 x 30 cm

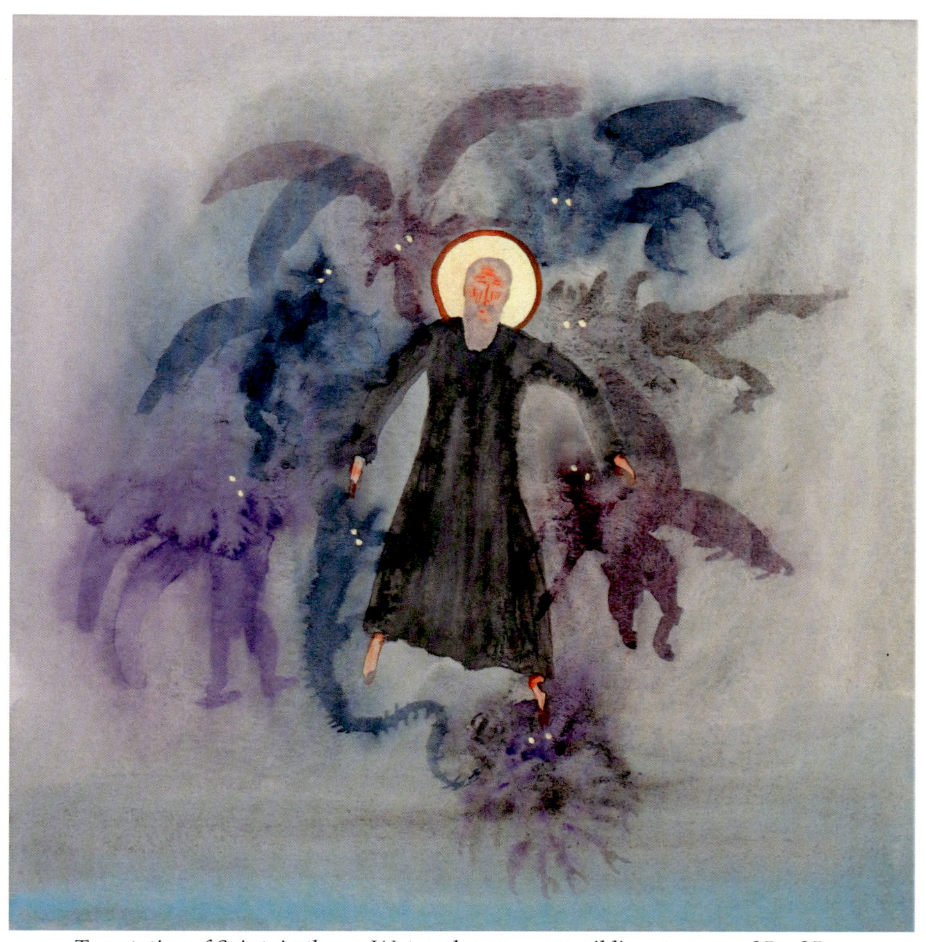

Temptation of Saint Anthony. Watercolor on paper, gilding, tempera. 35 x 35cm

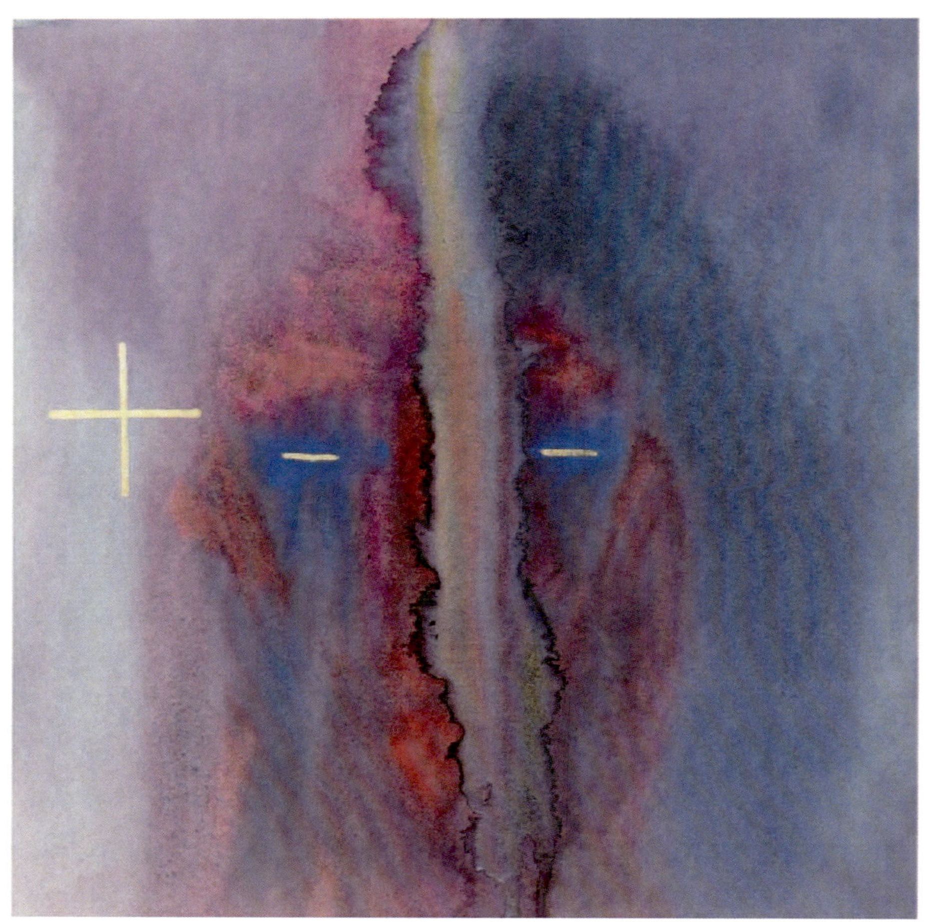

Change of Consciousness. 35 x 30 cm

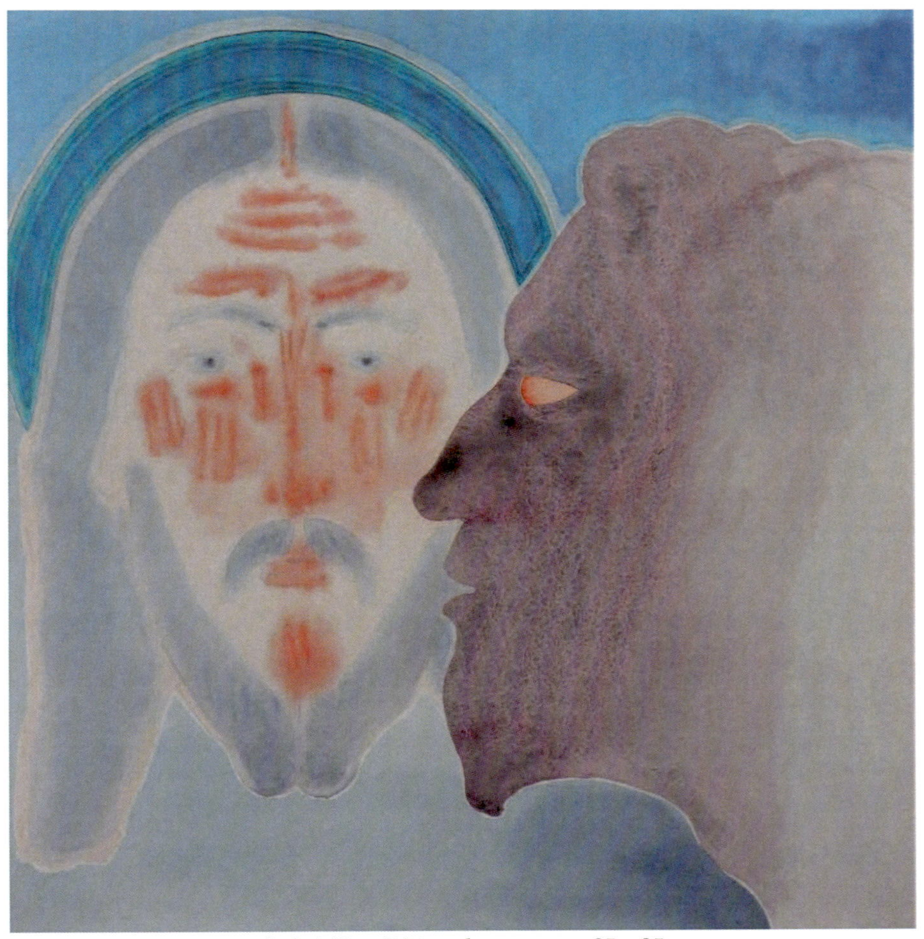

Judas' Kiss. Watercolor on paper. 35 x 35

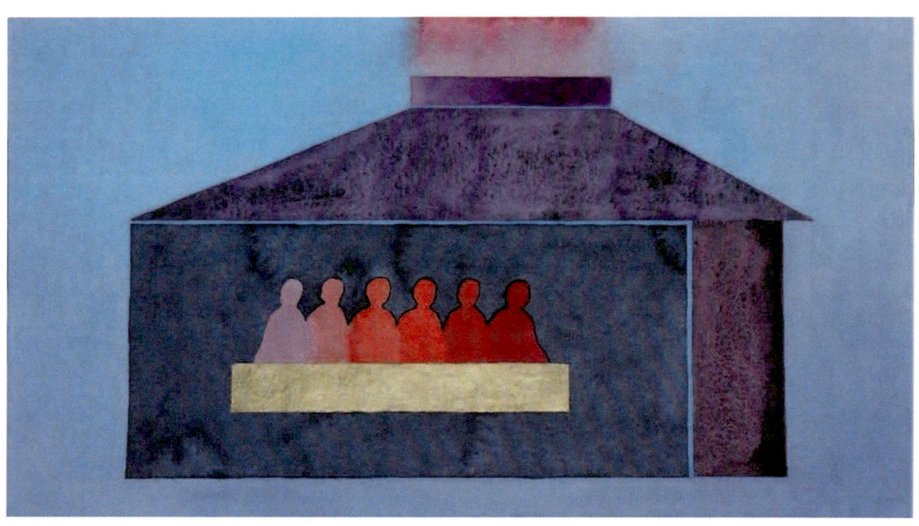

Dark Space. Watercolor on paper. 25 x 45 cm

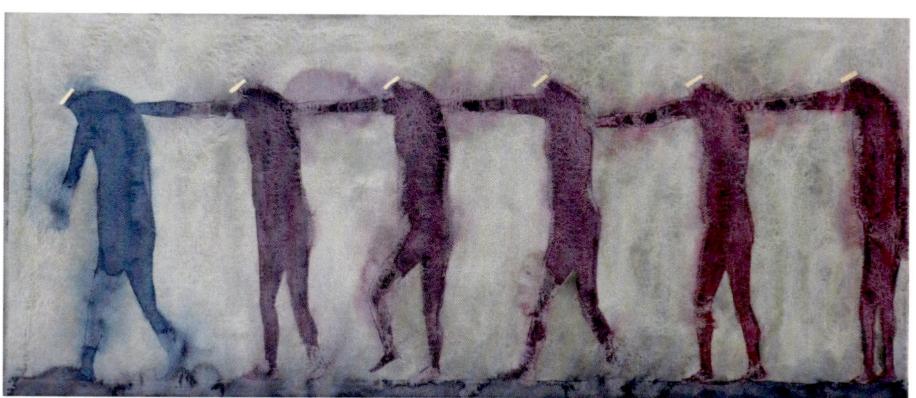

Procession of the Headless. Watercolor on paper, 30 x 70 cm

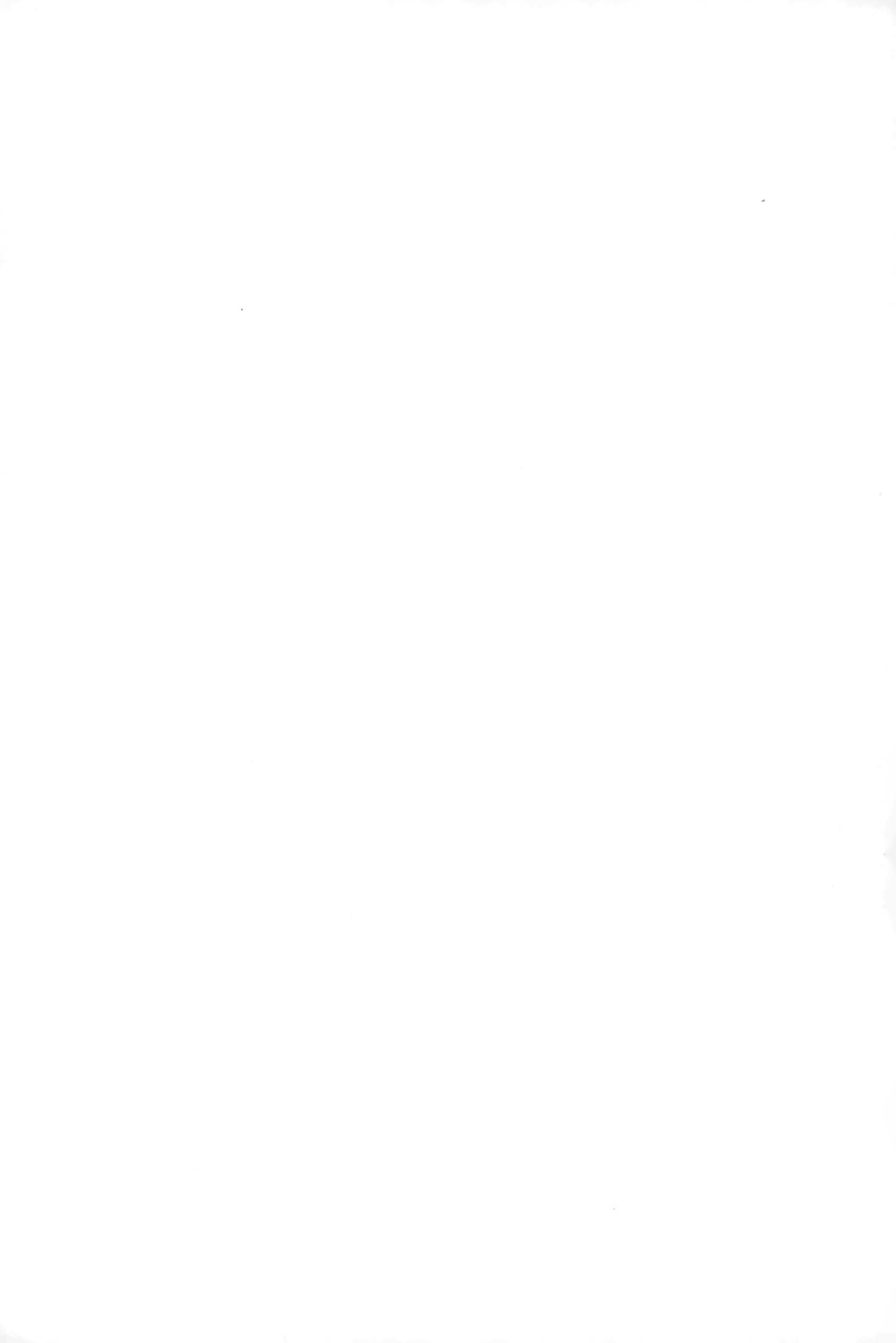

Details of the People Involved

Danylo Movchan

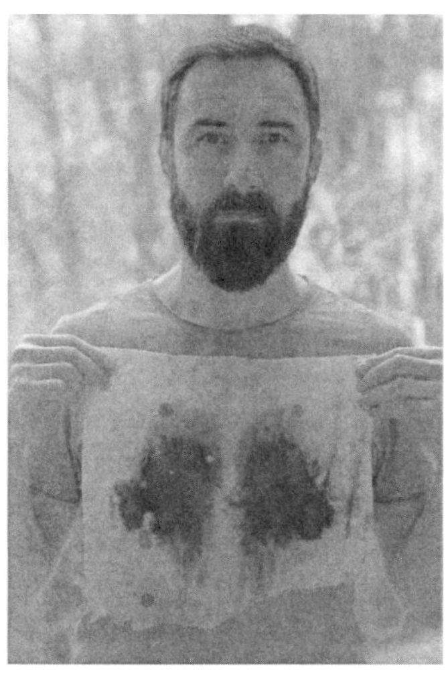

Born in Lviv in 1979. From 1995 to 2000, he studied at the Higher School of Decorative and Applied Arts in Lviv (named after I. Trush), in the Department of Restoration. From 2000 to 2006, he studied at the National Academy of Arts in Lviv (Department of Sacred Art). He creates icons and other paintings. He has been a member of the Ukrainian Union of Icon Painters since 2012. His work can be found in churches and private collections in Ukraine, Poland, Germany, Finland, and Italy, France, Canada, and the USA. He has participated in over one hundred group exhibitions and numerous international plein airs in Ukraine and abroad.

Personal exhibitions

2006	Sheptytsky National Museum	Lviv
2009	"Incarnation"	Ukrainian Catholic University, Lviv
2012	"Song of Songs"	Impart Art Center, Wroclaw
	"Heavenly"	Iconart Gallery, Lviv
	"Meal"	Detenpyla Gallery, Lviv
2013	"Man and Cherub"	Czestochowa, Poznan and Lodz, Poland
2014	"Lost Wings"	Sweet Art Gallery, Chernivtsi
2016	"On Paper"	Iconart Gallery, Lviv
	"Saints and the Body"	Gallery "At Jesuit", Pozna
2022	"The Color of War"	Dim Gallery, Warsaw
2023	"Where is you Sting"	National Art Museum, Odesa
2024	"Cross and Body"	Iconart Gallery, Lviv

Yaryna Movchan

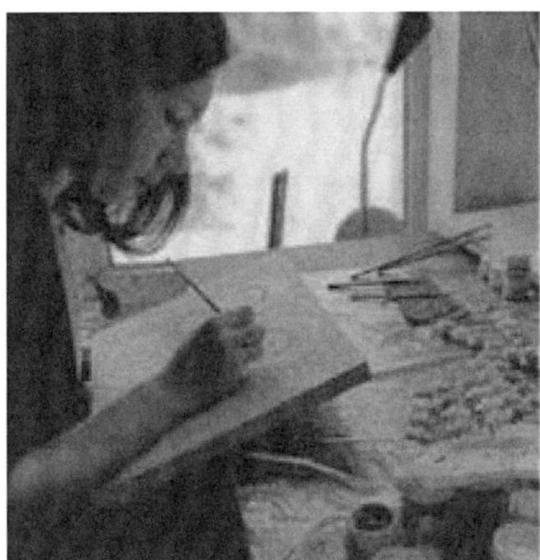

She was born in Lviv in 1982, graduated from the Department of Textiles at the I. Trush Academy of Arts in Lviv, and is the mother of two children. Her husband, Danylo, encouraged her to try the sacred painting technique of grounding on wood with tempera colors mixed with egg. She soon realized that this process, typical of icon painting, enabled her to achieve the desired emotional effects in her compositions and incorporate them into her style. In 2007, she had the extraordinary opportunity to participate in the international youth symposium for textile art, "ArcheNitka-Novo."

Some exhibitions

2006	International Salon "High Castle", Palace of Arts, Lviv
2008	Initiative Biennale, Ivano-Frankivsk, Chernivtsi, Uzhhorod, Ternopil, Lviv
	"Podlaskie Autumn", Podlaskie Opera and Philharmonic, European Center of Arts, Białystok, Poland
2010	Days of Ukrainian Culture in Warsaw; Green Sofa Gallery, Vienna
2010	“The Organic Streetscape Project”, Snowball Gallery, Toronto
2010	All-Ukrainian Triennial Painting 2010, Exhibition Rooms of the National Union of Artists of Ukraine, Kyjiw
2013	“The 50 most interesting artists of Western Ukraine”, Lubomirski Palace, Lviv
2024	Christmas, Exhibition, Green Sofa Gallery Lviv

Solomia Horyn

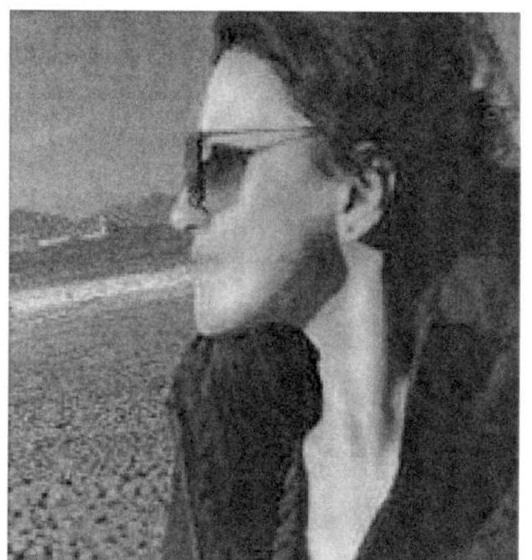

She was born in Lviv in 1973 and attended School No. 9, which offered extended German lessons. She later completed her language studies at Ivan Franko University. She also spent time in Dresden and Vienna. The current situation in the war and the independence of Ukraine get great concern to her. She met the artist Danylo Movchan at one of his exhibitions in the city of Lviv.

Dariusz Pado

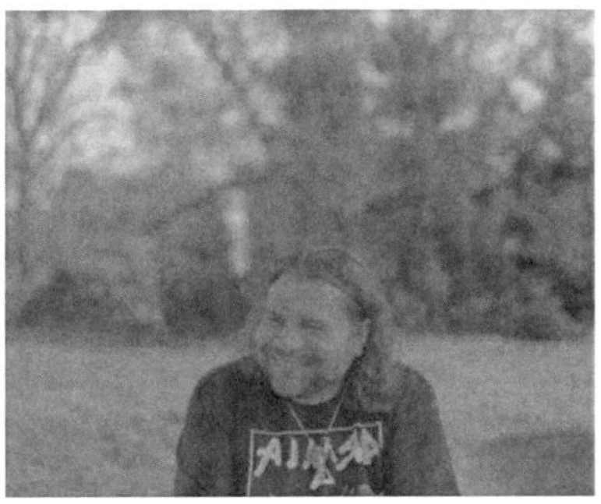

He was born in 1974 in Rzeszów, Poland. He is a poet and a lawyer. He is a contributor to the literary journals Kursywa and Arte. He has also published poems and articles in Noc poetów, Odra, Nowa Okolica Poetów, Gazeta Wyborcza, and RED, as well as Lampa. He is associated with the poetry website Nieszuflada, which he co-founded. He lives and works in Warsaw and Rzeszów.

Some works

2005 "Peripheries of Paradise," a volume of poetry, Warsaw

2006 Award in the second edition of the national literary competition "Golden Medium of Poetry" for the best poetry book debut of 2005

2020 Poetry collection "Urne", Association of Living Poets, Brzeg

Julian Chaplinsky

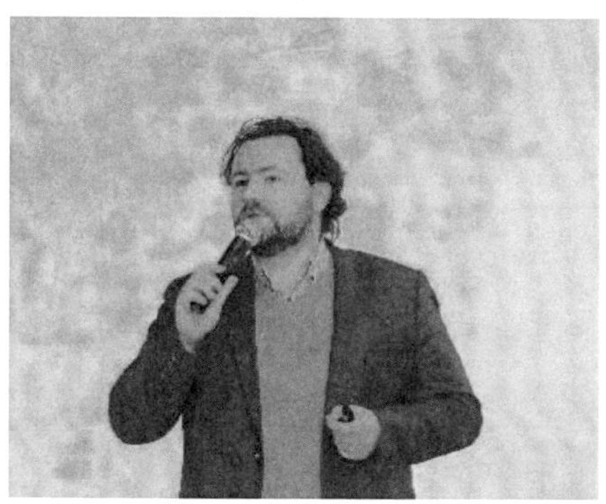

He was born in Lviv in 1982. He studied architecture at the Lviv Polytechnic. He is a Ukrainian architect, urbanist, politician, art lover, and wellknown public figure. In 2015, he collaborated with the world-renowned architect Stefan Behnisch on the project "Metropolitan Andrey Sheptytsky Center," an information and resource center for the Ukrainian Catholic University. The center includes several lectures and conference halls, a public cultural space, a café, and a library. The center was nominated for the 2019 Mies van der Rohe Architecture Prize of the European Union. During this time, he was invited to work in Stefan Behnisch's architectural office in Stuttgart, but he declined. While planning a new church in Lviv, he benefited from the knowledge and talent of the renowned Swiss architect Mario Botta. He later accepted an offer from the mayor of Lviv to become the city's chief architect. He blogs on YouTube about the problems of Ukrainian cities in the urban planning, architecture, and urbanism.

John A. Kohan

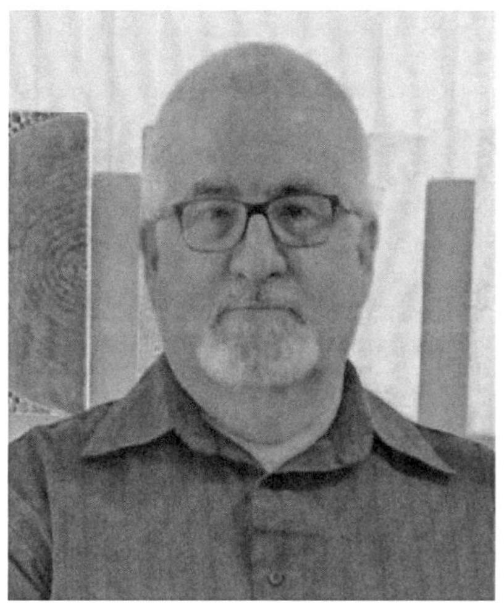

John Kohan holds a Master of Arts in Slavic Languages and Literatures from Columbia University. He worked for over twenty years as an associate editor, foreign correspondent, and Moscow bureau chief for Time magazine. He owns the Sacred Art Pilgrim Collection, curates exhibitions featuring artworks from his collection, and writes art columns for publications such as The Christian Century.[21]

21 http://www.sacredartpilgrim.com

Mateusz Sora

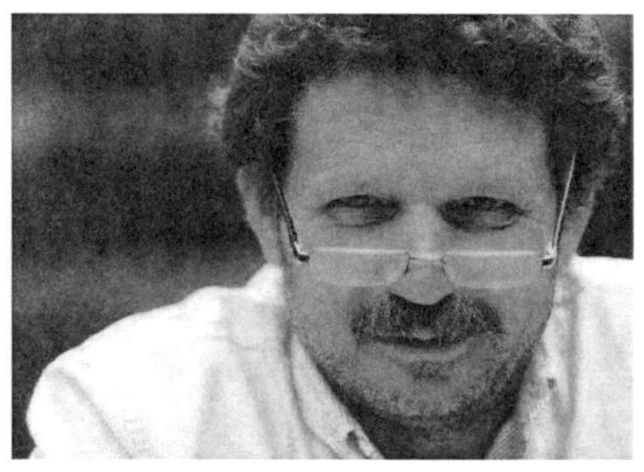

Born in Warsaw in 1965. He is a historian, museologist, and social activist who is particularly committed to helping the public understand history. Since 2017, he has been an employee of the Department of Education and Publishing of the Polish National Bank. He is the author of the concepts for the open-air exhibitions "History of the Zloty" and "100 Years of Bank of Poland SA," the former of which was awarded Historical Event of the Year in 2019. She is also the author of several publications on social and economic history and the editor of the NBP Money Center's educational library.

He is also the co-founder of the "Friends of Nowica" association, which has campaigned since 2000 to save the village school in Nowica, a small village in the Polish Carpathian foothills with a partly Ukrainian-speaking population. The "smallest school in Poland" continues to operate. An artists' initiative was created in this context that offers exhibitions, theater events, and concerts. This led to a cooperation agreement with the Lviv Oblast. The "Nowa Ikona" initiative was also developed there. It organizes annual workshops for a new kind of traditional iconography. Mainly professional artists from Ukraine and Poland take part in these workshops, including Danylo Movchan. Sora has curated around one hundred exhibitions in Ukraine, Poland, Belarus, Georgia, Armenia, Germany, Austria, and Switzerland. He publishes annual catalogs featuring new works, as well as comprehensive overviews.

Myroslav Marynovych

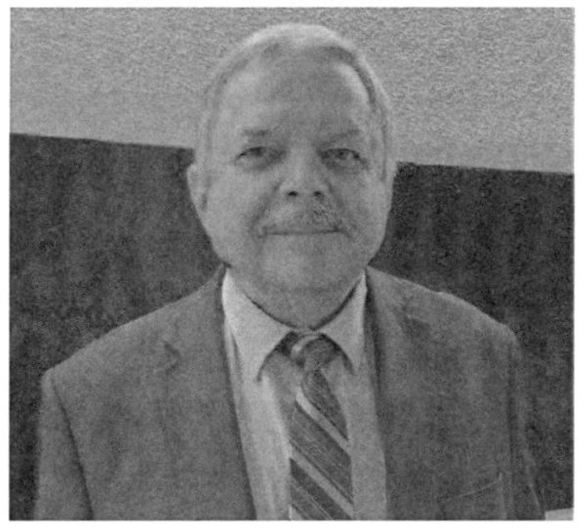

Myroslav Marynovych, born in 1949 in the Ukrainian village of Komarivychi near Lviv, is a Ukrainian human rights activist and co-founder of the Ukrainian Helsinki Group. He was a political prisoner and later became president of the Ukrainian branch of Amnesty International, a position he still holds today. He is also the Honorary President of the Ukrainian P.E.N. Center and has received the Order of Freedom of Ukraine and numerous other awards. Marynovych works as a publicist and religious scholar and is an advisor to the Ukrainian Catholic University in Lviv. Due to his involvement with the Ukrainian Helsinki Human Rights Group, he was imprisoned as a dissident in a labor camp for seven years and exiled to Kazakhstan for three years during the Brezhnev era. The group was the first legal, non-underground resistance movement to raise public awareness of the human rights situation in Ukraine during the Soviet era.[22]

22 Myroslav Marynovych: The Universe Behind the Barbed Wire—Memoirs of a Soviet Ukrainian Dissident. With a foreword by Timothy Snyder and an afterword by Max Hartmann. Ukrainian Voices, vol. 43, ibidem Press, 2023

Max Hartmann

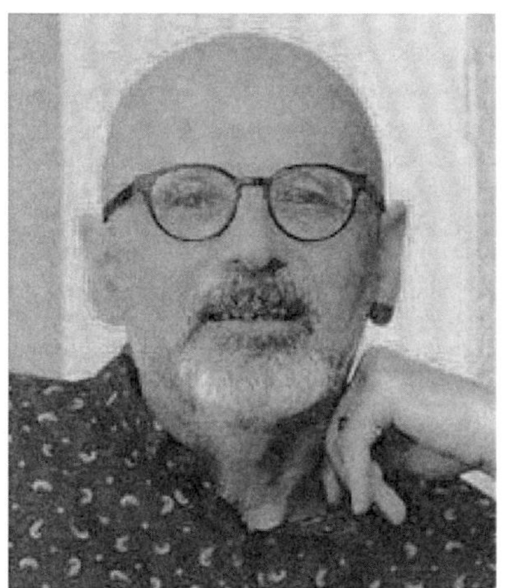

He was born in 1959 in Oftringen, Switzerland. He is married to Eva Hartmann-Kunz and has two daughters. From 1980 to 1986, he studied Protestant theology at the universities of Basel, Bern, and Zurich. From 1987 to 2022, he was a pastor in the Reformed Church. Since his youth, he has been interested in literature and events behind the Iron Curtain. Before the fall of the Berlin Wall, he visited the GDR several times, experiencing its gray reality and constant surveillance firsthand. During his first visit to Ukraine at the beginning of 2017, he became acquainted with the art of the "New Icon," which later led to meetings with some of these artists and an exhibition of their work in Switzerland. With the support of the publishing house ***ibidem***, he published his revised German translation of the memoirs “Das Universum hinter dem Stacheldraht” by the Soviet Ukrainian dissident Myroslav Marynovich. This work led to a friendship with Marynoych and a better understanding of Ukraine's history with Russia and the current war. He is also the author of the book “Der Weg zurück zum Leben—Die Geschichte meiner Depression”, published by “Mosaicstones” in 2021 and is involved in the publication “A Short Introduction to the World of Contemporary Icons: Examples and Contexts” which is forthcoming.

UKRAINIAN VOICES

Collected by Andreas Umland

1 *Mychailo Wynnyckyj*
Ukraine's Maidan, Russia's War
A Chronicle and Analysis of the Revolution of Dignity
With a foreword by Serhii Plokhy
ISBN 978-3-8382-1327-9

2 *Olexander Hryb*
Understanding Contemporary Ukrainian and Russian Nationalism
The Post-Soviet Cossack Revival and Ukraine's National Security
With a foreword by Vitali Vitaliev
ISBN 978-3-8382-1377-4

3 *Marko Bojcun*
Towards a Political Economy of Ukraine
Selected Essays 1990–2015
With a foreword by John-Paul Himka
ISBN 978-3-8382-1368-2

4 *Volodymyr Yermolenko (ed.)*
Ukraine in Histories and Stories
Essays by Ukrainian Intellectuals
With a preface by Peter Pomerantsev
ISBN 978-3-8382-1456-6

5 *Mykola Riabchuk*
At the Fence of Metternich's Garden
Essays on Europe, Ukraine, and Europeanization
ISBN 978-3-8382-1484-9

6 *Marta Dyczok*
Ukraine Calling
A Kaleidoscope from Hromadske Radio 2016–2019
With a foreword by Andriy Kulykov
ISBN 978-3-8382-1472-6

7 *Olexander Scherba*
Ukraine vs. Darkness
Undiplomatic Thoughts
With a foreword by Adrian Karatnycky
ISBN 978-3-8382-1501-3

8 *Olesya Yaremchuk*
Our Others
Stories of Ukrainian Diversity
With a foreword by Ostap Slyvynsky
Translated from the Ukrainian by Zenia Tompkins and Hanna Leliv
ISBN 978-3-8382-1475-7

9 *Nataliya Gumenyuk*
Die verlorene Insel
Geschichten von der besetzten Krim
Mit einem Vorwort von Alice Bota
Aus dem Ukrainischen übersetzt von Johann Zajaczkowski
ISBN 978-3-8382-1499-3

10 *Olena Stiazhkina*
Zero Point Ukraine
Four Essays on World War II
Translated from the Ukrainian by Svitlana Kulinska
ISBN 978-3-8382-1550-1

11 *Oleksii Sinchenko, Dmytro Stus, Leonid Finberg (compilers)*
Ukrainian Dissidents
An Anthology of Texts
ISBN 978-3-8382-1551-8

12 *John-Paul Himka*
Ukrainian Nationalists and the Holocaust
OUN and UPA's Participation in the Destruction of Ukrainian Jewry, 1941–1944
ISBN 978-3-8382-1548-8

13 *Andrey Demartino*
False Mirrors
The Weaponization of Social Media in Russia's Operation to Annex Crimea
With a foreword by Oleksiy Danilov
ISBN 978-3-8382-1533-4

14 *Svitlana Biedarieva (ed.)*
Contemporary Ukrainian and Baltic Art
Political and Social Perspectives, 1991–2021
ISBN 978-3-8382-1526-6

15 *Olesya Khromeychuk*
A Loss
The Story of a Dead Soldier Told by His Sister
With a foreword by Andrey Kurkov
ISBN 978-3-8382-1570-9

16 *Marieluise Beck (Hg.)*
Ukraine verstehen
Auf den Spuren von Terror und Gewalt
Mit einem Vorwort von Dmytro Kuleba
ISBN 978-3-8382-1653-9

17 *Stanislav Aseyev*
Heller Weg
Geschichte eines Konzentrationslagers im Donbass 2017–2019
Aus dem Russischen übersetzt von Martina Steis und Charis Haska
ISBN 978-3-8382-1620-1

18 *Mykola Davydiuk*
Wie funktioniert Putins Propaganda?
Anmerkungen zum Informationskrieg des Kremls
Aus dem Ukrainischen übersetzt von Christian Weise
ISBN 978-3-8382-1628-7

19 *Olesya Yaremchuk*
Unsere Anderen
Geschichten ukrainischer Vielfalt
Aus dem Ukrainischen übersetzt von Christian Weise
ISBN 978-3-8382-1635-5

20 *Oleksandr Mykhed*
„Dein Blut wird die Kohle tränken“
Über die Ostukraine
Aus dem Ukrainischen übersetzt von Simon Muschick und Dario Planert
ISBN 978-3-8382-1648-5

21 *Vakhtang Kipiani (Hg.)*
Der Zweite Weltkrieg in der Ukraine
Geschichte und Lebensgeschichten
Aus dem Ukrainischen übersetzt von Margarita Grinko
ISBN 978-3-8382-1622-5

22 *Vakhtang Kipiani (ed.)*
World War II, Uncontrived and Unredacted
Testimonies from Ukraine
Translated from the Ukrainian by Zenia Tompkins and Daisy Gibbons
ISBN 978-3-8382-1621-8

23 *Dmytro Stus*
Vasyl Stus
Life in Creativity
Translated from the Ukrainian by Ludmila Bachurina
ISBN 978-3-8382-1631-7

24 *Vitalii Ogiienko (ed.)*
The Holodomor and the Origins of the Soviet Man
Reading the Testimony of Anastasia Lysyvets
With forewords by Natalka Bilotserkivets and Serhy Yekelchyk
Translated from the Ukrainian by Alla Parkhomenko and Alexander J. Motyl
ISBN 978-3-8382-1616-4

25 *Vladislav Davidzon*
Jewish-Ukrainian Relations and the Birth of a Political Nation
Selected Writings 2013-2021
With a foreword by Bernard-Henri Lévy
ISBN 978-3-8382-1509-9

26 *Serhy Yekelchyk*
Writing the Nation
The Ukrainian Historical Profession in Independent Ukraine and the Diaspora
ISBN 978-3-8382-1695-9

27 *Ildi Eperjesi, Oleksandr Kachura*
Shreds of War
Fates from the Donbas Frontline 2014-2019
With a foreword by Olexiy Haran
ISBN 978-3-8382-1680-5

28 *Oleksandr Melnyk*
World War II as an Identity Project
Historicism, Legitimacy Contests, and the (Re-)Construction of Political Communities in Ukraine, 1939–1946
With a foreword by David R. Marples
ISBN 978-3-8382-1704-8

29 *Olesya Khromeychuk*
Ein Verlust
Die Geschichte eines gefallenen ukrainischen Soldaten, erzählt von seiner Schwester
Mit einem Vorwort von Andrej Kurkow
Aus dem Englischen übersetzt von Lily Sophie
ISBN 978-3-8382-1770-3

30 *Tamara Martsenyuk, Tetiana Kostiuchenko (eds.)*
Russia's War in Ukraine During 2022
Personal Experiences of Ukrainian Scholars
ISBN 978-3-8382-1757-4

31 *Ildikó Eperjesi, Oleksandr Kachura*
Shreds of War. Vol. 2
Fates from Crimea 2015–2022
With an interview of Oleh Sentsov
ISBN 978-3-8382-1780-2

32 *Yuriy Lukanov*
The Press
How Russia Destroyed Media Freedom in Crimea
With a foreword by Taras Kuzio
ISBN 978-3-8382-1784-0

33 *Megan Buskey*
Ukraine Is Not Dead Yet
A Family Story of Exile and Return
ISBN 978-3-8382-1691-1

34 *Vira Ageyeva*
Behind the Scenes of the Empire
Essays on Cultural Relationships between Ukraine and Russia
With a foreword by Oksana Zabuzhko
ISBN 978-3-8382-1748-2

35 *Marieluise Beck (ed.)*
Understanding Ukraine
Tracing the Roots of Terror and Violence
With a foreword by Dmytro Kuleba
ISBN 978-3-8382-1773-4

36 *Olesya Khromeychuk*
A Loss
The Story of a Dead Soldier Told by His Sister, 2nd edn.
With a foreword by Philippe Sands
With a preface by Andrii Kurkov
ISBN 978-3-8382-1870-0

37 *Taras Kuzio, Stefan Jajecznyk-Kelman*
Fascism and Genocide
Russia's War Against Ukrainians
ISBN 978-3-8382-1791-8

38 *Alina Nychyk*
Ukraine Vis-à-Vis Russia and the EU
Misperceptions of Foreign Challenges in Times of War, 2014–2015
With a foreword by Paul D'Anieri
ISBN 978-3-8382-1767-3

39 *Sasha Dovzhyk (ed.)*
Ukraine Lab
Global Security, Environment, and Disinformation Through the Prism of Ukraine
With a foreword by Rory Finnin
ISBN 978-3-8382-1805-2

40 *Serhiy Kvit*
Media, History, and Education
Three Ways to Ukrainian Independence
With a preface by Diane Francis
ISBN 978-3-8382-1807-6

41 *Anna Romandash*
Women of Ukraine
Reportages from the War and Beyond
ISBN 978-3-8382-1819-9

42 *Dominika Rank*
Matzewe in meinem Garten
Abenteuer eines jüdischen Heritage-Touristen in der Ukraine
ISBN 978-3-8382-1810-6

43 *Myroslaw Marynowytsch*
Das Universum hinter dem Stacheldraht
Memoiren eines sowjet-ukrainischen Dissidenten
Mit einem Vorwort von Timothy Snyder und einem Nachwort von Max Hartmann
ISBN 978-3-8382-1806-9

44 *Konstantin Sigow*
Für Deine und meine Freiheit
Europäische Revolutions- und Kriegserfahrungen im heutigen Kyjiw
Mit einem Vorwort von Karl Schlögel
Herausgegeben von Regula M. Zwahlen
ISBN 978-3-8382-1755-0

45 *Kateryna Pylypchuk*
The War that Changed Us
Ukrainian Novellas, Poems, and Essays from 2022
With a foreword by Victor Yushchenko
Paperback
ISBN 978-3-8382-1859-5
Hardcover
ISBN 978-3-8382-1860-1

46 *Kyrylo Tkachenko*
Rechte Tür Links
Radikale Linke in Deutschland, die Revolution und der Krieg in der Ukraine, 2013-2018
ISBN 978-3-8382-1711-6

47 *Alexander Strashny*
The Ukrainian Mentality
An Ethno-Psychological, Historical and Comparative Exploration
With a foreword by Antonina Lovochkina
Translated from the Ukrainian by Michael M. Naydan and Olha Tytarenko
ISBN 978-3-8382-1886-1

48 *Alona Shestopalova*
From Screens to Battlefields
Tracing the Construction of Enemies on Russian Television
With a foreword by Nina Jankowicz
ISBN 978-3-8382-1884-7

49 *Iaroslav Petik*
Politics and Society in the Ukrainian People's Republic (1917–1921) and Contemporary Ukraine (2013–2022)
A Comparative Analysis
With a foreword by Mykola Doroshko
ISBN 978-3-8382-1817-5

50 *Serhii Plokhy*
Der Mann mit der Giftpistole
Eine Spionageschichte aus dem Kalten Krieg
ISBN 978-3-8382-1789-5

51 *Vakhtang Kipiani*
Ukrainische Dissidenten unter der Sowjetmacht
Im Kampf um Wahrheit und Freiheit
Aus dem Ukrainischen übersetzt von Christian Weise
ISBN 978-3-8382-1890-8

52 *Dmytro Shestakov*
When Businesses Test Hypotheses
A Four-Step Approach to Risk Management for Innovative Startups
With a foreword by Anthony J. Tether
ISBN 978-3-8382-1883-0

53 *Larissa Babij*
A Kind of Refugee
The Story of an American Who Refused to Leave Ukraine
With a foreword by Vladislav Davidzon
ISBN 978-3-8382-1898-4

54 *Julia Davis*
In Their Own Words
How Russian Propagandists Reveal Putin's Intentions
With a foreword by Timothy Snyder
ISBN 978-3-8382-1909-7

55 *Sonya Atlantova, Oleksandr Klymenko*
Icons on Ammo Boxes
Painting Life on the Remnants of Russia's War in Donbas, 2014-21
Translated from the Ukrainian by Anastasya Knyazhytska
ISBN 978-3-8382-1892-2

56 *Leonid Ushkalov*
Catching an Elusive Bird
The Life of Hryhorii Skovoroda
Translated from the Ukrainian by Natalia Komarova
ISBN 978-3-8382-1894-6

57 *Vakhtang Kipiani*
Ein Land weiblichen Geschlechts
Ukrainische Frauenschicksale im 20. und 21. Jahrhundert
Aus dem Ukrainischen übersetzt von Christian Weise
ISBN 978-3-8382-1891-5

58 *Petro Rychlo*
„Zerrissne Saiten einer überlauten Harfe ...“
Deutschjüdische Dichter der Bukowina
ISBN 978-3-8382-1893-9

59 *Volodymyr Paniotto*
Sociology in Jokes
An Entertaining Introduction
ISBN 978-3-8382-1857-1

60 *Josef Wallmannsberger (ed.)*
Executing Renaissances
The Poetological Nation of Ukraine
ISBN 978-3-8382-1741-3

61 *Pavlo Kazarin*
The Wild West of Eastern Europe
A Ukrainian Guide on Breaking Free from Empire
Translated from the Ukrainian by Dominique Hoffman
ISBN 978-3-8382-1842-7

62 *Ernest Gyidel*
Ukrainian Public Nationalism in the General Government
The Case of *Krakivski Visti*, 1940–1944
With a foreword by David R. Marples
ISBN 978-3-8382-1865-6

63 *Olexander Hryb*
Understanding Contemporary Russian Militarism
From Revolutionary to New Generation Warfare
With a foreword by Mark Laity
ISBN 978-3-8382-1927-1

64 *Orysia Hrudka, Bohdan Ben*
Dark Days, Determined People
Stories from Ukraine under Siege
With a foreword by Myroslav Marynovych
ISBN 978-3-8382-1958-5

65 *Oleksandr Pankieiev (ed.)*
Narratives of the Russo-Ukrainian War
A Look Within and Without
With a foreword by Natalia Khanenko-Friesen
ISBN 978-3-8382-1964-6

66 *Roman Sohn, Ariana Gic (eds.)*
Unrecognized War
The Fight for Truth about Russia’s War on Ukraine
With a foreword by Viktor Yushchenko
ISBN 978-3-8382-1947-9

67 *Paul Robert Magocsi*
Ukraina Redux
Schon wieder die Ukraine ...
ISBN 978-3-8382-1942-4

68 *Paul Robert Magocsi*
L’Ucraina Ritrovata
Sullo Stato e l’Identità Nazionale
ISBN 978-3-8382-1982-0

69 *Max Hartmann*
Ein Schrei der Verzweiflung
Aquarelle von Danylo Movchan zu Russlands Krieg in der Ukraine
Mit einem Vorwort von Mateusz Sora
Paperback
ISBN 978-3-8382-2011-6
Hardcover
ISBN 978-3-8382-2012-3

70 *Vakhtang Kebuladze (Hg.)*
Die Zukunft, die wir uns wünschen
Essays aus der Ukraine
ISBN 978-3-8382-1531-0

71 *Marieluise Beck, Jan Claas Behrends, Gelinada Grinchenko und Oksana Mikheieva (Hgg.)*
Deutsch-ukrainische Geschichten
Bruchstücke aus einer gemeinsamen Vergangenheit
ISBN 978-3-8382-2053-6

72 *Pavlo Kazarin*
Der Wilde Westen Ost-Europas
Der ukrainische Weg aus dem Imperium
Aus dem Ukrainischen übersetzt von Christian Weise
ISBN 978-3-8382-1843-4

73 *Radomyr Mokryk*
Die ukrainischen »Sechziger«
Chronologie einer Revolte
ISBN 978-3-8382-1873-1

74 *Leonid Finberg*
My Ukraine
Rethinking the Past, Building the Present
ISBN 978-3-8382-1974-5

75 *Joseph Zissels*
Consider My Inmost Thoughts
Essays, Lectures, and Interviews on Ukrainian Matters at the Turn of the Century
ISBN 978-3-8382-1975-2

76 *Margarita Yehorchenko, Iryna Berlyand, Ihor Vinokurov (eds.)*
Jewish Addresses in Ukraine
A Guide-Book
With a foreword by Leonid Finberg
ISB 978-3-8382-1976-9

77 *Viktoriia Grivina*
Kharkiv—A War City
A Collection of Essays from 2022–23
ISBN 978-3-8382-1988-2

78 *Hjørdis Clemmensen, Viktoriia Grivina, Vasylysa Shchogoleva*
Kharkiv Is a Dream
Public Art and Activism 2013–2023
With a foreword by Bohdan Volynskyi
ISBN 978-3-8382-2005-5

79 *Olga Khomenko*
The Faraway Sky of Kyiv
Ukrainians in the War
With a foreword by Hiroaki Kuromiya
ISBN 978-3-8382-2006-2

80 *Daria Mattingly, Jonathon Vsetecka (eds.)*
The Holodomor in Global Perspective
How the Famine in Ukraine Shaped the World
With a foreword by Anne Applebaum
ISBN 978-3-8382-1953-0

81 *Olga Khomenko*
Ukrainians beyond Borders
Nine Life Journeys Through the History of Eastern Europe
With a foreword by Zbigniew Wojnowski
ISBN 978-3-8382-2007-9

82 *Mykhailo Minakov*
From Servant to Leader
Chronicles of Ukraine under the Zelensky Presidency, 2019–2024
With a foreword by John Lloyd
ISBN 978-3-8382-2002-4

83 *Volodymyr Hromov (ed.)*
A Ruined Home
Sketches of War, 2022–2023
ISBN 978-3-8382-2008-6

84 *Olha Tatokhina (ed.)*
Why Do They Kill Our People?
Russia's War Against Ukraine as Told by Ukrainians
With a foreword by Volodymyr Yermolenko
ISBN 978-3-8382-2056-7

85 *Mieste Hotopp-Riecke, Sarah Reinke (Hgg.)*
Die Krimtataren
Geschichte – Kultur – Politik
Mit einem Vorwort von Nariman Dschelal
ISBN 978-3-8382-1986-8

86 *Max Hartmann (ed.)*
A Cry of Despair
Danylo Movchan's Watercolors on the War in Ukraine
With a foreword by John A. Kohan and Matheusz Sora
ISBN 978-3-8382-2051-2

87 *Olha Marmilova, Yuliia Soroka (eds.)*
The Russian War Against Ukraine
Investigations of Its Social and Historical Context, 2014–2024
With a foreword by Ulrich Schmid
ISBN 978-3-8382-2035-2

88 *Mykola Davidyuk*
How Putin's Propaganda Works
Ukraine's Experience in Its War Against Russia since 2014
With a foreword by Roman Kostenko
ISBN 978-3-8382-1627-0

89 *Mikhail Minakov*
Der postsowjetische Mensch
Philosophische Betrachtungen zur Gesellschaftsgeschichte nach Ende der UdSSR
Mit einem Vorwort von Timm Beichelt
Aus dem Englischen übersetzt von Hermann Haushahn
ISBN 978-3-8382-2043-7

90 *Serhiy Kazimir, Vahur Laiapea*
This Is How It Was
A Ukrainian Officer's 691 Days In Russian Prisons
Translation by Tiiu Palumäe and Ott Palumäe
ISBN 978-3-8382-2077-2

91 *Anastasiia Simferovska (ed.)*
Confronting Catastrophes
The Art of Yohanan Petrovsky-Shtern
With an introduction by Andrew Horodysky
ISBN 978-3-8382-2163-2

92 *Сергій Казимир, Вагур Лайапеа*
Так Було
691 день українського офіцера в російських тюрмах
Переклад з російської на українську Тетяна Лач
ISBN 978-3-8382-2177-9

93 *Ilko-Sascha Kowalczuk*
Freedom Shock
A Different History of East Germany from 1989 to Today
ISBN 978-3-8382-2069-7

94 *Stephen Velychenko*
A Village in Revolutionary Ukraine
How Bolshevik Rule Changed a People: The Eyewitness Account of a Common Man, 1918–28
With a foreword by Yaroslav Hrytsak
ISBN 978-3-8382-2065-9

95 *Katerina Sergatskova*
Occupation and Migration in Eastern Europe
How Citizens Are Forced into Exile and Shaped by New Realities—Reports, Essays, Articles, 2014–25
With a foreword by Christopher Miller
ISBN 978-3-8382-2060-4

96 *Olena Bogatyrenko (ed.)*
What Did Russia's Occupation of Crimea Mean?
Twelve Women Report How They Experienced the Start of the Russo-Ukrainian War in 2014
With a foreword by Olena Bogatyrenko
ISBN 978-3-8382-2092-5

97 *Larisa Kalik*
Dress Rehearsal
How Transnistria Became Russia's Roadmap for Hybrid Wars in Ukraine and Beyond
With a foreword by Francis Farrell
Translated from the Ukrainian by Kate Tsurkan
ISBN 978-3-8382-2074-1

98 *Petro Rychlo*
Regenbogen über der Donau
Studien zu ukrainisch-deutschen Literaturbeziehungen
ISBN 978-3-8382-2093-2

Book series "Ukrainian Voices"

Sergiy Korsunsky, Kobe Gakuin University, Japan
Nadiia Koval, Kyiv School of Economics, Ukraine
Volodymyr Kravchenko, University of Alberta, Edmonton
Oleksiy Kresin, NAS Koretskiy Institute of State and Law, Kyiv
Anatoliy Kruglashov, Fedkovych National University, Chernivtsi
Andrey Kurkov, PEN Ukraine, Kyiv
Ostap Kushnir, Lazarski University, Warsaw
Taras Kuzio, National University of Kyiv-Mohyla Academy
Serhii Kvit, National University of Kyiv-Mohyla Academy
Yuliya Ladygina, The Pennsylvania State University, USA
Yevhen Mahda, Institute of World Policy, Kyiv
Victoria Malko, California State University, Fresno, USA
Yulia Marushevska, Security and Defense Center (SAND), Kyiv
Myroslav Marynovych, Ukrainian Catholic University, Lviv
Oleksandra Matviichuk, Center for Civil Liberties, Kyiv
Mykhailo Minakov, Kennan Institute, Washington, USA
Anton Moiseienko, The Australian National University, Canberra
Alexander Motyl, Rutgers University-Newark, USA
Vlad Mykhnenko, University of Oxford, United Kingdom
Vitalii Ogiienko, Ukrainian Institute of National Remembrance, Kyiv
Olga Onuch, University of Manchester, United Kingdom
Olesya Ostrovska, Museum "Mystetskyi Arsenal," Kyiv
Anna Osypchuk, National University of Kyiv-Mohyla Academy
Oleksandr Pankieiev, University of Alberta, Edmonton
Oleksiy Panych, Publishing House "Dukh i Litera," Kyiv
Valerii Pekar, Kyiv-Mohyla Business School, Ukraine
Yohanan Petrovsky-Shtern, Northwestern University, Chicago
Serhii Plokhy, Harvard University, Cambridge, USA
Andrii Portnov, Viadrina University, Frankfurt-Oder, Germany
Maryna Rabinovych, Kyiv School of Economics, Ukraine
Valentyna Romanova, Institute of Developing Economies, Tokyo
Natalya Ryabinska, Collegium Civitas, Warsaw, Poland
Darya Tsymbalyk, University of Oxford, United Kingdom
Vsevolod Samokhvalov, University of Liege, Belgium
Orest Semotiuk, Franko National University, Lviv
Viktoriya Sereda, NAS Institute of Ethnology, Lviv
Anton Shekhovtsov, University of Vienna, Austria
Andriy Shevchenko, Media Center Ukraine, Kyiv
Oxana Shevel, Tufts University, Medford, USA
Pavlo Shopin, National Pedagogical Dragomanov University, Kyiv
Karina Shyrokykh, Stockholm University, Sweden
Nadja Simon, freelance interpreter, Cologne, Germany
Olena Snigova, NAS Institute for Economics and Forecasting, Kyiv
Ilona Solohub, Analytical Platform "VoxUkraine," Kyiv
Iryna Solonenko, LibMod - Center for Liberal Modernity, Berlin
Galyna Solovei, National University of Kyiv-Mohyla Academy
Sergiy Stelmakh, NAS Institute of World History, Kyiv
Olena Stiazhkina, NAS Institute of the History of Ukraine, Kyiv
Dmitri Stratievski, Osteuropa Zentrum (OEZB), Berlin
Dmytro Stus, National Taras Shevchenko Museum, Kyiv
Frank Sysyn, University of Toronto, Canada
Olha Tokariuk, Center for European Policy Analysis, Washington
Olena Tregub, Independent Anti-Corruption Commission, Kyiv
Hlib Vyshlinsky, Centre for Economic Strategy, Kyiv
Mychailo Wynnyckyj, National University of Kyiv-Mohyla Academy
Yelyzaveta Yasko, NGO "Yellow Blue Strategy," Kyiv
Serhy Yekelchyk, University of Victoria, Canada
Victor Yushchenko, President of Ukraine 2005-2010, Kyiv
Oleksandr Zaitsev, Ukrainian Catholic University, Lviv
Kateryna Zarembo, National University of Kyiv-Mohyla Academy
Yaroslav Zhalilo, National Institute for Strategic Studies, Kyiv
Sergei Zhuk, Ball State University at Muncie, USA
Alina Zubkovych, Nordic Ukraine Forum, Stockholm
Liudmyla Zubrytska, National University of Kyiv-Mohyla Academy

Friends of the Series

[Please send requests for changes in, corrections of, and additions to, this list to andreas.umland@stanforalumni.org.]

ibidem*.*eu

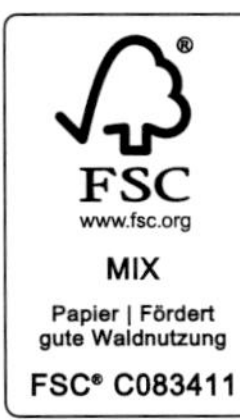

Zeitfracht Medien GmbH
Ferdinand-Jühlke-Straße 7
99095 Erfurt, Deutschland
produktsicherheit@kolibri360.de